Publications of the Center for Hellenic Studies
Bernard M. W. Knox, General Editor

Formula, Character, and Context

Formula, Character, and Context

Studies in Homeric, Old English,
and Old Testament Poetry

William Whallon

Published by the Center for Hellenic Studies,
Washington, D.C.

Distributed by Harvard University Press,
Cambridge, Massachusetts

1969

The lungs of Roland from the mountain tomb,
Shouting through thirty leagues within the horn,
Publish at last the embassy forsworn.
The grip of Beowulf, the massive room
A shambles, flings the ogre through the gloom,
His arm and axle from the body torn.
Job wishes dead the day that he was born
To trouble from the harbor of the womb.
Sometimes at sundown where the rose clouds change
To thick blue air above the watching lands,
Hurtles a meteor burning clear and strange:
So now Achilles runs across the sands.
The gates pull to, and by the open range
Prince of the broad-wayed city, Hector stands.

W.W.

Preface

This book is about verbal formulas and the ways in which they relate to characterization and to their contexts. The first two chapters are concerned with Homeric poetry but briefly draw in Old French poetry; the next two are concerned with Old English poetry but draw in Homeric and Old French poetry; the last two are concerned with Old Testament poetry but often draw in Homeric, Old English, and Old French poetry. The comparative method is used to define how the different traditions are analogous, and to propose corresponding solutions for corresponding problems. The questions that led me to write the book were these: (1) Are any of the Homeric epithets significantly true to individual character? (2) By what process did some of the Homeric epithets become true to character? (3) Are the Old English kennings similarly true to character, or are they pertinent to context? (4) Are the Old English words of religious sense formulaic and traditional? (5) What elements of Old Testament poetry are formulaic and traditional? (6) How do the

formulas of the Old Testament relate to their contexts?
(Since to create suspense has not been a part of my purpose,
the answers are given as the chapter headings.)

I have aimed chiefly at devising a few arguments not to be
found elsewhere. Though one of the poems under analysis is
in my opinion the finest ever composed, the kind of criticism
that isolates the good from the bad, or weighs different objects to put a price on them, has only rarely been taken as a
part of my subject. Nor do I discuss the larger number of
recent theories about Homeric, Old English, or Old Testament poetry; many scholars whose work is of outstanding
merit are not even mentioned. Here and there it has seemed
necessary or desirable to attack: my opponents are never
windmills, they are always real giants; and the three whom I
am conscious of speaking against most directly—Denys Page
in Chapter 2, Fr. Klaeber in Chapter 4, and Erich Auerbach
in Chapter 6—strike me as likely, for certain qualities
though not for all, to be regarded as, respectively, the
greatest Hellenist, Anglo-Saxonist, and comparatist, of their
day.

A substantial part of this book, perhaps the larger part,
appears here for the first time. But some of the material in
the first two chapters is from *Yale Classical Studies* 17 (1961)
97–142 and 19 (1966) 7–36; some in the next two, from
PMLA 76 (1961) 309–319 and 80 (1965) 19–23, and from
Modern Philology 60 (1962) 81–94 and 63 (1965) 95–104; and
some in the last two from *Comparative Literature* 15 (1963) 1–14
and 18 (1966) 113–131. For permission to re-use the material
I am indebted to the editors of the journals, and to the Yale
University Press, the Modern Language Association, the
University of Chicago Press, and the University of Oregon
Press, respectively. The chance to print the eight articles
singly was for many reasons of the greatest help to me; but

in this book I have modified or withdrawn several of my
earlier definitions and other statements. An appendix,
containing matter from a paper read at the meeting of the
International Comparative Literature Association in 1967,
lists a few topics that I should like to see taken up by other
hands.

For the *Iliad* and *Odyssey* I have used the edition by
Thomas W. Allen and David B. Monro, in the Oxford
Classical Texts series; for *Beowulf* and other Old English
poems, *The Anglo-Saxon Poetic Records*, edited by George
Philip Krapp and Elliott V. K. Dobbie; for the *Song of
Roland*, the revised edition by T. Atkinson Jenkins; for the
Edda, the text of Gustav Neckel, revised by Hans Kuhn;
and for the Old and New Testaments, the Authorized Version
for the numbers to chapter and verse, and the texts of Rudolf
Kittel, Constantin von Tischendorf, and Eberhard Nestle,
for readings from the Hebrew Old Testament, the Septuagint,
and the Greek New Testament, respectively. Greek iota
subscripts are printed as adscripts; and the Hebrew is trans-
literated—mainly into italic type, but with roman type used
to indicate the absence of *dāḡēš-lene* (as here). The translations
are my own except that for the Bible they have been taken
from the Authorized Version.

My obligations are so numerous that a list of them would
take up a disproportionate amount of space. Let me say only
that I outlined the book during a year as fellow at the Center
for Hellenic Studies and completed it during two terms as
research professor at Michigan State University.

I would greatly appreciate having every error, no matter
how small or large, called to my attention.

                                                      W.W.

East Lansing, Michigan
September 1967

Contents

Contents

Formula, Character, and Context

Animals, Gladiators, and Greed

One / The Homeric epithets are significantly true to individual character.

From a remark by Josephus (*Against Apion* 1.12) and a few other scraps of ancient opinion, certain Homerists of the eighteenth century—notably Robert Wood and Friedrich August Wolf—argued that the *Iliad* and *Odyssey* had been retold for a long while before being written down; the idea was never opposed systematically and became generally accepted. The tendency of lines to recur was well known to Aristarchus and his predecessors at the library of Alexandria; and in the nineteenth century the concordances compiled by Guy Lushington Prendergast (London 1875) and Henry Dunbar (Oxford 1880), together with the *Parallel-Homer* of Carl Eduard Schmidt (Göttingen 1885), made it possible to see the repeated phrases, lines, and passages very quickly. So the groundwork had been laid—in antiquity and then in the modern era—for Milman Parry, *L'Épithète traditionnelle dans Homère* (Paris 1928), to conclude that the Homeric idiom was traditional because its formulaic character could scarcely have been created by a single poet. He believed, I should say demonstrated, that as a rule the epithets were used not for their own sake, but to bring their nouns to more or less standardized lengths. In any context, "swift-footed Achilles" is to be regarded as above all a convenient way of saying "Achilles" and does not mean that the swiftness of foot is necessarily important, or even apparent, at the moment. What Parry neglected to discuss, and sometimes came close to denying, is that the epithets describe the essential and unchanging character of the men whose names they augment. My intention here is simply to provide for the omission. Some crucial details have already been emphasized by C. M. Bowra, *Tradition and Design in the Iliad* (Oxford 1930) 81, and Cedric H. Whitman, *Homer and the Heroic Tradition* (Cambridge, Mass. 1958) 113; but on the whole the subject is open to investigation.

I. ἄναξ ἀνδρῶν, κρείων for Agamemnon

The epithet ἄναξ ἀνδρῶν "king of men" is used, in the *Iliad* and *Odyssey* together, forty-seven times for Agamemnon and no more often than once for anyone else; the epithet κρείων "ruling" is used thirty times for Agamemnon, seven times for Poseidon, and no more often than once for anyone else; and the expanded form εὐρυκρείων "wide-ruling" is used twelve times for Agamemnon and once for Poseidon, and otherwise not at all. Since from these statistics alone we should have gathered that Agamemnon would be the commander-in-chief of the Achaeans, it is no surprise that his contingent of ships is the largest (*Il.* 2.580), or that he assembled the expedition and led it to Troy (*Il.* 4.179, 9.338). In the episode of the View from the Wall, Priam asks first about the man who looks so royal: he is like one who is a king (*Il.* 3.170); and Helen replies that it is Agamemnon. The

relationship here between the meaning of the epithets and
the nature of the man they so often describe is self-evident;
and yet a few further details ask to be mentioned.

Several of the major heroes are addressed (or apostro-
phized) with titles which fill the entire line; among these are
the following:

Ἀτρείδη κύδιστε ἄναξ ἀνδρῶν Ἀγάμεμνον
Atreides, most glorious, king of men Agamemnon
(eight times in the *Iliad*, twice in the *Odyssey*)

ὦ Ἀχιλεῦ Πηλῆος υἱὲ μέγα φέρτατ' Ἀχαιῶν
O Achilles, son of Peleus, by far the mightiest of the Achaeans
(twice in the *Iliad*, once in the *Odyssey*)

διογενὲς Λαερτιάδη πολυμήχαν' Ὀδυσσεῦ
Zeus-born Laertiades, Odysseus of many arts
(seven times in the *Iliad*, fifteen times in the *Odyssey*)

Ἀτρείδη Μενέλαε διοτρεφὲς ὄρχαμε λαῶν
Atreides Menelaus, Zeus-nurtured leader of the people
(once in the *Iliad*, five times in the *Odyssey*)

ὦ Νέστορ Νηληιάδη μέγα κῦδος Ἀχαιῶν
O Nestor Neleiades, great glory of the Achaeans
(four times in the *Iliad*, twice in the *Odyssey*)

Αἶαν διογενὲς Τελαμώνιε κοίρανε λαῶν
Ajax Zeus-born Telamonian, commander of the people
(three times in the *Iliad*)

Ἕκτορ υἱὲ Πριάμοιο Διὶ μῆτιν ἀτάλαντε
Hector, son of Priam, equal to Zeus in counsel
(twice in the *Iliad*)

Αἰνεία Τρώων βουληφόρε χαλκοχιτώνων
Aeneas, advisor of the bronze-shirted Trojans
(twice in the *Iliad*)

Since these lines are highly formulaic, any modification of

them is worth noting; let us list the instances that pertain to
Agamemnon. Reflecting upon the better luck of Achilles and
Odysseus, his shade replaces the usual vocatives with ὄλβιε
Πηλέος υἱὲ θεοῖς ἐπιείκελ' Ἀχιλλεῦ "fortunate son of Peleus,
godlike Achilles" (Od. 24.36) and ὄλβιε Λαέρταο πάι
πολυμήχαν' Ὀδυσσεῦ "fortunate child of Laertes, Odysseus
of many arts" (Od. 24.192); reflecting upon the better luck
of Agamemnon, Priam replaces the usual vocative with ὦ
μάκαρ Ἀτρεΐδη μοιρηγενὲς ὀλβιόδαιμον "O happy Atreides,
born to destiny, man of good fortune" (Il. 3.182). These exceptions are of some interest, but not of such interest as
another. When his refusal to return Chryseis is said, in the
first meeting of the Iliad, to be the cause of the plague,
Agamemnon agrees to give her up—on the condition that
another woman be found for him. And now Achilles speaks
in a manner we find impressive from our knowledge of the
epic idiom as a whole. Not Ἀτρεΐδη κύδιστε ἄναξ ἀνδρῶν
Ἀγάμεμνον "Atreides, most glorious, king of men Agamemnon," but Ἀτρεΐδη κύδιστε φιλοκτεανώτατε πάντων "Atreides,
most glorious, most covetous of all men" (Il. 1.122). I do not
know where we see more clearly the wrath announced in the
opening word of the poem.

One of the ordinary ways of expressing the concept king is
σκηπτοῦχος βασιλεύς "scepter-bearing king" (once in the
Iliad and twice in the Odyssey; cf. the plural σκηπτοῦχοι
βασιλῆες, likewise once in the Iliad, twice in the Odyssey). But
it would be wrong if that phrase occurred now, as a part of
the invective, and in fact it does not: Achilles speaks of
Agamemnon as a δημοβόρος βασιλεύς "folk-devouring king"
(Il. 1.231). To express the rancor of Achilles, the poet has
again departed from his usual idiom.

When Agamemnon has been denounced, in another meeting, for recommending that the war be abandoned, and

things are going badly for him, he is encouraged by Nestor, on the grounds of his being the "most royal" βασιλεύτατος (*Il.* 9.69), to take the lead in gathering ideas about what ought to be done; it is a diplomatic recommendation, not least in its use of this particular word. Soon afterwards, more privately, Nestor proposes that amends be promised to Achilles. Agamemnon makes the famous offer, and concludes: "Let him yield, and submit himself, since I am the more royal" βασιλεύτερος (*Il.* 9.160). Odysseus, Ajax, and Phoenix then go to the huts and the ships of the Myrmidons, and the offer is recounted—of many treasures, and Briseis, and one of Agamemnon's daughters in marriage, and seven cities. "Let him find another man for his daughter, one equal to him in rank, and more royal than I am" βασιλεύτερος (*Il.* 9.392) is the reply. The wrath of Achilles is now sullen, less passionate; but the matter of kingship is still the bone in his throat.

After Patroclus has been slain, and the Achaeans have convened in a further meeting, Achilles formally renounces his wrath, and Agamemnon repeats the offer of reconciliation. Nothing could be further from what Achilles wants at this time, and in asking that the army enter battle without delay he uses the formula Ἀτρείδη κύδιστε ἄναξ ἀνδρῶν Ἀγάμεμνον "Atreides, most glorious, king of men Agamemnon" (*Il.* 19.146, 19.199). It is significant that he does so; we may conclude that the relationship between them has been restored to what it ought to be. Agamemnon is truly, not in word only, the ἄναξ ἀνδρῶν among the Achaeans, and this fact pertains to the course of the *Iliad*.

Elsewhere we shall see other epithets that describe important figures with accuracy; unlike the phrase ἄναξ ἀνδρῶν Ἀγάμεμνον, however, they will not appear now used, now omitted, as the sense of the context demands.

II. πολύμητις for Odysseus

Not counting a single instance of the genitive πολυμήτιος, the epithet πολύμητις occurs eighty-six times, in the nominative only and for Odysseus alone. Since μῆτις means "counsel, plan" or "device, stratagem," πολύμητις may be taken in a good sense, "of many counsels," or in a bad sense, "of many devices," both applying well to the character of Odysseus. I shall consider him here solely with regard to what he says.

When Priam, in the View from the Wall, has learned to recognize Agamemnon, he asks who the man is that seems like a ram among ewes. (The simile is strong, even if we withhold judgment about whether the poet is alluding to the escape from the Cyclops' cave, in the *Odyssey*.) Helen replies that he is Odysseus, who knows all craft and cunning; and Antenor adds that in speech no one can equal him. "As he stands stiffly, his staff before him and his eyes downcast, you might take him for a clout; but when he speaks with his great voice from his chest, and his words fall like snowflakes on a winter's day, then no man is his like" (*Il.* 3.216–223, condensed). This estimate is actually similar to one made by Odysseus himself years later, when he distinguishes between ordinary-looking men whose grace lies in their words and men of extremely good looks who speak to no effect (*Od.* 8.167–175); the Phaeacian Euryalus he puts in the latter group, presumably thinking of himself in the former. Rightly so; no one else in the *Iliad*, not even Nestor, speaks with the same persuasiveness and force. When the Achaeans are rushing to the ships, it is Odysseus whom Athene urges to gather them back, and who reminds them of the prophecy that Troy should fall in the tenth year (*Il.* 2.166–332): it is good counsel and it saves an important day.

Odysseus' appeal to Achilles is a very fine speech indeed, emphasizing at both its start and its close the confidence of Hector (*Il.* 9.225–306); we were almost made to believe that things would turn out well. And just a few hours later the counsels or devices are brutally successful. Diomedes volunteers for a scouting mission, to hear some Trojan rumor or to catch some straggler, but asks for a companion since "the μῆτις of one man alone is often insufficient" (*Il.* 10.227). He is given the chance to name—from among the two Ajaxes, Meriones, Thrasymedes, Menelaus, and Odysseus—the man he wants to go with him, and decides that any choice other than Odysseus would be unreasonable. They overtake Dolon, and the questions are framed not by Diomedes, but by the man upon whose μῆτις he appeared to rely.

David B. Monro, ed. *Odyssey XIII–XXIV* (Oxford 1901) 291, suggested that the personal qualities of Odysseus, "the wisdom and eloquence by which he is distinguished in the *Iliad*, passed by an easy transition into the cleverness of a hero of adventures." Whether this is true or not, πολύμητις in the bad sense, "of many devices," does have some bearing on the lies of the *Odyssey*. Autolycus, a man known for his thievery and oaths, was allowed to name his new-born grandson, and replied: "I have come here angered against [ὀδυσσάμενος] many men and women throughout the fruitful earth; so let his name be Odysseus" (*Od.* 19.407–409). (The matter is elegantly discussed by George Dimock, "The Name of Odysseus," *The Hudson Review* 9 [1956] 52–70.) These are the beginnings from which we gather that Odysseus acquired the knack of lying as a matter of course. He lies to Polyphemus in the trick about Nobody (*Od.* 9.366–410), to Alcinous as well (*Od.* 7.304), and even to Laertes (*Od.* 24.244–279); and by repeatedly lying that he is a Cretan (*Od.* 13.256, 14.199, 19.172–181) he complicates the later

saying that all Cretans are liars. The words of Achilles or
Ajax we should always regard as true; those of Nestor or his
son Antilochus, as doubtful; those of Odysseus, as more
doubtful yet—indeed, we should often be judicious, from
what we know of him, in assuming they are untrue.

I do not believe anyone has remarked that the episode of
the Visit among the Dead may be partly a lie. According to
his account, Odysseus summoned up the shades by conjuring
in the manner Circe had recommended; Tiresias told him of
the dangers to be faced on the way home, and Anticleia told
of the ruinous conditions that we later find actually to exist
in Ithaca; then a procession of heroines filed past, as if in her
train. Here Odysseus breaks off his story, for the hour is late;
and during the following intermezzo in Scheria we have
the chance to reflect that the poet of the *Odyssey* has not been
describing the underworld in his own voice, though he will
do so later on (*Od.* 24.19–222). Alcinous raises the question
of veracity with great gentleness, declaring that those who
look at Odysseus do not regard him as a dissembler, or one
of those who create lies concerning the things that are not
common knowledge, but as a man whose words have form
and whose mind is steady (*Od.* 11.363–367). He compares
him to a bard—a remark perhaps to be explained from what
the Muses say to Hesiod: "We know how to speak many false
things that seem true, and also know how to speak true
things when we want to" (*Theogony* 27–28). Odysseus is now
asked to tell whether he also saw any of his comrades who
died at Troy, an invitation that cannot very well be declined;
and in the continuation certain inconsistencies have generally
been thought to appear.

Odysseus tells his listeners that he met Agamemnon,
Achilles, and Ajax, then saw Tityus, Tantalus, and Sisyphus
in their recurrent torment, and finally heard a gloomy

history from the wraith of Heracles—the wraith, because Heracles was actually among the gods all the while (*Od.* 11.602). There are difficulties here; for the great criminals are not pale spectres like Anticleia, but vigorous, full of life; and the idea that Heracles is in two places at once shatters whatever generalizations can be made about the Homeric ghost. The difficulties may be real; but we ought to consider that the narrative has been recounted by Odysseus, whose words are elsewhere no more than casually connected with the truth. If an untrustworthy witness, he is a charming guest; and in this episode, as throughout the *Iliad* and *Odyssey*, πολύμητις is a sign of his nature.

III. Τελαμώνιος for Ajax

Τελαμώνιος "Telamonian" is used for Ajax often, Τελαμωνιάδης "Telamoniades" and υἱὸς Τελαμῶνος "son of Telamon" less often; Τελαμώνιος and υἱὸς Τελαμῶνος are also used for Teucer. The oldest of these is almost certainly Τελαμώνιος. We can seldom or never estimate the *absolute* age of an epithet, or the phrase in which it occurs, but we can often speak confidently about *relative* age. For the Parry theory about the usefulness of the epithets (that they stretch out the names to standard sizes) depends largely upon phrases of $2\frac{1}{2}$ or $3\frac{1}{4}$ feet, in the nominative case. Because these two formula types appear to lie at the core of the formulaic style, a phrase belonging to either type is more likely to have engendered, than to have derived from, its synonyms of other lengths or in other cases. By this argument τλήμων Ὀδυσεύς "enduring Odysseus" is not so old as πολύτλας δῖος Ὀδυσσεύς "much-enduring brilliant Odysseus," nor πολυμήχαν' Ὀδυσσεῦ "Odysseus of many arts" so old as πολύμητις Ὀδυσσεύς "Odysseus of many counsels"; nor is Ἕκτορα

χαλκοκορυστήν "Hector of the bronze helmet" so old as
κορυθαίολος Ἕκτωρ "Hector of the flashing helmet." In
fact, κορυθαίολος Ἕκτωρ has a twofold claim to being of
great antiquity since it may, but need not, be augmented by
μέγας "great": κορυθαίολος Ἕκτωρ itself is 2½ feet in length,
μέγας κορυθαίολος Ἕκτωρ 3¼ feet. Precisely the same is true
for (μέγας) Τελαμώνιος Αἴας, which occurs nine times in the
briefer phrase and twelve more times in the longer. So in
assuming that Τελαμώνιος was used for Ajax before Τελαμωνιάδης and υἱὸς Τελαμῶνος were, we have every advantage.

Wilamowitz, *Homerische Untersuchungen* (Berlin 1884) 246,
conjectured that both Telamon and his post-Homeric grandson Eurysakes had names coined from the prominence of
Ajax as a shield warrior. Yet the names are not similar otherwise: while *Eurysakes* "Broadshield" is noble like most Greek
names, *Telamon* "Strap" refers to so minor a piece of equipment as to be unsuitable for a heroic figure. From this fact,
and from the fact of his obscurity, Telamon has been thought
to owe his existence to τελαμώνιος, which came to be understood as a patronymic, but originally referred to the telamon
of Ajax's shield; carrying a ponderous body shield he was a
huge and unmoving shield warrior. (See L. Preller,
Griechische Mythologie, vol. 2 *Die Heroen*, 4th ed. revised by
Carl Robert [Berlin 1923], book 3, part 2, p. 1039.) Yet a
quite different argument has equal merit. Since *Telamon* was
an architectural term for a colossal figure forming a pillar of
support, Telamon the father of Ajax had a noble name after
all, or else τελαμώνιος simply meant that Ajax himself was a
telamon—an enormous and impassive pillar or column, "a
giant, bulwark of the Achaeans" πελώριος, ἕρκος Ἀχαιῶν, as
he is said to be in the View from the Wall (*Il.* 3.229) and
elsewhere. (See Paul Girard, "Ajax fils de Télamon," *Revue
des études grecques* 18 [1905] 14–16.) But we have been dis-

cussing origins, and our question is what the epithet means
in the poetry. The Pelian ash of Achilles was cut from Mount
Pelion and given to Peleus (*Il*. 16.142–144 = 19.389–391);
these two facts are emphasized together and *Pelian* evidently
refers to both of them. So let much the same be said about
τελαμώνιος: the epithet is a patronymic, but it originally had,
and continues to have, one or more senses referring to the
shield for which Ajax is notable. (Nevertheless, I agree that
the *Iliad* contains some coincidences hardly to be explained—
in 13.693 the leader of the Phthians, a people ordinarily
under *Achilles*, is Ποδάρκης, the son of Iphiclus the son of
Phylacus.)

The telamon is a standard part of the Homeric shield
since, as many authorities have observed, in the two formulaic passages for the putting on of armor—the one used for
Paris (*Il*. 3.330–338), Agamemnon (*Il*. 11.17–43), Patroclus
(*Il*. 16.131–139), and Achilles (*Il*. 19.369–373); the other for
Teucer (*Il*. 15.479–482) and Odysseus (*Od*. 22.122–125)—
the shield is put on before the helmet. Such a procedure
would be irrational for arming with the hoplite shield, which
had no telamon and was always taken up last, an order of
events followed in the Hesiodic *Shield of Heracles*, 136–140. So
Ajax is not the only man whose shield hangs from a strap; on
the contrary, he resembles several others in this respect. But
he *is* the only man whose shoulder tires beneath the weight
of the shield (*Il*. 16.106–107), and the only man to be struck
where the two telamones—from his shield and from his
sword—cross on his chest (*Il*. 14.402–405). The equipment
mentioned by his epithet has indeed some bearing on his
career.

Nevertheless, it is the entire shield, not the telamon alone,
that Ajax is recognized by (*Il*. 11.527) and remembered for;
and the shield has the distinction of two special epithets. The

adverbial phrase ἠΰτε πύργον "like a tower" occurs only in
the repeated line Αἴας δ' ἐγγύθεν ἦλθε φέρων σάκος ἠΰτε
πύργον "and Ajax came near, carrying a shield like a tower"
(*Il.* 7.219 = 11.485 = 17.128); nothing similar is ever said
about anyone else, nor is anyone else spoken of as being a
tower himself (*Od.* 11.556). In the same way, the adjective
ἑπταβόειον "of seven oxen" is used repeatedly for Ajax's
shield, never for any other, and from the passage where its
occurrences are clustered (*Il.* 7.220–266) we learn that
Tychius, the best cutter of hides, made the shield, adding a
final layer of bronze—details of moment, since Hector's spear
shears through the bronze and the first six hides, but is
stopped by the *seventh* and last.

A fact of very great interest remains. (It was discovered by
J. G. Tayler, "Some Notes on the Homeric Shield,"
Classical Review 27 [1913] 222–225, and has more recently
been discussed by Hans Trümpy, *Kriegerische Fachausdrücke
im griechischen Epos* [Freiburg, Switz. 1950] 30–31.) The two
words for the shield, σάκος and ἀσπίς, are used with discrimination. The shield of Ajax is twenty-two times a sakos,
never an aspis. The shield of Achilles, made to replace the
one he has lost, is seventeen times a sakos, never the aspis that
Thetis asked for (*Il.* 18.458). Those of Hector and Aeneas,
mentioned thirteen and eight times respectively, are invariably aspides. This summary is impressive because no
other shield is referred to so often, except that Menelaus is
said eight times all told to have either a sakos or an aspis—
but the two words for his shield *never appear in the same passage*,
for the consistency in brief passages is absolute. There are
twenty-one instances in the *Iliad* where a given shield is
spoken of twice within five lines, and it is always a sakos or
an aspis, not both. (3.347–349 the aspis of Menelaus, 3.356–
357 the aspis of Paris, 5.297–300 the aspis of Aeneas, 7.219–

222 the sakos of Ajax, 7.250–251 the aspis of Hector,
7.270–272 the aspis of Hector, 8.267–268–272 the sakos of
Ajax, 11.434–435 the aspis of Odysseus, 12.402–404 the aspis
of Sarpedon, 13.157–160–163 the aspis of Deiphobus,
13.405–409 the aspis of Idomeneus, 13.561–565 the aspis of
Antilochus, 13.606–608 the sakos of Menelaus, 17.43–45 the
aspis of Menelaus, 17.128–132 the sakos of Ajax, 18.478–481
the sakos of Achilles, 18.607–608 the sakos of Achilles,
20.259–260–261 the sakos of Achilles, 20.274–277–278–281
the aspis of Aeneas, 21.164–165 the sakos of Achilles, 22.290–
291 the sakos of Achilles.) Only Paris (*Il.* 3.335–356) has a
sakos and an aspis within five hundred lines. One result of
the consistency is that the shields of different warriors can be
kept distinct. Menelaus and Paris, during their duel, do both
have aspides within eight lines (*Il.* 3.349–356), but within
seven lines the two words contrast without exception. In the
fourteenth book of the *Iliad* Nestor takes the sakos of Thrasymedes who has the aspis of his father (lines 9–11), and
Poseidon suggests that the better man with a small sakos
should take from the weaker man a large aspis (376–377).
In the thirteenth book Menelaus has a sakos (606–608) and
his opponent Peisander an aspis (611); in the twenty-third
book Diomedes has an aspis (818) and his opponent Ajax a
sakos (820). In the twentieth book Achilles has a sakos in
lines 259, 260, 261, and 268; then Aeneas an aspis in 274,
277, 278, and 281; then Achilles a sakos once more in 289.
In the seventh book Ajax has a sakos in 245, Hector an aspis
in 250 and 251, Ajax a sakos in 258, Hector an aspis in 260,
Ajax a sakos in 266, and Hector, finally, an aspis in 270 and
272. These statistics are not much of an addition to what we
knew before (Ajax and Achilles have sakea, Hector and
Aeneas aspides), but the contrasts show that the consistency
has its aesthetic value.

The sakea of Ajax and Achilles are the most important shields in the *Iliad*, and there is this connection between them: when the armor he lent to Patroclus has been lost, Achilles regards the sakos of Ajax as the only available piece that is adequate for his own needs (*Il.* 18.192–193). Otherwise the shields are dissimilar: the one is interesting for the episodes in which it figures, the other for the episodes in golden tableaux with which it is decorated. Teucer notches his arrows while crouching behind the shield of Ajax (*Il.* 8.266–272), and the two brothers regularly set out as a single engine of war (*Il.* 12.361–400); nothing could be more foreign to the character of Achilles. The companions of Ajax hold his shield when he is exhausted (*Il.* 13.709–711); but the shield of Achilles is not too heavy for him to have run with it a long time (see *Il.* 22.290, 22.314). So if the differences between the shields, or between the styles of shield warfare, are to be epitomized exactly, Idomeneus speaks for the *Iliad* as a whole: Ajax is equal to Achilles in close combat, but not in swiftness of feet (*Il.* 13.325)—a summary that answers to the implications of τελαμώνιος.

IV. ποδάρκης, πόδας ὠκύς for Achilles

Except for a single instance, from the *Odyssey*, of the accusative πόδας ὠκύν, the epithets πόδας ὠκύς and ποδάρκης, meaning "swift-footed" and occurring thirty and twenty-one times respectively, are limited to the *Iliad*, the nominative, and Achilles. But while saying that he is swift-footed they do not assert that all other men are slow. The *Iliad* as a whole tends to the same conclusion: as a fast runner Achilles may differ in degree but he does not differ in kind, and few things can be said about him that do not occasionally apply to someone else. He resembles a fast-running horse (*Il.*

22.22–24), but so do Paris and Hector (*Il.* 6.263–268 =
15.506–511); he trusts in his swiftness of foot (*Il.* 22.138), but
so does the sentinel Polites (*Il.* 2.792); and though he says
that Trojans flee before him (*Il.* 19.71–72), Diomedes says
more or less the same about himself (*Il.* 6.228). Yet Achilles
has this distinction: no one else gives chase in episodes of
such excitement and importance.

Let us consider an event for which we have two accounts,
one by the man who fled and one by him who pursued.
Coming upon Aeneas alone among the cattle, Achilles
chased him down Mount Ida (*Il.* 20.91, 20.188–189), and
Aeneas did not once look back (line 190). They ran to
Lyrnessus, which Achilles sacked, but Zeus helped Aeneas
and he escaped (92–93, 191–194). The incident did not end
with a spear between the shoulder blades; if asked who ran
the faster we may say it was Aeneas, not Achilles. Nevertheless, the intervention of Zeus has clouded the question, and
our impression is that in the normal course of things Aeneas
would have been not scot free but dead.

Not long after Aeneas has for a second time been rescued
from him by the gods, Achilles chases Agenor far afield,
while the other Trojans manage to reach the confines of the
city; yet once again we cannot say whether Achilles is the
faster, for it is actually not Agenor that he hounds, but
Apollo (*Il.* 21.600–22.13). Nor can we even tell conclusively
from the pursuit of Hector, for all the elegance of its similes,
whether πόδας ὠκύς and ποδάρκης are meaningless or apt.
The result is, Achilles does not catch him—"yet how could
Hector have escaped if Apollo had not made his knees
swift?" (*Il.* 22.204). We still have no proofs but only conceptions: mine is that the poet, though here concerned with
matters immeasurably more complex and momentous than
the characterization of men in accord with their epithets,

still regards the qualities denoted by the formulaic idiom as true.

Agamemnon is said to be ἄναξ ἀνδρῶν and κρείων, and in the View from the Wall we find that he really does look like a king on a battlefield of many princes. What we need to assess the accuracy of πόδας ὠκύς and ποδάρκης is similar testimony—and we have it in the remark of Idomeneus: "Ajax stands firm; not even to Achilles would he give way, at least in close fight, though in swiftness of foot no one compares with him" (*Il.* 13.324–325). It is true that Idomeneus himself is stiff-jointed and slow (*Il.* 13.512–515), but we do not have reason to suppose he has lost his sense of speed; and it happens that a fast man speaks about Achilles in much the same way. The smaller Ajax, who nine times has the epithet ταχύς "swift," and proves himself a good runner by his eminence in overtaking many Trojans (*Il.* 14.520–522), is one of the contestants in the foot race of the Funeral Games. Odysseus—whom we should not have regarded as a runner if he had not, in his night mission with Diomedes, chased the Trojan scout Dolon (*Il.* 10.360–364)—is another; and a third is Antilochus, who is said in a formulaic phrase to surpass other men in the swiftness of his running (*Od.* 3.112, 4.202; cf. *Il.* 23.756). We may perhaps expect swift Ajax to win, but Athene makes him slip on the dung from the bulls recently slain, and he comes in second, after Odysseus. That man has a green old age, says Antilochus in taking the last prize; "it would be hard for any Achaean to compete with him in racing, except Achilles" (*Il.* 23.791–792).

Throughout the larger part of the *Iliad* Achilles is not running but idle, and in many passages his epithets, if they make sense at all, can only mean that he is swift-footed by nature. Granted that he is, does he to our certain knowledge run faster than Aeneas or Hector or anyone else? No, he does not; we are less sure of his speed afoot than we are of his lineage or wrath or greatness as a warrior. Nevertheless, the epic matter leads us to believe that under ordinary circumstances no one is so ποδάρκης, πόδας ὠκύς as he.

V. κορυθαίολος for Hector

The epithet κορυθαίολος is used thirty-nine times for Hector and only once otherwise. The first element in the compound, κόρυς, means "helmet," though κορύσσεσθαι "to helm" can mean "to arm" with greaves, breastplate, sword, shield, helmet, and spear (Il. 16.130). The second element, αἰόλος, probably means "fast moving" in the phrase πόδας αἰόλος ἵππος "horse fast of foot" (Il. 19.404); and κορυθαίολος therefore seems to say that Hector has a helmet in rapid motion. Now his πήληξ "helmet" does shake as he fights (Il. 13.805, 15.608), but may not be unique in doing so, for Aeneas nods with his κόρυς (Il. 20.162) and so does Achilles (Il. 22.314). Even if the epithet refers to a helmet with a waving horsehair plume, Hector is no different from Paris, Agamemnon, Teucer, or Patroclus (Il. 3.337 = 11.42 = 15.481 = 16.138). But another meaning of αἰόλος, "flashing, glittering" like metal under the sun, is just as common in the Iliad (see 5.295, for example) and ought to be preferred here. For the distinctive epithets of a major figure tend to be synonyms (ποδάρκης and πόδας ὠκύς for Achilles are one instance among many), and κορυθαίολος can be explained from χαλκοκορυστής "of the bronze helmet," which is used seven times for Hector and only once else. Yet the individuality we expected to find is still missing. When Hector is struck on the head by the spear of Diomedes, bronze turns away bronze (Il. 11.351); but Damasus, Hippothous, Demoleon, and Eupeithes all have helmets with

2

cheekpieces of bronze (*Il.* 12.183, 17.294, 20.397, *Od.* 24.523). The line βῆ δὲ διὰ προμάχων κεκορυθμένος αἴθοπι χαλκῶι "helmeted in blazing bronze he went among the foremost" is used most often for Hector (*Il.* 5.681, 17.87, 17.592), but also used twice for Menelaus (*Il.* 5.562, 17.3) and once each for Aeneas (*Il.* 20.111, cf. 20.117) and Odysseus (*Il.* 4.495). And though Hector is rather frequently described as being φλογὶ εἴκελος "like a flame" (*Il.* 13.53, 13.688, 17.88, 18.154, 20.424), a phrase used elsewhere only once (*Il.* 13.330), Athene kindles a flame from the κόρυς and shield of Diomedes (*Il.* 5.4) and then still more resplendently from the bare head of Achilles (*Il.* 18.206–214, 18.225–227).

Nor will further analysis of the formulaic epic diction show clearly what makes Hector's helmet remarkable. Unlike Ajax's shield it has no special epithet. Unlike Ajax's shield and even Hector's own shield, it is not always referred to by a special noun: usually a κόρυς, as would be expected from κορυθαίολος, it is sometimes a πήληξ instead, or τρυφάλεια. And a survey of the episodes themselves is no more informative. Ajax's shield is of a known maker and known construction, and it holds our interest in certain passages about shield combat; Hector's helmet is not comparable in any of these respects. The truth may be that helmets as means of defence do not lead to heroic action—in the most striking incident where one is crucial to a man's life it works to his disadvantage: Menelaus drags Paris by the helmet until Aphrodite cuts the strap below the chin and saves him (*Il.* 3.369–376). Our results are negative so far: we have decided that κορυθαίολος refers, primarily, to a helmet of bronze, though perhaps also to a helmet somehow in motion; but we have not seen that the epithet pertains in any meaningful way to Hector. Only one passage is worth attention, and its force is entirely emotional: "Hector reaches to take

Astyanax, but the little boy pulls back to the bosom of his
nurse, crying, frightened by the bronze and by the horsehair
plume nodding from the helmet; then Hector laughs and
lays the helmet, brightly shining, on the ground, and kisses
the boy and caresses him" (*Il.* 6.466–474, condensed).
Astyanax loves his father, but as a father rather than a
soldier; Hector unsoldiers himself by putting the helmet
aside; and this episode, where the flashing helmet is memorable, goes far towards explaining why we have greater
sympathy, greater concern, for Hector than for anyone else
in the *Iliad*.

VI. $\iota\pi\pi\acute{o}\delta\alpha\mu o s$ for Diomedes and $\iota\pi\pi\acute{o}\tau\alpha$ for Nestor

Six epithets that refer to mastery over horses—$\iota\pi\pi\acute{o}\delta\alpha\mu o s$,
$\iota\pi\pi\acute{o}\tau\alpha$, $\iota\pi\pi\eta\lambda\acute{a}\tau\alpha$, $\iota\pi\pi\epsilon\acute{v}s$, $\iota\pi\pi o\kappa\acute{\epsilon}\lambda\epsilon\upsilon\theta o s$, and $\pi\lambda\acute{\eta}\xi\iota\pi\pi o s$—are
used (in the aggregate) far more often for Nestor than for
anyone else, and next most often for Diomedes. Not surprisingly, these two men are prominent where horses figure
in the *Iliad*, and it is to them that we shall restrict ourselves,
though $\iota\pi\pi\acute{o}\delta\alpha\mu o s$ and its synonyms are also used with fairly
notable frequency for Patroclus, Peleus, and Hector, men
whose association with horses is sometimes significant.
Neither the horses of Nestor nor those of Diomedes have the
celebrity of the twelve known to us by name (Aethe, Aethon,
Arion, Balius, Pedasus, Phaethon, and two each named
Lampus, Xanthus, and Podargus), except that Arion belonged to Diomedes' father-in-law, Adrestus; but they do
occasionally have the distinction of special epithets. The
gods drive $\chi\rho\upsilon\sigma\acute{a}\mu\pi\upsilon\kappa\alpha s$ $\iota\pi\pi o\upsilon s$ "horses with frontlets of
gold," not mere $\kappa\rho\alpha\tau\epsilon\rho\acute{\omega}\nu\upsilon\chi\alpha s$ $\iota\pi\pi o\upsilon s$ "horses with strong
hooves"; the horses of Nestor are $N\eta\lambda\acute{\eta}\iota\alpha\iota$ $\iota\pi\pi o\iota$ "mares of
Neleus" (*Il.* 11.597), not mere $\kappa\alpha\lambda\lambda\acute{\iota}\tau\rho\iota\chi\epsilon s$ $\iota\pi\pi o\iota$ "horses of

fair mane"; and those of Diomedes are Τρώιοι ἵπποι or
ἵππους ... Τρωιούς "horses of Tros" (*Il.* 8.106, cf. 23.378;
and 23.291), probably instead of μώνυχες ἵπποι "horses of
undivided hooves" and ἵππους ... ξανθούς "horses of sandy
color." This last example is especially provocative; let us recall how the horses of the horse-breaking Trojans came into
the possession of Diomedes, breaker of horses.

On his day of great success in battle, Diomedes stands
against the chariot driven by Phegeus and Idaeus; he kills
Phegeus and sends the horses to the Achaean ships (*Il.* 5.26).
Soon afterwards he kills Echemmon and Chromius in their
chariot, and gives the horses to his comrades, to be sent to
the ships. He is not without horses of his own—Pandarus
identifies him to Aeneas by his shield and helmet and horses
(*Il.* 5.183)—but he fights all the while on foot. (On the lack
of chariot combat in the *Iliad*, see G. S. Kirk, *The Songs of
Homer* [Cambridge 1962] 124.) Horses of great worth are
now near by, and Diomedes proposes to Sthenelus that they
capture them. Erichthonius, the father of Tros, was famous
for horses that could gallop over the breakers of the sea
(*Il.* 20.221–229), and to Tros, in recompense for Ganymedes,
Zeus gave the finest horses under the sun—from these were
bred the horses of Aeneas, which are the ones Diomedes
wishes to take as prizes of war (*Il.* 5.265–273). Standing
against the chariot driven by Aeneas and Pandarus, he
cripples the one after killing the other, and Sthenelus sends
the horses to the ships. Horses of Tros now belong not only
to the Trojans (see *Il.* 16.393), but to Diomedes as well, and
will pull his chariot in later adventures.

The other Achaeans are retreating, and Nestor, his
chariot unmanageable because one of the horses has been
struck in the brain with an arrow, is about to lose his life;
but Diomedes saves him: "Climb into my chariot, and see

how well the horses of Tros know the plain" (*Il.* 8.106). They
drive against Hector, and Diomedes kills his charioteer; but
a flash of lightning frightens their horses, and Nestor, after
dropping the reins, urges that they turn back. Is Diomedes
unmatched for his horsemanship? Perhaps not, but he is the
eminent horseman among Ajax, Odysseus, and most of the
others.

On a scouting mission at night, Diomedes and Odysseus
overtake the Trojan spy Dolon, and learn the whereabouts
of the Thracians, whose king, Rhesus, has horses whiter than
snow. Diomedes kills Dolon, they strip him, and Odysseus
puts the clothing and weapons on a tamarisk bush (*Il.*
10.466). They enter the Thracian camp, where every man
has his horses beside him, Rhesus with his horses in the
midst—this is the pair (for the number see line 530) that
Diomedes and Odysseus intend to take as spoils. Diomedes
kills the men one by one, and Odysseus drags off the bodies,
so that the horses, when led away, will not be perplexed.
Last of all they come to Rhesus, and Diomedes kills him too,
while Odysseus, forgetting to take a whip from the chariot,
drives off the horses with his bow (line 500). They return to
the tamarisk bush, and Diomedes takes up what they had
left there, giving it to Odysseus; finally both ride horseback
(see line 541) to the ships. What is the connection between
this episode and the epithet ἱππόδαμος? It lies chiefly in the
conclusion: Odysseus puts the clothing and weapons of
Dolon on the stern of his ship, after the horses of Rhesus have
been taken to the trough of the horses of Diomedes (line 568).

In the chariot race honoring Patroclus, the foremost con-
tenders are Diomedes, with the horses of Tros (*Il.* 23.291),
and Eumelus, with the best of the horses the Achaeans had
brought to Troy, mares Apollo had raised in Pereia (*Il.*
2.764–766). Eumelus is at once in the front, Diomedes is

about to overtake him, Apollo knocks the lash from the hand of Diomedes, and Athene breaks the yoke in the chariot of Eumelus (*Il.* 23.392); the result is no longer in doubt. Why has not Eumelus won? There are general principles involved: Athene is ordinarily more successful than Apollo, and the better-known man more successful than the less well known. But a further principle, one more decisive yet, is involved here: the character or nature or accomplishment of a major figure is significantly related to his epithets, not always but very often. In a later story, Dido will ask what the horses of Diomedes were like (*Aeneid* 1.752)—a question that turns upon the suitability of ἱππόδαμος in the *Iliad*.

Nestor is a connoisseur of horses, for it is he, rather than any other Achaean, who admires the quality of the horses of Rhesus brought back by Diomedes and Odysseus. But he is competent still as a horseman himself, and at times we see him with his chariot in the foremost part of the battle: once he almost loses his life when one of his horses has been struck with an arrow (*Il.* 8.81), and on another occasion he drives the wounded Machaon to the ships (*Il.* 11.17–20). But his greatest deeds are those he tells of, deeds that happened, if at all, in the past. When he was a young man, the Epeians had slain his brothers, and Augeias, the king of Elis, had kept back four fine horses belonging to Neleus. The Pylians drove off cattle and sheep in reprisal, and in the local war that followed, Nestor was eminent among the horsemen—even though he was on foot, since Neleus had hidden away his horses. On that day Nestor was the first to kill an enemy and take his horses; and this accomplishment he repeated fifty times before the battle dispersed and the horses were driven to Pylos. The sons of Actor escaped, for Poseidon saved them; but nothing else marred the success of the morning (*Il.* 11.692–761). This is the man he was; but in the events now

taking place his role is to advise the charioteers and en-
courage them, since old age has come upon him (*Il.* 4.293–
323).

When Antilochus has entered the chariot race in honor of
Patroclus, Nestor warns him that his horses are slow, and
that he must compete by ingenuity rather than strength, and
take advantage when he has the chance to do so. Antilochus
does then drive in this manner, making the best use of irregu-
larities in the road, and from his skill and aggressiveness he
carries off the second prize. It is altogether an exciting race,
partly because of Diomedes and Eumelus, but equally because of Antilochus and Menelaus; and the epithets that
describe Nestor as a horseman are confirmed by the results
of his advice.

To him, now past the age of an athlete, Achilles gives the
last prize, unclaimed. Nestor takes it gladly, and tells how
years before, in other funeral games, he won every contest,
except that the sons of Actor—who here as elsewhere are a
bad memory—competed strenuously, we gather unfairly, in
the chariot race, and won the richest prize of all (*Il.* 23.626–
640). It is perhaps not unreasonable to assume that from this
experience Nestor learned the tactics he recommended to
Antilochus.

VII. ἑκάεργος for Apollo

The roughly synonymous epithets ἑκάεργος, ἕκατος,
ἑκηβόλος, ἑκατηβόλος, and ἑκατηβελέτης are used, as a group,
with considerable frequency, and always for Apollo. Though
what some of them meant originally is uncertain, it is not
seriously inaccurate to translate them as "far working" or
"far shooting." Apollo is also described as ἀργυρότοξος "of
the silver bow," and we hear about his silver bow in other

lines besides. Similarly, ἰοχέαιρα is restricted to Artemis, and may be translated approximately as "shooter of arrows." These descriptions all pertain to the idea that Apollo brings death to men (e.g. *Od.* 3.279, 7.64), and Artemis to women (e.g. *Il.* 6.428, *Od.* 11.172, 11.198, 11.324, 15.478; but see *Od.* 5.123). Niobe said that her children were more numerous than the two of Leto, and these two killed them all, Apollo the sons and Artemis the daughters (*Il.* 24.602–609); Hector lies fresh as dew, like one slain by the gentle arrows of Apollo (*Il.* 24.758).

In the Homeric idiom, "I wish Artemis would strike me" (*Od.* 18.202, 20.60, 20.80), "I wish Artemis had struck her" (*Il.* 19.59), and "I hope Apollo strikes him" (*Od.* 17.251, 17.494) are so conventional as to need no comment. Yet the last of these is at one point a matter of consequence: "If ever I burned to you the thighs of bulls or goats, avenge my tears with your arrows." Apollo comes from Olympus with his bow and quiver, the arrows rattling as he makes his way. Sitting down apart from the ships he releases an arrow, and the silver bow is terrible to hear. First he strikes the mules and dogs, but then the men; and the pyres of the dead burn everywhere (*Il.* 1.37–52). In this passage his archery is not alluded to; it is a fact; and nothing we know about Apollo is more descriptive of his nature or more important.

When Chryseis has been returned, her father prays that the pestilence be averted; Apollo hears him; and the Achaeans make sacrifice and sing the paean (*Il.* 1.473), a song bearing the name of Paean, the healer of the gods (*Il.* 5.401, 5.899–900). We may conclude that in one of his aspects Apollo himself is a healer, not only here but as a rule, and such in fact he appears to be (see *Il.* 16.529–530). He sends the plague and withdraws it, inflicts wounds and binds them up. The one art leads to the other, and from his role as the far worker or far archer is derived the Oath of Hippocrates: "I swear by Apollo the Physician." But why do the Achaeans *sing* the paean, why is the paean a song? Perhaps because Apollo himself is a musician, laying aside his bow for a lyre (*Il.* 1.603)—one stringed instrument for another.

The career of Apollo is not summed up by the epithets that refer to his archery: certainly they have nothing to do with his concern for the horses of Eumelus (*Il.* 2.763–767, 23.383–384). Nevertheless, as Artemis makes true the arrows of the hunter (see *Il.* 5.49–54), Apollo has the right to guide those of the warrior; and this general truth explains a good deal. We all know perfectly well what it will be that causes the death of Achilles: it will be Paris, and an arrow in the heel. But Thetis said it would be the arrows of Apollo (*Il.* 21.276–277), and Hector believes it will be Paris and Apollo together (*Il.* 22.359–360). The whole fact of the matter is that Paris will release the arrow and Apollo send it to the mark. And since Pandarus himself had killed the goat from whose horns his bow was made (*Il.* 4.105–111), that Apollo gave him the bow (*Il.* 2.827) must mean that he gave him the skill of an archer; so it is right that Pandarus should pray to Apollo for aid (*Il.* 4.119–121, cf. 4.101–103) and credit to him his own measure of success (*Il.* 5.105). Such prayer is important: the difference between Meriones and Teucer, in the archery contest in the Funeral Games, is that the one remembers Apollo and the other does not (*Il.* 23.861–881)— with the result that Meriones takes up the double axes which are the first prize. These incidents are all vivid, some will say unforgettable; but if we ask what association of ideas (see *Od.* 19.573–578, 21.76–421) may have led the poet to choose *axes* as the prize, we recall where Apollo and archery have their closest connection of all.

Whereas Idas appears to have done well in taking the bow

to withstand Apollo for the sake of Marpessa (*Il.* 9.558–560), Eurytus challenged him to an archery contest from presumption alone, so far as we can tell, and Apollo killed him in anger (*Od.* 8.226–228). Eurytus left his bow to Iphitus, who gave it to Odysseus in friendship (*Od.* 21.31). He did not take it to Troy, however (*Od.* 21.38–40)—the bow he uses there (*Il.* 10.513–514) was lent to him by Meriones (*Il.* 10.260)—and when it comes into his hands again he examines it all over to see whether worms have eaten the horn in his absence (*Od.* 21.393–395). These details mesh together—and there is one more, no less significant. *When* does he take up his bow again, on what day of the year? It is on the feast day of Apollo (*Od.* 20.276–278, 21.258). At a critical moment Odysseus hopes for his aid (*Od.* 22.7), and the rest does not need retelling.

VIII. Further examples and exceptions

The epithets we have been examining pertain to unchanging character but not necessarily to context: ἱππότα "horseman" is a good description for Nestor because he surpasses most other men in his knowledge of horses; but it would be wrong to say that he is described as ἱππότα in precisely those situations where his knowledge becomes most clearly evident. Now several additional epithets, worthy of being mentioned only hurriedly, are similarly true to character, though not necessarily relevant to context. Zeus is always and by nature a νεφεληγερέτα "cloud-gatherer," and wraps Hera about with a golden cloud (*Il.* 14.342–351) to hide their love-making from the sight of the sun. Hephaestus is rightly said to be κυλλοποδίων "crook-footed" and κλυτοτέχνης "famous workman," since his mother once wished to hide him for being a cripple (*Il.* 18.395) and since

he forges the shield of Achilles. Poseidon is ἐνοσίχθων and
ἐννοσίγαιος, both meaning "shaker of the earth," and he does
shake the earth on occasion (*Il.* 20.57–63). Eumaeus is said
to be ὑφορβός, συφορβός, and συβώτης, all meaning "swine-
herd," and he does in fact tend swine (*Od.* 13.407–410).
Eurycleia has the epithet τροφός "nurse, wet-nurse," and
was the wet-nurse of Odysseus (*Od.* 19.482–483). Aegisthus
is δολόμητις "of deceitful plan," and about all we know of
him is that he prepares death for Agamemnon. Circe is
πολυφάρμακος "adept in drugs," and Phoenix, παλαιγενής
"greybeard"; we do not need to say why. Such longer
epithets as Ἑλένης πόσις ἠϋκόμοιο "husband of fair-tressed
Helen" for Paris, and Θέτιδος πάϊς ἠϋκόμοιο "child of fair-
tressed Thetis" for Achilles, also belong to this class. So do
all the epithets that are patronymic; so also do ναυσικλυτοί
"famed for ships," δολιχήρετμοι "of long oars," and φιλήρετ-
μοι "fond of the oar," for the Phaeacians; and likewise with
a great number of others.

We may have reservations about saying the same for
θεοειδής "godlike." Nearly all the epithets we have inspected
are largely or absolutely limited to one figure. An exception
is ἱππόδαμος "breaker of horses," which is used in the singular, in the *Iliad* and *Odyssey* together, eight times for
Diomedes, but also five times for Hector, and once or twice
each for several other men. Yet θεοειδής is used even more
widely and evenly: ten times for Paris, but also eight times
for Priam, and five times each for Telemachus and Theoclymenus, as well as once or twice each for several others.
In being described as θεοειδής, Paris is by no means unusual;
and yet the epithet does apply very well to his particular
character. Hector twice chafes him for being a man whose
courage does not match his εἶδος, or appearance (*Il.* 3.45,
3.55), and twice else addresses him with the full line Δύσπαρι

εἶδος ἄριστε γυναιμανὲς ἠπεροπευτά "Paris of bad name, very
fine to look at, woman-mad, seducer" (Il. 3.39, 13.769), a
formulaic vocative that is, for Paris, the counterpart of
"Atreides, most glorious, king of men Agamemnon"—and it
too is once replaced, but by an even more forcible synonym,
spoken by Diomedes: τοξότα λωβητὴρ κέραι ἀγλαὲ παρθενο-
πῖπα "bowman, braggart, curly-locks, ogler at girls" (Il.
11.385). The first time we see Paris in the Iliad he wears a
panther hide about his shoulders, along with a bow and a
sword, and brandishing two spears he challenges the
Achaeans to battle (Il. 3.17–20). Though inadequate for
close combat his costume is very good looking, and θεοειδής,
whether or not it describes others besides, has its merits for
him. All the same, whatever features the epithet denotes, they
belong to many men. Hector himself is stung into bravery
by the words εἶδος ἄριστε "very fine to look at" (Il. 17.142),
and later the Achaeans marvel at the εἶδος of his corpse
(Il. 22.370). Judged according to his εἶδος, Euryalus is
second among the Phaeacians, after Laodamas (Od. 8.116),
and Ajax is second among the Achaeans, after Achilles (Il.
17.280 = Od. 11.470 = 11.551 = 24.18). The quality is
generic for heroes; would not the epithet be consistent with
what we know of Odysseus? Such a demurrer must be filed;
θεοειδής for Paris is not one of the great epithets, but it is a
good one.

Because the epithet βοὴν ἀγαθός "good at the war cry" is
used often for Menelaus or Diomedes, and seldom for anyone else, we might expect that these two would shout more
loudly than other men, or to greater effect; but the predic-
tion would be wrong. It is true that Ajax—rather than do so
himself—asks Menelaus to call for reinforcements (Il. 17.236–
247), and it is true that Diomedes not only shouts at
Aphrodite (Il. 5.347) but shouts so as to be recognized by

his *voice* as he drives his horses down the return stretch in the chariot race of the Funeral Games (*Il.* 23.452). But Hector (*Il.* 8.160, 17.183, 18.156), Agamemnon (*Il.* 8.227), Odysseus (*Il.* 11.461), and many others shout effectively; Stentor has a voice like bronze; and when Achilles shouts the Trojan horses are thrown into confusion (*Il.* 18.217–231). We cannot say that Menelaus and Diomedes are distinguished among warriors in the way their epithet implies. Nor do we have evidence that the use of καλλιπάρῃος "lovely of cheek" for Briseis is either especially fitting or especially poignant; she tears her breast and neck and beautiful face in grief (*Il.* 19.284–285), but to do so seems customary (see *Il.* 2.700, 11.393). The epithet γλαυκῶπις "of the bright eyes" tells us little about Athene that is relevant to Homeric poetry. She does have bright eyes, ὄσσε φαεινώ (*Il.* 21.415), but so do Zeus (*Il.* 13.3–7, 14.236, 16.645) and Menelaus (*Il.* 17.679); and though Achilles recognizes her by her eyes (*Il.* 1.200), Helen recognizes Aphrodite in the same way (*Il.* 3.397). And Menelaus, who has a strong claim upon ξανθός "sandy," must share the sandy color of his hair, if that is what the epithet denotes, with both Achilles (*Il.* 1.197, 23.141) and Odysseus (*Od.* 13.399–431). These epithets—βοὴν ἀγαθός, καλλιπάρῃος, γλαυκῶπις, and ξανθός—refer to qualities that are not possessed in an unusual manner by the figures so described. In addition, several epithets—such as ἄλκιμος "valiant," κρατερός "powerful," μενεπτόλεμος "staunch in war," μενεχάρμης "staunch in battle," μεγαλήτωρ "greathearted," and ἀντίθεος "equal to the gods"—are so vague, so generally heroic, as to denote qualities shared by a great number of men in either epic. Yet I do not claim that all the epithets are exemplified, or illustrated, in episodes, but only that many of them are (and among these, several of the most memorable). When every limitation and caveat is given its due weight, Odysseus continues to strike us as a man more deserving of πολύμητις than anyone else, and so with κορυθαίολος and the other epithets we have considered at length.

Parry, *L'Épithète traditionnelle* 182–183, reasoned that ἄναξ ἀνδρῶν "king of men," which describes certain minor figures in the *Iliad*, must have described several more in the entire domain of the oral tradition, and therefore had no special pertinence to Agamemnon. But in reply we note that κυδιάνειρα "where men win glory" does not appreciably lose its distinction, as an epithet for battle, by being once applied to the assembly. Since ἄναξ ἀνδρῶν is used, in the *Iliad*, nine times as often for Agamemnon as for the sum of other men, and forty-four times as often for him as for any one of them, our initial assumption ought to be that the title is his. Only if we discovered that, in another poem, it regularly accompanied the name of some further *major* figure, would there be reason to change our minds. But no one is ἄναξ ἀνδρῶν in the *Odyssey* besides Agamemnon, and no one at all is κορυθαίολος or ποδάρκης. So far as we can reach a decision it must be that a man of importance did not share his chief epithets with another man of importance, either in the same poem or anywhere else in the entire tradition. That Aeneas is once ἄναξ ἀνδρῶν can therefore be taken to mean that he was never of the first rank. But from the restriction of πολύτλας "much-enduring" to Odysseus, and from the rather poor sense it makes in the *Iliad*, we should have been able to postulate the existence of an *Odyssey* if none had survived.

Parry, *L'Épithète traditionnelle* 232–235, found no reason why ἱππόδαμος "breaker of horses," which describes Diomedes and several others, was not also used, instead of ἀντίθεος "equal to the gods," for Odysseus. But would the epithets really apply as well to one man as to another? To some extent they would indeed; yet their promiscuity has its limits, and we can see why Diomedes is ἱππόδαμος but Odysseus not, even though they both ride horseback on return from the night mission (*Il.* 10.541). For Diomedes proves himself a fine charioteer in the Funeral Games, his corral at Troy contains many fine horses, and his homeland Argos is ἱππόβοτος "good pasture for horses." But Odysseus has no horses at Troy, so far as we know, *nor are there ever any mentioned as being in Ithaca,* an island explicitly unfit for them (*Od.* 4.606–608, 13.242). To replace the final member of Ὀδυσῆος ἀμύμονος ἀντιθέοιο "of faultless Odysseus, equal to the gods" (*Od.* 19.456) with ἱπποδάμοιο would be as senseless as to make the same change in Κύκλωπος . . . μεγαλήτορος ἀνδροφάγοιο "of the Cyclops . . . great-hearted man-eater" (*Od.* 10.200).

The epithets in two other phrases—Ἀλέξανδρος θεοειδής "godlike Paris" and Ἀντίλοχος μενεχάρμης "Antilochus staunch in battle"—are reasonable; but Ἀλέξανδρος μενεχάρμης "Paris staunch in battle" would be a contradiction in terms. No less so would be Τηλέμαχος δουρικλυτός, a composite of Τηλέμαχος πεπνυμένος "Telemachus the wise" and Ἰδομενεὺς δουρικλυτός "Idomeneus spear-famed." Hector is known for his helmet and Ajax for his shield, so κορυθαίολος Ἕκτωρ "Hector of the flashing helmet" and τελαμώνιος Αἴας "Ajax of the shield strap" are admirable, whereas τελαμώνιος Ἕκτωρ and κορυθαίολος Αἴας would be difficult to understand.

My last examples are taken from πόδας ὠκὺς Ἀχιλλεύς "swift-footed Achilles," πολύμητις Ὀδυσσεύς "Odysseus of many counsels," γλαυκῶπις Ἀθήνη "Athene of the bright eyes," and ἑκάεργος Ἀπόλλων "far working Apollo." Omitting γλαυκῶπις, we have nine new combinations; let us comment on them quickly. ἑκάεργος Ἀθήνη, meaningless.

ἑκάεργος 'Οδυσσεύς, strangely felicitous but inferior to
πολύμητις 'Οδυσσεύς. ἑκάεργος 'Αχιλλεύς, false (Achilles is a
spearman, not a bowman). πόδας ὠκὺς 'Απόλλων, acceptable
(Apollo in the guise of Agenor leads Achilles in chase) but
inferior to ἑκάεργος 'Απόλλων. πόδας ὠκέ' 'Αθήνη, meaningless. πόδας ὠκὺς 'Οδυσσεύς, acceptable (Odysseus wins the
foot race in the Funeral Games) but inferior to πολύμητις
'Οδυσσεύς. πολύμητις 'Απόλλων, acceptable but inferior to
ἑκάεργος 'Απόλλων. πολύμητις 'Αθήνη, excellent. πολύμητις
'Αχιλλεύς, ruinously false (Achilles is an athlete in pursuit of
those who flee before him. He is certainly not a man of counsels or devices. We cannot refer to the words with which he
rejects the offer of the embassy—"Hateful to me as the gates
of Hades is the man who hides one thing in his mind and says
another" [Il. 9.312–313]—for Odysseus declares much the
same in bad faith [Od. 14.156–157]; we remark only that
Achilles does not need to deceive and never does). What
could be less Homeric than πολύμητις 'Αχιλλεύς, or κορυθαίολος Αἴας, or Τηλέμαχος δουρικλυτός, or 'Αλέξανδρος
μενεχάρμης? Must we go so far as to take from Aphrodite the
epithet "laughter-loving" and consider φιλομμειδὴς 'Αγαμέμνων?

I have not considered here whether the epithets are relevant to context, nor have I denied that they were useful for
filling out a line. I agree that the poet did not continually ask
himself, "Would *much-enduring brilliant Odysseus* or *Odysseus of
many counsels* make the better sense?" My conclusion—that
a major epithet is true to the character of the figure whose
name it accompanies—is not a contradiction against but an
addition to the formula theory. And the conclusion may well
affect our idea of how the *Iliad* and *Odyssey* were created.

Two / The epithets for the heroes of the *Iliad* influenced their characterization.

In the sixth chapter of his *History and the Homeric Iliad* (Berkeley and Los Angeles 1963), Denys Page argues two closely related theses: that certain phrases describing old-fashioned objects—such as σάκος ἑπταβόειον "shield of seven oxen" and σάκος ἠύτε πύργον "shield like a tower," both for the shield of Ajax—have lain imbedded in the formulaic style ever since the Mycenaean era, and that many of the personal epithets—such as κορυθαίολος "of the flashing helmet" and χαλκοκορυστής "of the bronze helmet," both for Hector—record historical truths about men who fought at Troy. One of the most careful reviewers—Sterling Dow in the *American Journal of Philology* 83 (1962) 97—remarks that the chapter is perhaps the best in the book. On the contrary, it is perhaps far from the best; but it would be the best in most Homer books, and to discredit the sections on Ajax and Hector, as I shall try to do, will be no easy task. I must make the attempt, however, by way of laying the groundwork for a theory of another kind.

I. The age of ἑπταβόειον and ἠύτε πύργον as special descriptions for the shield of Ajax

Page comments (p. 234) upon the fact that Ajax is the only man whose shield is ἑπταβόειον "of seven oxen" and carried ἠύτε πύργον "like a tower": "This remarkable consistency is not fortuitous: what the traditional phrases have preserved is not only the Mycenaean shield but also the name of the Mycenaean hero with whom alone it is associated." This implies, and may state explicitly, that the phrases σάκος ἑπταβόειον and σάκος ἠύτε πύργον were restricted to the shield of Ajax *during the Mycenaean era*. Though much can be said in favor of such a conclusion, our first long objective is to decide against it: we shall see that the *Iliad* refers to shields with an exactitude almost certainly unknown in the poetry of the earlier age.

a. Do the monuments define the sakos and the aspis?

The standard authority was Wolfgang Reichel, *Homerische Waffen* (Vienna 1901); now it is H. L. Lorimer, *Homer and the Monuments* (London 1950) 132–192; and the details I cite are taken from her work and ultimately from his. As judged by their appearance from the back, the shields on the "lion-hunt" dagger blade, from Late Helladic I or ca. 1600 B.C., are of two varieties: the "figure-of-eight" narrows in its middle; the "tower" has straight sides and an arched top. Where shown in profile here and elsewhere (on plaque-bead and signet ring), both varieties curve about the body of the warrior. No grip is visible on either, and none seems needed; each hangs by a *telamon* or strap over the *left* shoulder of a right-handed man. Ajax too carries his sakos ἠύτε πύργον "like a tower," and its weight causes his *left* shoulder to tire

(*Il.* 16.106–107). Two round and apparently flat types of shield are to be seen on the Warrior Vase from Mycenae, of LH 3 or ca. 1200 B.C. (but the smaller is warped along the bottom and may be the figure-of-eight shield folded for transport: see John L. Myres, "The Structure and Origin of the Minoan Body-Shield," *Man* 39 [1939] 39). One of the larger size has a grip not in use and must consequently be presumed to be hanging by a telamon: a right-handed man would hold the grip in his left hand, and the telamon might conceivably lie over his *right* shoulder. Diomedes, for example, cools the wound irritated by the sweat beneath the telamon of his ἀσπίδος εὐκύκλου "well-rounded shield" (*Il.* 5.797), after his *right* shoulder has been injured by an arrow (5.98). Certain provisional identifications can be made accordingly: the sakos (of Ajax) with the "tower" dagger-blade shield, the aspis (of Diomedes) with the larger Warrior Vase shield, and neither the sakos nor the aspis with the shield of the hoplite.

So neat an hypothesis is regrettably untenable. Ajax carries his sakos ἠύτε πύργον "like a tower" in *Iliad* 17.128 but uses a σάκος εὐρύ "broad shield" to cover Patroclus four lines later; Aeneas is struck on his ἀσπίδα πάντοσ' ἐΐσην "shield in all ways equal" in *Iliad* 20.274, two circles being ripped from the ἀσπίδος ἀμφιβρότης "shield that covers the body on both sides" seven lines later. The one shield is broad at the same time as it is tall; the other bends about the body even while being round. Nor do the two nouns themselves, quite aside from their epithets, denote shields of two clearly different kinds. The aspis that flays the neck and ankles of Hector (*Il.* 6.117) and the aspis that Periphetes trips over (*Il.* 15.646)—though I am unable to see why they cannot be like those depicted on the Warrior Vase—are generally thought similar to the shields of the dagger blade and hence to the sakos carried ἠύτε πύργον "like a tower." Achilles holds

his sakos ἀπὸ ἕο "away from himself," as if it has a grip
(*Il.* 20.261); Deiphobus holds his aspis ἀπὸ ἕο in just the same
manner (*Il.* 13.163). The monuments tell us a great deal that
is important about the Homeric shield, but they do not say
how the sakos may be unlike the aspis. The difficulty is that
there are sakea of at least two kinds and aspides of at least
two kinds. So any argument that defines these words further
is most welcome, especially one based upon the theory of a
continuous oral tradition.

b. Do their epithets distinguish the sakos from the aspis?

In a paper on "Homeric Epithets for Things," *Classical
Quarterly* 41 (1947) 109–121, D. H. F. Gray examines all the
epithetic phrases used for the sea, the helmet, and the shield,
initially classifying them as "traditional" (that is, common)
or "individual" (that is, uncommon), but modifying this
straightforward dualism later on. In discussing the shield she
implies three general theorems and draws their specific con-
sequences. First, a phrase must be unusually modern if its
epithet is widely used with other nouns; hence unusual
modernity can be assigned to all the phrases that speak of
the shield as being metallic. Secondly, a phrase must be
archaic if it occurs rarely and if its epithet is seldom used
with other nouns; hence σάκος ἠύτε πύργον "shield like a
tower" and ἀσπίδος ἀμφιβρότης "shield that covers the body
on both sides," which apparently refer to the dagger-blade
varieties of the body shield, are of exceptionally remote
antiquity. Thirdly, a phrase must have been coined when the
formulas were at their greatest intensity of development and
standardization if it occurs often and if its epithet is seldom
used with other nouns; hence σάκος μέγα τε στιβαρόν τε
"shield both large and tough," σάκος ἑπταβόειον "shield of

seven oxen," σάκος εὐρύ "broad shield," ἀσπίδος εὐκύκλου
"well-rounded shield," ἀσπίδα πάντοσ᾽ ἐίσην "shield in all
ways equal," and ἀσπίδος ὀμφαλοέσσης "bossed shield" (together with their variants in case or number) are all roughly
contemporary with each other. Miss Gray then sums up
these six frequently recurring phrases so as to define "two
types of shield, a large and strong leather σάκος of unspecified
shape but, unlike the body-shield, broad rather than high,
and a round ἀσπίς with a conspicuous boss or bosses"—the
important reasoning here being that the "consistent grouping
of epithets round ἀσπίς and σάκος is against assuming a single
type which combined the attributes of both" (p. 121 and
n. 1). The objectivity of these contentions is greatly in their
favor; still, they cannot be accepted without comment.

(It may be noticed that the six frequently recurring phrases
sort out the sakea from the aspides, if at all, on the basis of
their dimensions, shields of the one kind being broad but
perhaps not round, and those of the other kind being round
but perhaps not broad. The six phrases do not, except from
silence, distinguish the sakea from the aspides by their lack
or possession of a boss, or by their being leather or metallic.
ἀσπίδος ὀμφαλοέσσης "bossed shield" says that the aspis has
a boss and σάκος ἑπταβόειον "shield of seven oxen" says that
the sakos is leather, but there are no phrases in this special
group that say whether the sakos has a boss or whether the
aspis is leather. Since Miss Gray argues that no, the sakos
does not have a boss, we should have expected her to argue
that no, the aspis is not leather: as she infers from a bossed
aspis an unbossed sakos, she might have inferred from a
sakos of leather an aspis of metal. Instead, she holds that
"outstanding beauty of ornament or substantial use of
metal" [p. 121] is no more absent from the one than from
the other. This decision, which is important if correct,

depends partly on its compatibility with a reasonable but unsupported corollary [the phrases that speak explicitly of the
shield as being metallic are unusually modern because they
contain only such epithets as occur widely with other nouns],
but depends chiefly on the belief that the epithets for a
metallic shield ought to speak about metal—a belief that is
unwarranted. For the question faced by the poet was not
"What part of the aspis is the most elegant?" but "How
does the aspis differ from other things?" If many works of
war—greaves, breastplate, helmets, swords, and spears—
were metallic, the aspis could not be made interesting so well
by epithets saying that it, too, was metallic, as by epithets
saying that it was πάντοσ' ἐΐση "in all ways equal" and
ὀμφαλόεσσα "bossed," whether or not the sakos was alike in
these respects. So it is not by any means certain that the
aspis was nonmetallic when the most frequently recurring
phrases for the shield were being created.)

But the chief problem we face here is whether the sakos
and the aspis are alike in dimension. From the group of
special phrases that she has walled up, Miss Gray believes
not; but two fissures catch the eye. First, it is worrisome that
even a preliminary inspection should emphasize disparities
of so minor an order: σάκος εὐρύ "broad shield" and
ἀσπίδος εὐκύκλου "well-rounded shield," since they occur
four times each, are listed as *traditional*, but σάκος . . . τετραθέλυμνον "shield of four layers" and ἀσπίδα θοῦριν "furious
shield," since they occur only twice each, as *individual*. Such
a statistical method is invalidated by the stricture that
T. B. L. Webster, *From Mycenae to Homer* (London 1958)
277–282, has brought against an argument of a similar
nature. Secondly, it is doubtful whether the frequencies with
which two formulas recur, no matter how great the difference, bear in any way directly on their relative ages. If σάκος

ἠύτε πύργον "shield like a tower" is a relic from an extremely early day, σάκος μέγα τε στιβαρόν τε "shield both large and tough" may be a relic of exactly the same kind.

Neither of these objections can be brought against my conclusion that their epithets were never intended to distinguish the sakos from the aspis. σάκος ἠύτε πύργον "shield like a tower" and ἀσπίδος ἀμφιβρότης "shield that covers the body on both sides" have been synonymous from the beginning, since they apparently refer to one or both varieties of the dagger-blade body shield. σάκος μέγα τε στιβαρόν τε "shield both large and tough" has never said that aspides are small and weak; and σάκος ἑπταβόειον "shield of seven oxen" has never implied that every sakos is more leathern than any aspis, unless ἀσπίδα ταυρείην "shield of bull's hide" has implied the contrary. σάκος εὐρύ "broad shield" has always meant much the same as both ἀσπίδα πάντοσ' ἐίσην "shield in all ways equal" and ἀσπίδος εὐκύκλου "well-rounded shield"—not only because anyone accustomed to the body shield, which was predominantly tall, would think that the round shield was predominantly broad, but also because a shield *greater* in breadth than in height is repugnant to common sense. σάκος εὐρύ "broad shield," ἀσπίδα πάντοσ' ἐίσην "shield in all ways equal," and ἀσπίδος εὐκύκλου "well-rounded shield" all differ in meaning from σάκος ἠύτε πύργον "shield like a tower" and ἀσπίδος ἀμφιβρότης "shield that covers the body on both sides," but they do not differ among themselves, and have never done so. Miss Gray thinks that σάκος and ἀσπίς once meant the same (when the phrases for the body shield were coined), then differed (when the most frequently recurring phrases for the shield were established), and then meant the same again (when the poetry reached its present form). I myself—while agreeing that some σάκος phrases, and some ἀσπίς phrases, are older than others—find

it easier to say that no arrangement of the epithets will con-
jure up a time when the sakos and the aspis were not alike.

The *Iliad* certainly does not regard their epithets as a sign
of any distinction between them. σάκος μέγα τε στιβαρόν τε
"shield both large and tough," if it said that sakea were
larger and tougher than aspides, would be contradicted by
the lines "whoever has a small sakos ought to find a large
aspis" (14.376–377). σάκος ἑπταβόειον "shield of seven oxen,"
if it implied that sakea were more leathern than aspides,
would be at odds with the shield of Achilles, which is invariably a sakos but metallic in every detail. The sakos of
Ajax was made by a cutter of hides who added a layer of
bronze (7.221–223), the aspis of Sarpedon by a worker in
bronze who stitched its hides (12.295–297): both are of
leather and metal together; so the sakos cannot consistently
be distinguished from the aspis on the basis of their materials.
ἀσπίδα πάντοσ' ἐίσην "shield in all ways equal" and ἀσπίδος
εὐκύκλου "well-rounded shield" do not prove that the aspis
is rounder than the sakos, since the only shield we know to
have a threefold rim around it (18.479–480) and to gleam
like the moon (19.374) is not an aspis at all, but the sakos of
Achilles. ἀσπίδος ὀμφαλοέσσης "bossed shield" asserts that
the aspis has a boss, but does not deny that the sakos has one
as well—the sakos of Ajax is struck μέσσον ἐπομφάλιον "in the
middle of its boss" (7.267). There is no way to define the
two words with respect to each other; the facts all seem to
indicate that σάκος and ἀσπίς are entirely synonymous.

Miss Gray observes that although πόντος may not refer to
the same part of the sea as ἅλς does, θάλασσα contains all the
meanings of both—the epithets of πόντος and ἅλς not being
shared with θάλασσα merely because verbal connections
"usually prevented the exchange of epithets between nouns
even when there was no obstacle of sense or metre" (pp.

112–113). True; and a like statement must hold for the shield. Miss Gray therefore seems to me mistaken in asserting that both the distribution of their epithets and the use of the two nouns imply a latent awareness of a difference in meaning "between ἀσπίς and σάκος combined with a willingness to treat them as alternatives in most contexts" (p. 113). I should say that there was no difference, and that nevertheless they were not treated as alternatives in most contexts, or used as synonyms generally. If they *had been* used as synonyms when their epithets were created, the likelihood of a distinction between them, as we shall see, is more remote than ever.

c. How do σάκος ἑπταβόειον and σάκος ἠύτε πύργον compare with the other phrases for the shield?

Parry observed that two laws governed the epic diction: the law of scope, *there are many expressions for any concept, used as exact synonyms of each other*; and the law of economy, *expressions used as synonyms differ from each other in meter*. The laws are equally important, but the second is the more interesting. It explains why "Odysseus" and "Laertiades," which are used as synonyms, differ in meter, and why θεὰ γλαυκῶπις Ἀθήνη "goddess Athene of the bright eyes" and Χάρις λιπαροκρήδεμνος "Charis of the glistening veil," which do not differ in meter, are not used as synonyms. Violations are uncommon; yet they do occur. βέλος "missile"—spear or arrow—has the epithets ὀξύ "sharp" and ὠκύ "swift" (in the phrases βέλος ὀξύ and βέλος ὠκύ, ὀξὺ βέλος and ὠκὺ βέλος), which appear to have been regarded as alike in both scansion and sense. We could say that a missile ought to be "swift" when in flight and "sharp" when extracted from a wound; but the idea is ours, it was not the poet's; there is no

reliable basis for determining why either was preferred to
the other. δόρυ and ἔγχος, both meaning spear, have the
epithets μείλινον "ash" and χάλκεον "bronze" (in the
phrases δόρυ μείλινον and δόρυ χάλκεον, μείλινον ἔγχος and
χάλκεον ἔγχος), which are likewise distributed as if by chance.
Among those who have an ash spear (δόρυ μείλινον or
μείλινον ἔγχος), Menelaus, Aeneas, Ajax, Hector, and
Achilles have a bronze spear (δόρυ χάλκεον or χάλκεον ἔγχος)
somewhere else, and only Tlepolemus and Euphorbus do
not. In brief passages the epithets—μείλινον or χάλκεον—for a
given spear may (Il. 13.595–597), inconsistently but in-
terestingly, be different, or they may (16.608–610), consistently but uninterestingly, be the same (on this example
and others, see Page, p. 274). The terms for the shield show
no violation that deserves so much attention, but we do find
it hard to say why δεινὸν σάκος ἑπταβόειον "terrible shield of
seven oxen" competes with σάκος αἰόλον ἑπταβόειον "dazz-
ling shield of seven oxen," and φαεινὴν ἀσπίδα "shining
shield" with παναίολον ἀσπίδα "all-dazzling shield" (further,
see Page, p. 271). Behind most of the elements in the epic
diction there is some rhyme or reason, but here there is
neither.

Other elements of the same meter might have been, but
are not, used as synonyms, and therefore might have con-
stituted, but do not constitute, violations of economy; these
elements all maintain distinctions faithfully. αἴθοπι χαλκῶι
"ruddy bronze" and σάκος ἑπταβόειον "shield of seven oxen"
could always replace (though they could never be replaced
by) ὀξέι χαλκῶι "sharp bronze" and σάκος ἠΰτε πύργον
"shield like a tower," respectively, without any noticeable
error in sense. πάντοσ' εἴσην "in all ways equal," an epithet
for the aspis, could replace or be replaced by θυσσανόεσσαν
"fringed," an epithet for the aegis; and in several forms

ἀσπίς and αἰγίς themselves could each replace the other: ἀσπίδα and αἰγίδα, ἀσπίδα θοῦριν "furious aspis" and αἰγίδα θοῦριν "furious aegis," ἀσπίδα πάντοσ᾽ ἐίσην "aspis in all ways equal" and αἰγίδα θυσσανόεσσαν "fringed aegis," ὣς εἰπὼν οὔτησε κατ᾽ ἀσπίδα πάντοσ᾽ ἐίσην "so saying he struck upon the aspis in all ways equal" (Il. 11.434 = 17.43) and ὣς εἰπὼν οὔτησε κατ᾽ αἰγίδα θυσσανόεσσαν "so saying he struck upon the fringed aegis" (21.400). Here the poet holds to set procedures; unlike ὀξύ and ὠκύ (for βέλος), and μείλινον and χάλκεον (for δόρυ and ἔγχος), the alternatives are not a matter of indifference to him. And we can see intellect behind his choices, as we could not with δεινὸν σάκος and σάκος αἰόλον, φαεινὴν ἀσπίδα and παναίολον ἀσπίδα. For ὀξέι "sharp" is far clearer, as an epithet for bronze in the sense of spear, than αἴθοπι "ruddy" would be, and ἠύτε πύργον "like a tower" has an adverbial meaning even more colorful in its contexts than the adjectival meaning of ἑπταβόειον "of seven oxen" would be; πάντοσ᾽ ἐίσην "in all ways equal" and θυσσανόεσσαν "fringed" distinguish the aspis from the aegis; and the use of ἀσπίς for our shields but αἰγίς for theirs distinguishes men from the gods.

The nouns δόρυ, ἔγχος, and ἐγχείη, all meaning spear, plus χαλκός "bronze," plus βέλος "missile," are all capable, as used in the Iliad, of referring to any spear whatsoever, with no restriction and no consistency. It is true that the spear of Hector may be a δόρυ in each of four consecutive lines (16.861–864) and that the use of a single word for any one spear in each of two consecutive lines is common enough (10.369–370, the δόρυ of Diomedes; 11.95–96, the δόρυ of Agamemnon; 13.441–442, the δόρυ of Idomeneus; 20.437–438, the δόρυ of Hector; 13.177–178, the ἔγχος of Teucer; 16.309–310, the ἔγχος of Patroclus). But in consecutive lines, too, the spear of a given man may be a χαλκός, and then a βέλος (5.18, Diomedes; 16.480, Patroclus), an ἔγχος (8.535, Hector), or a δόρυ (16.346, Idomeneus). A spear may also be an ἐγχείη in one line and an ἔγχος in the next (5.279–280, Pandarus), or it may, in three consecutive lines, be a δόρυ, a βέλος, and an ἔγχος (22.291–293, Hector). Hector (6.319 = 8.494) and Meriones (13.570) each have a spear that is an ἔγχος and then a δόρυ in the same line; Diomedes (10.372–373) and Aeneas (16.610–611, 20.259–260) each have one that is an ἔγχος and then a δόρυ in the next line; Agamemnon (5.537–538), Hector (13.183–184, 17.304–305), Deiphobus (13.403–404, 13.518–519), Menelaus (13.583–584), Antilochus (16.317–318), Patroclus (16.504–505), and Ajax (17.295–296) each have one that is a δόρυ and then an ἔγχος in the next line. The spear of Hector is a δόρυ, an ἔγχος, and a δόρυ in three consecutive lines (17.525–527); that of Sarpedon, a δόρυ, an ἔγχος, and a δόρυ within eight feet (12.394–395).

Since these words are used indiscriminately for any spear, we cannot foresee that two of them will contrast with each other so as to distinguish one spearman even slightly from his opponent. The actual distribution, then, is quite unexciting. In a repeated passage (except for the names, 5.16–19a = 16.478–481a) Phegeus, or Sarpedon, does have an ἔγχος in the line where Diomedes, or Patroclus, has a χαλκός; but in another repeated passage (3.347b–350 = 17.43b–46) the opponent of Menelaus—Paris, or the son of Panthous—has a χαλκός in one line while he himself has a χαλκός in the next; and in a further instance (20.272–273) Aeneas has an ἔγχος in one line, Achilles an ἔγχος in the next. Three consecutive lines (22.271–273) may have the ἔγχος of Achilles, the ἔγχος of Hector, the ἔγχος of Achilles, or (17.303–305) the δόρυ of Ajax, the δόρυ of Hector, the ἔγχος of Hector. This last example fairly sums up the manner in which βέλος, χαλκός, δόρυ, ἔγχος, and ἐγχείη behave: they do not contrast one spear with another, and there is no consistency in their usage for any single spear. They are used as synonyms and differ from each other in meter.

The same is true for nearly all the epithetic phrases for the spear. δόρυ μακρόν "long spear" and δολιχόσκιον ἔγχος "far-shadowing spear" are not just convenient ways of referring to the δόρυ and the ἔγχος, respectively, when there is room for elements of these larger sizes: they are, instead, convenient ways of referring to any spear whatsoever. Some elements are used as synonyms even though they do not differ in meter—μείλινον "ash" and χάλκεον "bronze" as applied to the δόρυ and ἔγχος; ὀξύ "sharp" and ὠκύ "swift" as applied to the βέλος—but they are a small minority. In general we shall say that all the forms and phrases of δόρυ, ἔγχος, and ἐγχείη, as well as χαλκός and βέλος in the sense of spear, mean so nearly the same that they are chosen according to the metrical needs they provide for. In the *Odyssey* the noun μελίη "ash" is a further member of the group, a most useful member though not encountered very often; but in the *Iliad*—where it is used ten times for the spear of Achilles, never for any other—μελίη is an exception, and we shall speak about it again.

Most of the recurring phrases for the sakos are also evidently used as synonyms: σάκος . . . τετραθέλυμνον "shield of four layers" refers once each to the shields of Teucer and Odysseus (in the repeated passage *Il.* 15.479b–482a = *Od.* 22.122b–125a); σάκος μέγα τε στιβαρόν τε "shield both large and tough" refers three times to the shield of Achilles (*Il.* 18.478, 18.608, 19.373), the last of these being a formulaic line also used for the shields of Paris and Patroclus (*Il.* 19.373 = 3.335 = 16.136); and σάκος εὐρύ "broad shield" refers once each to the shields of Antilochus, Menelaus, Ajax,

and Laertes (*Il.* 13.552, 13.608, 17.132, *Od.* 22.184). Since
these forms differ in meter their failure to distinguish one
shield from another is easily understood. We could add either
σάκος ἑπταβόειον "shield of seven oxen" or σάκος ἠύτε πύργον
"shield like a tower" to the group if they, too, were used
generously, for they take care of an additional metrical need;
but we could not add both, since they scan entirely alike. In
actuality neither can be added as a further general term for
the sakos on account of their being used for the shield of
Ajax, five and three times respectively, but never for any
other. Like μελίη they are an exception and must be treated
apart.

The recurring phrases for the aspis are used as synonyms
almost without exception. ἀσπίδ' . . . κρατερῆι "strong shield"
is indeed limited to Menelaus in a repeated passage (*Il.*
3.347b–350 = 17.43b–46), but all the others are divided
widely and evenly. ἀσπίδι (-α) πάντοσ' ἐίσηι (-ην) "shield in
all ways equal" together with ἀσπίδι (-α) . . . πάντοσ' ἐίσηι
(-ην) occurs sixteen times and is used for the shields of eleven
different men, no more often than three times for any one of
them. φαεινὴν ἀσπίδ' (-α) "shining shield" together with
ἀσπίδος . . . φαεινῆς occurs six times and is used for the
shields of five different men; ἀσπίδος ὀμφαλοέσσης "bossed
shield," together with ἀσπίδα . . . ὀμφαλόεσσαν, five times,
for those of four different men. ἀσπίδος ἀμφιβρότης "shield
that covers the body on both sides" is used for the shields of
two different men, once each, and in a single instance refers
to those of men unnamed. ἀσπίδα θοῦριν "furious shield,"
preceded by another epithet or not, is also used for the shields
of two different men, once each, as is ἀσπίδι (-α) ταυρείηι (-ην)
"shield of bull's hide." No pattern of usage for these phrases
is discernible. A half dozen men have a partial claim on two
or more of them, but the half dozen collections do not re-

semble one another. So we predict confidently, and with complete accuracy, that these phrases, like most of the terms for the spear, will provide for dissimilar problems in meter. Among the recurring phrases for the aspis, as among those for the sakos, none characterizes its owner so forcefully as do the two phrases restricted to Ajax. The same applies to the phrases for the aegis: they are used as synonyms and differ in meter. Not only are σάκος ἑπταβόειον "shield of seven oxen" and σάκος ἠύτε πύργον "shield like a tower" limited to one particular shield: in being so limited they have, among the repeated phrases for the shield, a most unusual distinction.

d. Were σάκος and ἀσπίς used as synonyms?

Menelaus has a sakos three times, in *Il.* 13.606–646, and an aspis five times, in 3.347–349 and 17.7–45; Odysseus, a sakos once, in 10.149, and an aspis three times, in 11.434–457; Paris, a sakos once, in 3.335, and an aspis three times, in 3.356–357 and 6.322; Patroclus, a sakos once, in 16.136, and an aspis twice, in 16.704–803. Since the arms of the slain are sometimes taken as trophies, the leading heroes are likely, by the tenth year of the war, to own more than a single shield each; so it could perhaps be argued that a man might use different shields at different times, now a sakos and now an aspis. This handy explanation does not, however, turn out to be helpful; for Paris has no time to change a sakos for an aspis in 3.335–356, and both the sakos and the aspis of Patroclus, in 16.136–803, are the shield he borrowed from Achilles. The two words are capable of being used as different ways of saying the same thing; and they do not scan in the same manner—even if we consider elements that occur only once, no form or epithetic phrase of *sakos* is metrically equal to any form or epithetic phrase of *aspis*. The same is

true for *sakos* and *aegis*: both words refer to the shields of the
gods (*Il.* 15.125, 2.447, etc.), and they provide for different
metrical needs. The results are precisely what we expected
from the theory: *aspis* and *aegis* do not differ in meter and
are not used as synonyms of each other; *sakos* is occasionally
used as a synonym for both and differs from both in meter.

Parry has explained these results; Miss Gray agrees im-
plicitly ("the principle of epic economy," p. 111; "where
ἀσπίς and σάκος could be used indifferently," p. 113; "poet
who uses the noun which fits the line," p. 116); Page agrees
emphatically ("The law of economy prevails in general over
the whole group," p. 271 with a brief list of the exceptions,
omitting only δεινὸν σάκος and σάκος αἰόλον, ἀσπίδα ταυρείην
and ἀσπίδα Νεστορέην). Yet the law of economy is of little
further use to us here; it would apply more widely if *sakos*
and *aspis* were used as synonyms ordinarily, but they are not
so used—Menelaus, Odysseus, Paris, and Patroclus are the
only men in the *Iliad* whose shields are referred to as both.
The shield of Ajax is unique for being said to be made of
seven oxen and to be carried like a tower; it is equally interesting as the shield mentioned more often than any other;
but the really notable fact lies in its being always a sakos,
never an aspis, and we must decide whether the distribution
is fortuitous. If *sakos* and *aspis* occurred equally often in a
random assortment, a man who carried the sakos on one
occasion would have an even chance to carry it on the next,
and an even chance again for the occasion after that. The
odds against his carrying the sakos twenty-two times, the
aspis never, would be roughly two million to one. So we
should decline to wager heavily, even if we did not know that
Achilles (seventeen times) had a sakos but never the aspis
Thetis asked for, that Hector (thirteen times) and Aeneas
(eight times) had aspides but never sakea, and that within

twenty lines the shield of any man was a sakos or an aspis but
not both.

Miss Gray finds it significant that the shield of Ajax is
always a sakos (p. 113), and Page implies his consent
(p. 272); but neither says what it is significant of. The
answer is this: *sakos* and *aspis* are distributed from a desire
for verbal consistency in the terms referring to the most important shields, and for verbal contrast in the episodes of
shield combat; or else they are distributed from some further,
undiscovered motive; but certainly *their arrangement has little
to do with the Parry theory*. Like μελίη for the spear of Achilles,
and σάκος ἑπταβόειον or σάκος ἠΰτε πύργον for the shield of
Ajax, *sakos* and *aspis* are an exception. Now μελίη is not so
extraordinary, after all, since it is not the only word for its
object; in addition to being this "ash" the spear of Achilles
is also a βέλος ὀξύ "sharp missile," ὀξὺ δόρυ "sharp spear,"
δόρυ μακρόν "long spear," δόρυ μείλινον "ash spear," μείλινον
ἔγχος "ash spear," χάλκεον ἔγχος "bronze spear," δολιχόσκιον ἔγχος "far-shadowing spear," and ἔγχος ἀκαχμένον
"capped spear." Similarly, σάκος ἑπταβόειον and σάκος ἠΰτε
πύργον do not prevent the shield of Ajax from being a σάκος
εὐρύ "broad shield"—and *of themselves* they do not even prevent it from sharing in the wealth of phrases for *aspis*. What
is truly remarkable, for the insights it gives us into the aims
and methods of the poet, is the fact that the greatest shield
warriors invariably have sakea, and their great opponents,
aspides. For referring to the shields of Ajax and Achilles the
poet never uses ἀσπίς, ἀσπίδος, ἀσπίδος εὐκύκλου, ἀσπίδος
ἀμφιβρότης, ἀσπίδος ὀμφαλοέσσης, ἀσπίδι (-α), ἀσπίδι (-α)
ταυρείηι (-ην), ἀσπίδι (-α) πάντοσ᾽ ἐΐσηι (-ην), or ἀσπίδα θοῦριν.
For referring to those of Hector and Aeneas, never σάκος,
σάκος εὐρύ, σάκος μέγα τε στιβαρόν τε, σάκος ... τετραθέλυμνον, or σάκος ἑπταβόειον. And yet in no single instance

3

could *sakos* and *aspis* replace each other so well as *aspis* and
aegis. This is Tayler's principle—*Classical Review* 27 (1913)
222–225—and I have added nothing new except by saying
that it largely replaces, for the shield, the law of economy.

The law of economy means that expressions used as synonyms differ from each other in meter and that expressions
not differing from each other in meter are not used as
synonyms. The law can never be construed to mean that
expressions not used as synonyms do not differ in meter or
that expressions differing in meter are used as synonyms. In
their distribution σάκος and ἀσπίς, σάκος ἑπταβόειον or
σάκος ἠΰτε πύργον, and μελίη do not *violate* the law (as δεινὸν
σάκος and σάκος αἰόλον do); they are exceptional merely for
not being governed by it. We now face two possibilities:
either it is meaningless and a delusion—a snare laid for the
theorist—that *sakos* (with all its forms and phrases) never
scans in the manner of *aspis* (with its own forms and phrases);
or else *sakos* and *aspis* were used as synonyms while their
forms and phrases were being established in the epic diction.
The former is compatible with the theory, advanced by Miss
Gray and warmly accepted by Page, that the most frequently recurring epithetic phrases for *sakos* and *aspis*—σάκος
μέγα τε στιβαρόν τε "shield both large and tough," σάκος
ἑπταβόειον "shield of seven oxen," σάκος εὐρύ "broad
shield," ἀσπίδος εὐκύκλου "well-rounded shield," ἀσπίδα
πάντοσ' ἐΐσην "shield in all ways equal," and ἀσπίδος
ὀμφαλοέσσης "bossed shield"—were coined when the two
nouns did not refer to shields of the same kind. For if they
did not mean the same thing there was good reason to distri-
bute them with consistency—*sakos* for the shields of Ajax and
Achilles, *aspis* for those of Hector and Aeneas—as they are
distributed in the *Iliad*. But the possibility is most unattractive, because poets who did not believe that *sakos* and *aspis*

meant the same thing, and did not intend to use them as synonyms, would have coined families of phrases—one with *sakos*, another with *aspis*—that were as interchangeable as possible. So as to turn their backs on any temptation to use the wrong term they would have approximated for *sakos* and *aspis* the metrical identity of *aspis* and *aegis*, just as they approximated for *Hector* and *Achilles* the metrical identity of *Achilles* and *Odysseus*. And yet we look in vain for a single example of a *sakos* phrase and an *aspis* phrase that correspond so well as do ἀσπίδα πάντοσ' ἐΐσην and αἰγίδα θυσσανόεσσαν— or ὄβριμος Ἕκτωρ and ὠκὺς Ἀχιλλεύς, φαίδιμος Ἕκτωρ and δῖος Ἀχιλλεύς, κορυθαίολος Ἕκτωρ and πόδας ὠκὺς Ἀχιλλεύς, μέγας κορυθαίολος Ἕκτωρ and ποδάρκης δῖος Ἀχιλλεύς. If the chief phrases for *sakos* and *aspis* were coined when the two nouns were *not* used as synonyms, the economy of the *sakos-aspis* system was created by poets for their own great inconvenience.

So we shall accept the other possibility and say that σάκος and ἀσπίς *were* used as synonyms when the phrases were being established. But here we have to reject Miss Gray's theory that the chief epithets for the shield were conceived with the intention of distinguishing between the two nouns. For poets who used *sakos* and *aspis* as synonyms, often going from one to the other in succeeding lines (as the *Iliad* goes from δόρυ to ἔγχος in referring to the same spear), cannot have thought that the words denoted shields of different kinds. And poets who intended to *continue* using σάκος and ἀσπίς as synonyms cannot possibly have produced epithets designed to tell them apart. It would have been the same as describing Odysseus in terms expressly chosen for keeping him distinct from Laertiades. It is unreasonable to accept any interpretation other than this: *sakos* and *aspis* were regarded as useful ways of saying the same thing when all, or nearly all, their recurring phrases were brought into being. σάκος ἠύτε πύργον "shield like a tower" and ἀσπίδος ἀμφιβρότης "shield that covers the body on both sides" were created when the body shield was in vogue, or else later when a poet, having heard of such a shield or having seen such a relic as the lion-hunt dagger blade, wished to archaize for color. (See G. S. Kirk, *The Songs of Homer* [Cambridge 1962] 109 and 112; and consider how Herodotus [1.171] came to know that instead of being held by a grip the shield once hung on a strap that crossed over the left shoulder.) σάκος εὐρύ "broad shield" and ἀσπίδα πάντοσ' ἐίσην "shield in all ways equal" were created when the round shield shown on the Warrior Vase was the more common. Until this time was reached and passed, *sakos* and *aspis* were used as synonyms; neither Ajax nor anyone else had always a sakos, neither Hector nor anyone else always an aspis.

In like manner either σάκος ἑπταβόειον or σάκος ἠύτε πύργον, and the former is the more likely as being adaptable to the greater number of lines, was also once used as a synonym for all the other ways of referring to a shield, and was not limited to the special shield of Ajax. And, similarly, μελίη was once not limited to the special spear of Achilles. For μελίη and σάκος ἑπταβόειον (or σάκος ἠύτε πύργον) share with *sakos* and *aspis* themselves the property of metrical uniqueness, among the expressions for the spear and the shield, respectively, except that ἑπταβόειον and ἠύτε πύργον are duplicates of each other. These nouns and one or the other of the epithets became restricted only after the epic diction was well formed—when entire passages could be worked over for greatest force and clarity, and when lines were created with attention to their consistency with the epic as a whole. When the restriction of σάκος and ἀσπίς, ἑπταβόειον and ἠύτε πύργον, and μελίη had taken place, only then was the passage about the Pelian ash of Achilles created, was the shield of Ajax described part by part, and was Ajax himself spoken of as the tower his shield suggested.

If no *sakos* form or phrase was ever interchangeable with any *aspis* form or phrase, how did the poet manage to restrict these nouns so elegantly? He worked with elements of larger size—and by recasting the formulas we are able to give the σάκος ἑπταβόειον "shield of seven oxen" to Achilles or Hector, and the σάκος μέγα τε στιβαρόν τε "shield both large and tough" or the ἀσπίδα πάντοσ᾽ ἐΐσην "shield in all ways equal" to Ajax.

καὶ βάλεν Αἴαντος δεινὸν σάκος ἑπταβόειον   (*Il.* 7.245),
καὶ βάλε Πηλεΐδαο μέσον σάκος οὐδ᾽ ἀφάμαρτε   (22.290),
  and
καὶ βάλε Πριαμίδαο κατ᾽ ἀσπίδα πάντοσ᾽ ἐΐσην   (3.356 =
7.250)—

can be combined as καὶ βάλε Πηλεΐδαο (Πριαμίδαο) μέσον σάκος ἑπταβόειον "and struck in the midst of Peleides' (Priamides') shield of seven oxen."

χάλκεον, αὐτὰρ ἔπειτα σάκος μέγα τε στιβαρόν τε   (3.335 =
16.136 = 19.373),
ὣς εἰπὼν οὔτησε κατ᾽ ἀσπίδα πάντοσ᾽ ἐΐσην   (11.434 =
17.43), and
Αἴαντος δ᾽ ἀλέεινε μάχην Τελαμωνιάδαο   (11.542)—

can similarly be combined as Αἴαντος δ᾽ οὔτησε σάκος μέγα τε στιβαρόν τε "and struck Ajax's shield both large and tough" or as Αἴαντος δ᾽ οὔτησε κατ᾽ ἀσπίδα πάντοσ᾽ ἐΐσην "and struck on Ajax's shield in all ways equal."

$Aἴας\ δ'\ ἐγγύθεν\ ἦλθε\ φέρων\ σάκος\ ἠύτε\ πύργον$ (7.219 =
    11.485 = 17.128) and
$"Εκτωρ\ δ'\ ἐν\ πρώτοισι\ φέρ'\ ἀσπίδα\ πάντοσ'\ ἐΐσην$ (11.61)—

can even more easily be combined by trading the one name
for the other: "and Ajax (Hector) came near, carrying a
shield like a tower"; "and Hector (Ajax) among the foremost carried a shield in all ways equal." But some exchanges
of *sakos* for *aspis* are very difficult, *and the epic diction is not
likely to have been shaped so as to make them necessary.* We cannot
believe that in the Mycenaean era the shield of Ajax was
always a sakos, never an aspis, and in the same way we cannot believe that both $σάκος\ ἑπταβόειον$ and $σάκος\ ἠύτε\ πύργον$
were used, in the Mycenaean era, for the shield of Ajax
alone, and not once for any other. This fulfils our first objective.

II. The historicity of $κορυθαίολος$, $χαλκοκορυστής$ as special descriptions for Hector

Taking two ideas that had become widely accepted—that
the *Iliad* and *Odyssey* were created (at least in part) during an
age of illiteracy, and that they contain an extraordinary
degree of repetition—Parry found a most important connection between them: formulas would indeed have been
useful to an oral poet. With the same brilliance, by taking
two other ideas—that the highly stereotyped epithets for the
helmet (with a single exception) fail to speak of it as being
metallic, and that Hector is (almost) the only figure to have
the epithets $κορυθαίολος$ "of the flashing helmet" and
$χαλκοκορυστής$ "of the bronze helmet"—Page concludes that
"If Hector alone is distinguished as wearing a bronze helmet,
the likeliest reason for the distinction is that it reported a

truth, a matter of common knowledge at the time" (p. 255).
Our next long objective is to impugn this belief that κορυθαίολος and χαλκοκορυστής are authentic clues to the past.

  a. What can be decided from the epithets for a non‐
  metallic helmet?

Page's bold and original assertion is actually the fusion of
two arguments. They may be sorted out and arranged sym‐
metrically as follows:

The argument from the epithets for a nonmetallic helmet:	The argument from the restriction of κορυθαίολος and χαλκοκορυστής:
1. The distinctive and regular epithets for an object were all coined during the creative stage of the epic diction.	1. An epithet restricted to one man has been restricted to him ever since the creative stage of the epic diction.
2. They fully indicate the nature the object had at that time.	2. It indicates how he was meant to differ from other men at that time.
3. The distinctive and regular epithets for the ordinary helmet indicate that it was nonmetallic.	3. κορυθαίολος and χαλκοκορυστής indicate that Hector was meant to differ by having a metallic helmet.
4. So the epithets for the ordinary helmet indicate that any metallic helmet was unusual.	4. So κορυθαίολος and χαλκοκορυστής indicate that other men were thought to have nonmetallic helmets.

That the arguments complement each other so neatly is an
enormous advantage. Nevertheless, no single one of the

premises or conclusions is entirely reliable. They can be opposed point by point:

Contra the argument from the epithets for a nonmetallic helmet.

1. The distinctive and regular epithets for the helmet may be fossils from the same deep stratum as σάκος ἠΰτε πύργον "shield like a tower" and ἀσπίδος ἀμφιβρότης "shield that covers the body on both sides." If several centuries older than κορυθαίολος and χαλκοκορυστής, they do not imply that Hector's helmet was unusual.

2. Even if most of the regular epithets for the helmet were contemporaneous with κορυθαίολος and χαλκοκορυστής, they need not have been meant to describe the ordinary helmet as nonmetallic. They merely imply that it was not metallic in any unusual manner. If all armor was metallic the helmet would have been distinguished less well by numerous epithets saying that it, too, was metallic, than by epithets saying that it

Contra the argument from the restriction of κορυθαίολος and χαλκοκορυστής:

1. An epithet now largely restricted to one man may at first have been common property. Hector shares κορυθαίολος (once) with Ares and χαλκοκορυστής (once) with Sarpedon: he was either giving up or acquiring his special right to them, and we lack sufficient evidence for deciding which. Nor need an epithet restricted to one man have belonged to him from the beginning. Ἕκτορα ποιμένα λαῶν "Hector shepherd of the people" competes with Ἕκτορα χαλκοκορυστήν, and we cannot say which is the older (see Page, p. 288, n. 91): either a traditional distinction was being lost as ποιμένα λαῶν was replacing χαλκοκορυστήν, or a distinction was being created as (Ἕκτορα) χαλκοκορυστήν was replacing (Ἕκτορα) ποιμένα λαῶν; similarly with (Ἕκτορος) ἱπποδάμοιο "breaker of horses" and (Ἕκτορος) ἀνδροφόνοιο "man-slaying."

2. Even if an epithet restricted to one man was always so re-

was, for example, ἱπποδάσεια "plumed with horse hair."

3. Even if most of the regular epithets for the helmet imply that it was ordinarily non-metallic, χαλκοπάρῃος "with bronze cheek-pieces" says very clearly that it was partly metallic (see Page, p. 289, n. 97).

4. Even if χαλκοπάρῃος is un-important or spurious, a metal-lic helmet could have been imagined.

stricted, it may have been meant to distinguish him not from other men, but from other things than men—such as women, lions, and ships.

3. Even if κορυθαίολος and χαλκοκορυστής were meant to distinguish Hector from other men, the difference may have been not in kind but in degree or moment. πόδας ὠκύς "swift-footed" does not imply that Achilles was a fast runner in the company of slow ones, but that he could run even faster than anyone else or to greater purpose.

4. Even if κορυθαίολος and χαλκοκορυστής were meant to distinguish Hector in kind from all other men, his metallic helmet may be fictional.

The evidence would be compatible with, but does not lead to, the conclusion that there really was a day when a single metallic helmet, the helmet of Hector, flashed conspicuously in battle at Troy. The question is whether the conclusion will be arrived at by other reasoning. Page (pp. 255–256) thinks it will; he is persuaded that only the force of an unusual historical fact (or occasionally, perhaps, a popular belief) can have given a rare and distinctive epithet to anyone—since "the technique of oral poetry would have automatically suggested" the conventional and merely ornamental epithet instead. Here is the assumption that *variety is contrary to the nature of the epic diction*, with which I disagree.

b. Is the epic diction as meager as possible?

Achilles and *Odysseus*, like *aspis* and *aegis*, do not differ in
meter and are not used as synonyms. Consequently, many of
the epithets attached to these nouns—such as πόδας ὠκύς and
πολύμητις, or πάντοσ᾽ ἐίσην and θυσσανόεσσαν—also do not
differ in meter and are not used as synonyms. But neither
the law of scope (which requires many expressions for any
concept) nor the law of economy (which requires them to
provide for different metrical needs), nor yet any other aspect
of the Parry theory, can be invoked to explain why Odysseus
has flourished *along with* Achilles and the aegis along with the
aspis, or why πολύμητις has survived *in addition to* πόδας ὠκύς,
and θυσσανόεσσαν in addition to πάντοσ᾽ ἐίσην. Here we stand
in need of the principle of variety. The great number of
names, or other special nouns, provides amplitude; the great
number of epithets, color. With a considerable loss of either,
the tradition would be impoverished. The idea of variety
does not oppose the ideas of scope and economy; it only sup-
plements them. For complexity and refined distinction,
elements could always be added; but they had to behave in
an orderly manner.

The theory that the restricted epithets had a basis in
history (or cult worship) does not suffice to explain why they
exist, but fails unless supported by this principle of variety.
For even if πόδας ὠκύς "swift-footed," πολύμητις "of many
counsels," γλαυκῶπις "of the bright eyes," and ἑκάεργος
"far working" (epithets for Achilles, Odysseus, Athene, and
Apollo, respectively) were thought true to character, μεγάθυμος "great-spirited" could have served as a Jack-of-all-
trades—μεγάθυμος Ἀχιλλεύς (*Il.* 23.168), Ἀχιλλῆος μεγαθύμου
(*Il.* 20.498, *Od.* 3.189), μεγαθύμου Πηλείωνος (*Il.* 18.226,
19.75), Ὀδυσσῆος μεγαθύμου (*Od.* 15.2), and μεγάθυμον

'Αθήνην (*Od.* 8.520, 13.121) do actually occur. Why did not μεγάθυμος replace the other epithets of its length?

(Why μεγάθυμος 'Αχιλλεύς has once replaced πόδας ὠκύς 'Αχιλλεύς is a different problem. It may be that μεγάθυμος in *Iliad* 23.168 was thought more relevant to context than πόδας ὠκύς would have been, though μεγάθυμος would also have been more relevant, or less irrelevant, than πόδας ὠκύς in 1.58, 9.196, 24.138, and many places elsewhere. It may be that μεγάθυμος was used to avoid the iteration of πόδας [ὠκύς] with πόδας in the line following [*Il.* 23.169]—and this answer seems to me the best—though 'Αχιλλῆος μεγαθύμου [which occurs in the middle of *Il.* 20.498] does not replace 'Αχιλλῆος θείοιο [at the end of *Il.* 19.297] even after θείοιο in the line preceding. Parry, *L'Épithète traditionnelle* 64, thought that μεγάθυμος began with a double consonant but πόδας ὠκύς with a single consonant, so that μεγάθυμος 'Αχιλλεύς and πόδας ὠκύς 'Αχιλλεύς answered to πτολίπορθος 'Οδυσσεύς and πολύμητις 'Οδυσσεύς; but as a matter of fact, μεγάθυμος 'Αχιλλεύς occurs only where a double consonant would rather have been avoided than sought after—δημὸν ἑλὼν ἐκάλυψε νέκυν μεγάθυμος 'Αχιλλεύς [*Il.* 23.168]—and does not replace πόδας ὠκύς 'Αχιλλεύς where a double consonant would have obviated a *nu* movable [*Il.* 11.112, 23.776]. This problem— Why has μεγάθυμος 'Αχιλλεύς once replaced πόδας ὠκύς 'Αχιλλεύς?—may have no solution. Let us return to what we were asking before. Why has not μεγάθυμος replaced πόδας ὠκύς, πολύμητις, γλαυκῶπις, and ἑκάεργος altogether?)

Because a major figure, sometimes a minor figure, was apt to insist on having his own epithet; otherwise his role could be played by someone else. If Hector had been the only man to wear a metallic helmet—and I state the possibility as contrary to fact because it seems to me unlikely—he could still have been described not as κορυθαίολος but as θεοείκελος

Ἕκτωρ "godlike Hector" (as in the first line of *The Fall of Troy* by Quintus of Smyrna), and not as χαλκοκορυστήν but as ποιμένα λαῶν (as occasionally in the *Iliad*); or else others could have become κορυθαίολος and χαλκοκορυστής as well as he, so that no distinction was left. The argument for variety is necessary, which denies that the argument for history is sufficient. We therefore aim at denying that the argument for history is necessary, which will mean (there being no other factors to consider) that the argument for variety is sufficient.

Several lines in the *Iliad* contain τόν "him" or τήν "her," followed by a particle and a masculine participle, then by the verb προσέφη "said," and finally by an epithet and a personal name (see also Parry, *L'Épithète traditionnelle* 18–19):

				Frequency
τὸν	δ᾽ ἀπαμειβόμενος	προσέφη	πόδας ὠκὺς Ἀχιλλεύς	11
τὴν			πολύμητις Ὀδυσσεύς	5
			κορυθαίολος Ἕκτωρ	1
			Τελαμώνιος Αἴας	2
			κρατερὸς Διομήδης	2
			κρείων Ἀγαμέμνων	5
			Πρίαμος θεοειδής	1
			νεφεληγερέτα Ζεύς	8
	δ᾽ ἄρ᾽ ὑπόδρα ἰδὼν		πόδας ὠκὺς Ἀχιλλεύς	4
			πολύμητις Ὀδυσσεύς	2
			κορυθαίολος Ἕκτωρ	3
			κρατερὸς Διομήδης	3
			νεφεληγερέτα Ζεύς	1
	δὲ μέγ᾽ ὀχθήσας		πόδας ὠκὺς Ἀχιλλεύς	4
			ξανθὸς Μενέλαος	1
			νεφεληγερέτα Ζεύς	3
			κρείων Ἐνοσίχθων	1
			κλυτὸς Ἐννοσίγαιος	1

		Frequency
δ’ ἐπιμειδήσας	πολύμητις ’Οδυσσεύς	1
	κρείων ’Αγαμέμνων	1
	νεφεληγερέτα Ζεύς	1
δ’ οὐ ταρβήσας	κορυθαίολος ῞Εκτωρ	1
	κρατερὸς Διομήδης	2
δὲ βαρὺ στενάχων	πόδας ὠκὺς ’Αχιλλεύς	2
δ’ ὀλιγοδρανέων	κορυθαίολος ῞Εκτωρ	2
δ’ ἐπιθαρσύνων	ξανθὸς Μενέλαος	1
καὶ φωνήσας	κρείων ’Αγαμέμνων	1
δὲ καταθνήσκων	κορυθαίολος ῞Εκτωρ	1
δ’ ἐπικερτομέων	πόδας ὠκὺς ’Αχιλλεύς	1
καὶ νεικείων	ξανθὸς Μενέλαος	1

The list has by definition been brought to reasonable size. But many other examples are very similar: the elements δὲ βαρὺ στενάχων, δ’ ὀλιγοδρανέων, and δ’ ἐπικερτομέων all occur within the framework τὸν ... προσέφης Πατρόκλεες ἱππεῦ.

The particles made the participles metrically interchangeable, as the epithets made the names metrically interchangeable. The participles were chosen for their own sake and are always relevant to context; the epithets were chosen for the sake of their names and are often irrelevant to context. So the participles are not entirely analogous to the epithets, *but there are more of both than the meter required.* Economy caused various men in similar situations to speak (δ’ ἄρ’) ὑπόδρα ἰδών "with stern looks," or (δὲ) μέγ’ ὀχθήσας "greatly troubled," or (δ’) ἐπιμειδήσας "with a smile"—as it caused Achilles to be repeatedly πόδας ὠκύς "swift-footed," Hector

κορυθαίολος "of the flashing helmet," and Menelaus ξανθός
"sandy." But variety caused men in special situations to
speak in a sharply defined manner, not just (δ') ἀπαμειβόμενος "answering" or (καὶ) φωνήσας "saying"—as it
caused Achilles and Odysseus, Hector and Ajax, and
Menelaus and Diomedes, to have six different epithets
rather than just the three the scansion demanded. So with
respect to economy and variety, the participles and the
epithets correspond very well. Let us therefore test the argument for history by applying it to the participles. Does the
greatness of their number mean that they are accurate records of the past? It ought to be clear what we are asking:
not whether the *Iliad* has a core of truth, but whether it is
true in every episode.

c. Is comparable epic poetry fictional?

Jean Rychner, *La Chanson de geste* (Geneva and Lille 1955)
126–153, has extended the Parry theory so as to comment
powerfully upon the nature of the epics in Old French. For
example, when a man spurs his horse in the *Song of Roland*,
or the other chansons of the genre, the spurs may be cutting
or burnished or golden or made of mother-of-pearl, the
choice among these adjectives (or epithets) depending on the
assonance of the laisse. The comparative analysis of the two
traditions is rewarding; and if here the *Iliad* must lend,
elsewhere it may be able to borrow. The *Roland* tells of an
attack, brought about by the treachery of the Frankish
nobleman Ganelon, upon the rearguard of Charlemagne's
army, by a battalion of Saracens; and of the vengeance taken
upon them and the traitor. It is a holy war: "pagans are
wrong, and Christians are right" (line 1015) is the belief of
the one force, and the converse the belief of the other. But

what really happened, according to the nearly contemporary historian Eginhardt, is that Roland and the rearguard, on return from having supported certain Saracen princes against their Caliph, were attacked by (Christian) Gascons, or Basques. This is a very clear instance of how an historical occurrence has been changed, almost beyond recognition, by the poets who kept it from being forgotten; and Rhys Carpenter, *Folk Tale, Fiction and Saga in the Homeric Epics* (Berkeley and Los Angeles 1946) 39–40, asks whether what took place at Troy is not likely to have been distorted similarly. The answer he gives is surely the best: some details from the *Iliad* may be accurate, and no one can say whether they are few or many; others may ring true and yet be false. So the προσέφη participles from our list are not likely to be historical every one; the principle of variety will wholly account for their number; and from the analogy we assumed let the epithets be explained similarly. To justify the restriction of κορυθαίολος and χαλκοκορυστής, the argument for variety is both necessary and sufficient; the argument for history is neither. It is possible that Hector was once unique for his metallic helmet; but he may have had no unusual feature and been assigned one arbitrarily; or he may have been created by the poetic imagination and given an epithet implying an imaginary distinction: there is no way of deciding. This fulfils our second objective.

III. The effect of the epithets upon the poetic imagination

The epithets are significantly true to individual character —partly, perhaps, because they contain a nugget of history; but I have argued that most of the explanation must come from elsewhere. Let us ask whether the epithets, used not for

their own meaning but for stretching out their nouns to convenient length, may not have stimulated the mind of the
poet.

a. When are the epithets explained in context?

Agamemnon orders the "clear-voiced" heralds not to
shout in calling the men to assembly (*Il.* 9.10–12) when the
Trojans are camped near by; and "howling" dogs do not
bark but wag their tails (*Od.* 16.4–5) when they recognize
the man approaching as a friend—readers of the Sherlock
Holmes story "Silver Blaze" will recall "the curious incident
of the dog in the night-time." In both instances the poet used
conventional epithets—"clear-voiced heralds" occurs in four
other passages, "howling dogs" in one other—and then decided, as if from afterthought, to negate them. Similarly, the
"swift" dog of Odysseus used to run after goats and rabbits,
but now has no longer the strength even to stir himself; for
old age has come upon him (*Od.* 17.291–304): once more,
the poet has righted the small wrong done by a timeworn
phrase. ("Swift," or Argus, has often, always?, been regarded by modern readers as the dog's name, but until the
end of the episode—lines 326–327, which may be a very
great interpolation—we have no reason, other than the
paroxytone in the text, not to take it as the ordinary epithet:
for other "swift dogs" see *Il.* 1.50, 18.283, *Od.* 2.11, 17.52,
20.145.) And finally, the question "How could Hector have
escaped if Apollo had not made his knees swift?" (*Il.* 22.202–
204) tells why the man who is dozens of times said to be
swift-footed (see lines 188 and 193) has not overtaken him.
The heralds and the dogs should normally be heard afar, the
dog and Achilles should normally be preeminent in chase:
so much the epithets lead us to infer. Aware of the contradic-

tions, the poet has glossed them over. The epithets in "Ennomus the diviner from birds" (*Il.* 2.858) and "Scamandrius the skillful in hunting" (*Il.* 5.49)—the former of these phrases being found elsewhere, the latter not—are also commented upon, right after their occurrence: good divining did not save the one man, nor good hunting the other. And the phrase "Polymele the fair in the dance" (*Il.* 16.180) is followed by an account of how, while on the dance floor, she quickened the desire of Apollo. It would seem that the poet was not oblivious to the epithets but at times immediately justified them or expanded upon them. The number of such examples is not great, however, and they should not detain us longer. It is more important, as well as more interesting, that the poet gave heed to the epithets even when they were not at hand; and we can see (or speculate) about why he did so.

b. When are the epithets explained out of context?

As a rule, an epithet refers to its noun and lacks a special association with any context, while other elements refer to their contexts and lack a special association with any noun. Everyone knows that Ajax is τελαμώνιος but no one recalls whether he ever speaks (δὲ) βαρὺ στενάχων "groaning greatly." Furthermore, the names of the men and gods differ from most other nouns by not alluding to the world of common experience, and the epithets accompanying these names consequently differ from most other epithets by not being true intuitively. That Ajax is τελαμώνιος is legendary but that the spear is δολιχόσκιον "far-shadowing" is clear to see. For these reasons it seems to me that the poet was induced to create and retain episodes fulfilling the epithets of his chief figures. From the influence of τελαμώνιος, Ajax

continued to be a Telamon or gigantic immobile shield
warrior, and the telamon or strap of his shield continued to
be an important piece of his equipment: both ideas were
brought to mind by the epithet and could never be forgotten.
His shield came to be referred to with a special noun that
had special epithets which themselves were given prominence
in special descriptions or allusions. He also became $T\epsilon\lambda\alpha$-
$\mu\omega\nu\iota\acute{\alpha}\delta\eta\varsigma$ "Telamoniades" and $\upsilon\acute{\iota}\grave{o}\varsigma$ $T\epsilon\lambda\alpha\mu\hat{\omega}\nu o\varsigma$ "son of
Telamon" as $\tau\epsilon\lambda\alpha\mu\acute{\omega}\nu\iota o\varsigma$ was regarded as a patronymic.
There was no reason why any of these details should replace
the others, and at the end of the tradition $\tau\epsilon\lambda\alpha\mu\acute{\omega}\nu\iota o\varsigma$ was in
all ways more accurate than at the beginning. None of this
could have happened, though, if the epithet had not been
largely restricted. Other men—especially anyone with a
name the same size as Ajax's (and even more especially a
second Ajax)—had to be described differently. Here, then,
is a single instance of an epithet explained out of context.
But we need a general theorem, even if it is full of uncertain-
ties (the parentheses show how one example may be sub-
stituted for another).

    Immediately upon its coinage the epithet $\kappa o\rho\upsilon\theta\alpha\acute{\iota}o\lambda o\varsigma$
($\pi\acute{o}\delta\alpha\varsigma$ $\grave{\omega}\kappa\acute{\upsilon}\varsigma$) was recognized as interesting; soon afterwards
it may have been used with any name of appropriate length.
The epithet may or may not have existed before it was used
with the name of Hector (Achilles), who may or may not
have been already famous for the helmet (swiftness of foot).
The phrase $\kappa o\rho\upsilon\theta\alpha\acute{\iota}o\lambda o\varsigma$ $"E\kappa\tau\omega\rho$ ($\pi\acute{o}\delta\alpha\varsigma$ $\grave{\omega}\kappa\grave{\upsilon}\varsigma$ $'A\chi\iota\lambda\lambda\epsilon\acute{\upsilon}\varsigma$) was
sooner or later used in a context where the epithet was not
clearly relevant, and here $\kappa o\rho\upsilon\theta\alpha\acute{\iota}o\lambda o\varsigma$ ($\pi\acute{o}\delta\alpha\varsigma$ $\grave{\omega}\kappa\acute{\upsilon}\varsigma$) con-
veyed that the helmet (swiftness of foot) had some enduring
connection with Hector (Achilles). All poets began to use
the phrase $\kappa o\rho\upsilon\theta\alpha\acute{\iota}o\lambda o\varsigma$ $"E\kappa\tau\omega\rho$ ($\pi\acute{o}\delta\alpha\varsigma$ $\grave{\omega}\kappa\grave{\upsilon}\varsigma$ $'A\chi\iota\lambda\lambda\epsilon\acute{\upsilon}\varsigma$), not
for the epithet but merely as a metrical variant of the name:

they associated the sound of the epithet with the sound of the name and the meaning of the epithet with the man referred to by the name. As a consequence of its affinity with Hector (Achilles), κορυθαίολος (πόδας ὠκύς) was restricted to him alone. Episodes involving the helmet (swiftness of foot) and Hector (Achilles) together were exceptionally likely to be created and to survive: for this reason κορυθαίολος (πόδας ὠκύς) can be said to have influenced the shape of the epic matter. The epithet thus came to have greater contextual relevance than would have been the result of average luck, and also became more than ever true to the singular nature, or ability, or appearance, of Hector (Achilles). All major, more or less distinctive, and highly colorful epithets of men and gods acquired these relationships with the figures whose names they accompanied—except that πολύμητις "of many counsels" and πολύτλας "much-enduring," for Odysseus; πόδας ὠκύς or ποδάρκης, both "swift-footed," for Achilles; κρείων "ruling" or ἄναξ ἀνδρῶν "king of men," for Agamemnon; κορυθαίολος "of the flashing helmet," for Hector; ἱππότα "horseman," for Nestor; and ἑκάεργος "far working," for Apollo, were more handsomely illustrated than ξανθός "sandy," for Menelaus, or γλαυκῶπις "of the bright eyes," for Athene.

Page's view of the epithets is largely at odds with my own; yet in some ways they are identical, and in some others compatible. He believes that Hector's metallic helmet was once historically unique, but does not say whether κορυθαίολος bears significantly on the *Iliad*. I am skeptical of the helmet's being historically unique, but am convinced that κορυθαίολος is relevant to—it may possibly have been coined from (but more probably led to the creation of)—a scene from the sixth book. He believes that πόδας ὠκύς and ποδάρκης either record a historical fact or were coined from an early version

of the twenty-second book, but does not say whether they
bear significantly on the other episodes of the *Iliad*. I am
uncertain whether they record a historical fact, or were
coined from an early version of the twenty-second book, or
led to the creation of that book, but am convinced that they
led to the creation of other episodes in which the swiftness of
Achilles is manifest or remarked upon.

c. What are the aesthetic effects of the epithets?

First, those many epithets that recur without particular
relevance to context—Andromache tells how her brothers
were killed "among the white sheep and the rolling-gaited
oxen" (*Il.* 6.424)—call attention unpredictably to the
special excellence of all things; C. S. Lewis, *A Preface to
Paradise Lost* (Oxford 1942) 30, summed it up in his phrase
"the unwearying, unmoved, angelic speech of Homer."
Second, the epithets are convincing by virtue of their recurrence: we are quite sure that the aegis is θυσσανόεσσα
"fringed" and Menelaus ξανθός "sandy." Third, they provide certain valuable distinctions: the aegis and the aspis—
Menelaus and Diomedes, Hector and Ajax, Achilles and
Odysseus—might to a far greater degree have been described as alike. Fourth, some epithets are relevant to context because they were chosen with no less care than the
προσέφη participles were: μειλιχίοις (ἐπέεσσι) "with soft
(words)" and κερτομίοις (ἐπέεσσι) "with hard (words),"
since they are identical in meter, were used according to
sense; and, except that alternatives referring to the man
alive are not so easy to find, the same is true for (Πατροκλῆος)
δειλοῖο "wretched (Patroclus)," (Μενοιτιάδαο) θανόντος
"dead (Menoetiades)," and (Πατρόκλοιο) θανόντος "dead
(Patroclus)." Fifth, some epithets are relevant to context

because they are commented upon where they occur: we recall Polymele "fair in the dance" (*Il.* 16.180) and the "clear-
voiced" heralds (9.10). Sixth, some are true to character
because—or so I am convinced—they affected the poet's
conception of his heroes: if not for πόδας ὠκύς and ποδάρκης,
why should Idomeneus have been given to say that in
swiftness of foot no one could match Achilles?

Frederick M. Combellack, "Milman Parry and Homeric
Artistry," *Comparative Literature* 11 (1959) 193–208, argues
that as a rule there is no telling whether an epithet was used
largely for its sense or solely to lengthen the noun it had
become associated with: the poet may have said less what he
wanted to than what he could. The poetry remains the same;
we merely recognize that the quality of a passage may be
partly due to the quality of the traditional diction. But if the
epithets were not usually determined by their contexts, they
may now and then have determined those contexts. Consider the line that occurs more often than any other in
Homeric poetry: τὸν δ᾽ ἀπαμειβόμενος προσέφη πολύμητις
᾽Οδυσσεύς "and answering him said Odysseus of many
counsels." Does πολύμητις here announce, and was it in any
way intended to announce, the eloquence of the speech that
follows? The epithet serves to express the name in a phrase
of the required size, and, having done so very frequently, it
has become prominent among the reasons (all the others
being beyond the domain of analysis) why—to the poet and
hence to ourselves—Odysseus is a man whose words are of
special persuasiveness or force. From time to time πολύμητις
is not only metrically valuable and true to character but
relevant to context as well: Odysseus is of many counsels in
actuality just when the appropriate epithet happens to
occur.

But I do not wish to suggest that the distinctive epithets of

the major heroes are relevant to context very often; for they
are not. I am more concerned with emphasizing that, even
when not relevant to context, they give the impression of
being true to character—not merely because they are tied
firmly to their names, but also, and chiefly, because the men
denoted by the names really do have, here or there in the
Iliad, a special claim on the traits and arms that the epithets
repeatedly speak of. Are the episodes that show us the counsels of Odysseus, the swiftness of Achilles, the helmet of
Hector, the shield of Ajax, the kingship of Agamemnon, and
the horsemanship of Nestor, forcibly and inevitably brought
to mind by the various occurrences of πολύμητις, πόδας ὠκύς,
κορυθαίολος, τελαμώνιος, ἄναξ ἀνδρῶν, and ἱππότα? No, not
forcibly and inevitably. And yet I think that now and then
an epithet resembles, in its effect, the upraised finger of
Thomas in *The Last Supper* by Leonardo.

Three / The kennings for Beowulf rank high in relevance to context, but low in economy, when measured against the epithets for the Homeric heroes.

Old English and Greek epic both appear to describe the narration of verse in the heroic age. Hrothgar's court bard sings of the encounters at Finnsburg (*Beowulf* 1068–1159) and improvises the tale of Beowulf's exploits in a complimentary comparison of the Geatish visitor with Sigemund (871–892); Alcinous' court bard sings of the discovered adultery of Ares and Aphrodite (*Odyssey* 8.266–366) and takes up a tale of Odysseus while the Ithacan wanderer listens on (*Od.* 8.499–520). Nothing in all this is autobiographical: unlike the poets of *Deor* and *Widsith*, the poet of *Beowulf* is not concerned with his own identity; the poet of the *Odyssey*, reputed blind, reveals himself not at all in singing of blind Demodocus. Since none of these glimpses into the making of poetry without the use of writing is intended to incorporate a signature into the epic matter, there is prima-facie evidence that *Beowulf* and the Homeric poems each derive from an oral tradition. Furthermore, it has long been undeniable that both works are somewhat formulaic. The *Angelsächsischer Sprachschatz* of C. W. M. Grein

(Göttingen 1864), revised by F. Holthausen and J. J. Köhler (Heidelberg 1912), isolates repeated phrases quite as clearly as do the Prendergast (1875) and Dunbar (1880) Homeric concordances; and *Die wörtlichen Wiederholungen im Bêowulf* by Richard Kistenmacher (Greifswald 1898) lists the phrases much in the manner of Schmidt's *Parallel-Homer* (1885).

That *oral* and *formulaic* mean somewhat the same thing has also been established for half a century by the summary of H. Munro Chadwick, *The Heroic Age* (Cambridge 1912) 320:

Thus in the first part of Beowulf eight speeches out of thirteen by the hero himself are introduced by the formula: *Beowulf maþelode bearn Ecgþeowes*, while three of Hrothgar's seven speeches follow the words: *Hroðgar maþelode helm Scyldinga*. In the Iliad we may compare the constant repetition of such formulae as: τὸν δ' ἀπαμειβόμενος προσέφη κρείων Ἀγαμέμνων or: τὸν δ' ἡμείβετ' ἔπειτα Γερήνιος ἱππότα Νέστωρ. The explanation of such formulae is probably to be found in the fact that both sets of poems were designed for preservation by oral tradition. In literary poems such as the Aeneid they seem to be avoided.

Yet it is possible to go a short but important distance further, so as to say that only an oral poet would have found a formulaic style necessary. This refinement in theory was developed in the Homeric studies of Milman Parry, extended to Serbo-Croatian by Parry and Albert B. Lord, and further extended to Old English by Lord and Francis P. Magoun, Jr.: Lord in his 1949 Harvard dissertation, published in revised form as *The Singer of Tales* (Cambridge, Mass. 1960), and Magoun in "Oral-Formulaic Character of Anglo-Saxon Narrative Poetry," *Speculum* 28 (1953) 446–467. Credit due primarily to Parry has sometimes been given to Lord; credit due primarily to Lord has often been given to Magoun.

Parry—"Studies in the Epic Technique of Oral Verse-Making, I," *Harvard Studies in Classical Philology* 41 (1930) 118–121—took passages from the *Iliad* and *Odyssey* and underlined all the elements recurring elsewhere in either poem. Lord (p. 201 of his dissertation, p. 199 of *The Singer of Tales*) and Magoun (pp. 464–467 of the *Speculum* essay) follow him by taking passages from Old English poetry and underlining all the elements that recur in the same corpus. The results have been widely admired, but they are not reliable or discriminating, or analytical. They are not reliable because there is always doubt whether the specimen underlined is typical: *Iliad* 8.381–396 is heavily formulaic since every one of its lines recurs within *Il.* 5.720–767, whereas *Il.* 2.188–238 is less formulaic since none of its lines recurs in either the *Iliad* or the *Odyssey*; and in the same way some passages from *Beowulf* (for example, lines 1492–1500) have a far greater proportion of elements repeated elsewhere in extant Old English poetry than do some others (for example 1146–1159a). The results are not discriminating because the underlining impedes rather than furthers comparison: Lord and Magoun imply that Homer and *Beowulf* are formular while Virgil and Chaucer are not; but with regard to brief phrases the truth is that, whereas Homer has a much higher order of repetition than Virgil, *Beowulf* does not have a much higher order of repetition than Chaucer: see the 1966 Michigan State University dissertation of Edward J. Wolff. Finally, the results are not analytical because the underlining obscures rather than highlights the formula type: the exceptionally powerful summations that Parry began with—*L'Épithète traditionnelle dans Homère* (Paris 1928) 50–51—have no analogue in the Old English studies of Lord and Magoun. Let us therefore make a new start.

I. When compared with the *Iliad* or the *Song of Roland*, *Beowulf* has few repeated lines and passages.

According to Schmidt, *Parallel-Homer* (1885) viii, over eighteen hundred different lines recur without the slightest change in the *Iliad* and *Odyssey*. But we cannot expect to find two hundred different lines recurring in *Beowulf*, though it is a ninth as long, for when a work increases in size the proportion of its repeated elements increases even more rapidly. Nor can we in all fairness offer a comparison from the entire corpus of Old English poetry, since the Homeric poems are far more similar than are, say, the *Rune Poem* and the *Meters of Boethius*. So we shall ask instead whether more or fewer lines recur within the first 3182 lines of the *Iliad* than do within the 3182 lines of *Beowulf*. The answer here will be as dependable as any we could come to. In deciding whether similar lines are to be regarded as identical, we shall be strict in dealing with the *Iliad* but permissive in dealing with *Beowulf*. The presence or absence of a *nu* movable at the end of the line will not be taken into account when we add up the repeated lines in the *Iliad*, but otherwise we shall not overlook any variation whatsoever: ὣς ἄρα φωνήσασ᾽ ἀπεβήσετο, τὸν δὲ λίπ᾽ αὐτοῦ (*Il.* 1.428) and ὣς ἄρα φωνήσας ἀπεβήσετο, τὸν δ᾽ ἔλιπ᾽ αὐτοῦ (*Il.* 2.35) will be regarded as different, even though when pronounced they must have sounded the same. On the other hand, in drawing up the list from *Beowulf* we shall include all instances of consecutive half-lines (a *b* half-line with either a preceding or a following *a* half-line) where the accented syllables are alike, or almost alike, and in the same order.

A total of one hundred fifteen different lines, some occurring in identifiably formulaic passages and some not, are used at least twice each in the first 3182 lines of the *Iliad*. They are as follows, passages preceding single lines: 1.13–16 = 1.372–375, 1.22–25 = 1.376–379, 1.37–38 = 1.451–452, 1.458–461 = 2.421–424, 1.464–469 = 2.427–432 (1.468 = 1.602 = 2.431), 2.23–32 = 2.60–69 (2.13–15 = 2.30–32 = 2.67–69), 2.161–162 = 2.177–178, 2.164–165 = 2.180–181, 2.373–374 = 4.290–291, 3.71–72 = 3.92–93, 4.66–67 = 4.71–72, 4.102–103 = 4.120–121, 4.196–197 = 4.206–207, 4.534–535 = 5.625–626; 1.43 = 1.457, 1.68 = 1.101 = 2.76, 1.73 = 1.253 = 2.78 = 2.283, 1.130 = 1.285 = 2.369 = 4.188, 1.196 = 1.209, 1.201 = 2.7 = 4.312 = 4.369, 1.232 = 2.242, 1.356 = 1.507 = 2.240, 1.361 = 5.732, 1.517 = 4.30, 1.538 = 1.556, 1.551 = 4.50, 1.552 = 4.25, 2.17 = 2.168, 2.45 = 3.334, 2.47 = 2.187, 2.52 = 2.444, 2.72 = 2.83, 2.91 = 2.464, 2.113 = 2.288, 2.158 = 2.174, 2.167 = 4.74, 2.173 = 4.358, 2.271 = 4.81, 2.313 = 2.327, 2.341 = 4.159, 2.371 = 4.288, 2.516 = 2.680 = 2.733, 2.524 = 2.747, 2.534 = 2.545 = 2.630 = 2.644 = 2.710 = 2.737 = 2.759, 2.541 = 4.464, 2.568 = 2.652, 2.703 = 2.726, 2.785 = 3.14, 2.790 = 3.129, 2.860 = 2.874, 3.15 = 5.14 = 5.630, 3.29 = 5.494, 3.73 = 3.256, 3.75 = 3.258, 3.86 = 3.304, 3.127 = 3.131 = 3.251, 3.136 = 3.253, 3.262 = 3.312, 3.266 = 3.341, 3.276 = 3.320, 3.287 = 3.460, 3.297 = 3.319, 3.343 = 4.80, 3.355 = 5.280, 3.358 = 4.136, 3.374 = 5.312, 4.39 = 5.259, 4.47 = 4.165, 4.89 = 5.169, 4.90 = 4.201, 4.92 = 5.123, 4.284 = 4.337, 4.292 = 4.364, 4.411 = 5.251, 4.495 = 5.562 = 5.681, 4.496 = 5.611, 4.504 = 5.42 = 5.540, 5.31 = 5.455, 5.84 = 5.627, 5.101 = 5.283, 5.179 = 5.229, 5.274 = 5.431, 5.317 = 5.346.

Since the list from *Beowulf* is much shorter, we may write out the examples, taking special notice of the widest deviations from word-for-word identity. Here again the passages precede single lines.

se wæs moncynnes   mægenes strengest
on þæm dæge   þysses lifes (196–197)
he was of mankind   of might the strongest
on that day   of this life

se þe manna wæs   mægene strengest
on þæm dæge   þysses lifes (789–790)
he who of men was   in might the strongest
on that day   of this life

(197 = 790 = 806)

on þære medubence   maþðum gesealde
yrfelafe   (1052–1053a)
on the mead-bench   treasure gave
an heirloom

on meodubence   maþme þy weorþa
yrfelafe   (1902–1903a)
on [the] mead-bench   by the treasure worthier
an heirloom

manigre mægþe   geond þisne middangeard (75 = 1771)
to many a tribe   throughout this mid-yard

mære mearcstapa   se þe moras heold (103)
famous waste-stepper   who moors held

micle mearcstapan   moras healdan (1348)
great waste-steppers   moors hold

ond þa cearwylmas   colran wurðaþ (282)
and the care-wellings   cooler become

æfter cearwælmum   colran weorðað (2066)
after care-wellings   cooler become

Hroðgar maþelode   helm Scyldinga (371 = 456 = 1321)
Hrothgar spoke   helm of the Scyldings

seon sibbegedriht   samod ætgædere (387)
the band of kinsmen to see   all together

swefan sibbegedriht   samod ætgædere (729)
the band of kinsmen to sleep   all together

þe æt fotum sæt   frean Scyldinga (500 = 1166a)
who at the feet sat   of the Scyldings' lord

Beowulf maþelode   bearn Ecgþeowes (529 = 631 = 957
                                    = 1383 = 1473 = 1651 = 1817 =
                                    1999 = 2425)
Beowulf spoke   child of Ecgtheow

þa wæs on salum   sinces brytta (607)
then was in joy   [the] wealth's giver

sinces brytta   þu on sælum wes (1170)
wealth's giver   be thou in joy

þæt mihtig god   manna cynnes (701 = 1725)
that mighty god   mankind

inwidsorge   þe hie ær drugon (831)
evil sorrow   which they earlier endured

inwitniþas   þe hie ær drugon (1858)
evil afflictions   which they earlier endured

swiðhicgende   to sele þam hean (919 = 1016)
stout-hearted   to the high hall

gimfæste gife   ðe him god sealde (1271 = 2182)
ample gift   which god gave him

næfne he wæs mara   þonne ænig man oðer (1353)
except that he was bigger   than any other man

buton hit wæs mare   ðonne ænig mon oðer (1560)
save that it was bigger   than any other man

swylce þu ða madmas   þe þu me sealdest (1482)
also thou the treasures   that thou didst give me

Ic him þa maðmas   þe he me sealde (2490)
I him the treasures   that he gave me

ær he þone grundwong   ongytan mehte (1496 = 2770)
before he the ground-plain   might perceive

forbarn brodenmæl   wæs þæt blod to þæs hat (1616)
burnt up the intricate sword   the blood was so hot

forbarn brogdenmæl   swa þæt blod gesprang (1667)
burnt up the intricate sword   so that blood sprang

þæs þe hi hyne gesundne   geseon moston (1628)
so that they him sound   might see

þæs ðe ic ðe gesundne   geseon moste (1998)
so that I thee sound   might see

hæle hildedeor   Hroðgar gretan (1646 = 1816)
hero battle-fierce   Hrothgar to greet

ond þegna gehwylc   þinra leoda (1673)
and every one of the thanes   of thy people

ond þegna gehwam   þara leoda (2033)
and to each of the thanes   of the people

ðæm selestan   be sæm tweonum (1685 = 1956)
the best   between the seas

æfter hæleþa hryre   hwate Scyldungas (2052 = 3005)
after the fall of heroes   valiant Scyldings

no ðy ær suna sinum   syllan wolde (2160)
not the earlier to his son   would give

nu ic suna minum   syllan wolde (2729)
now I to my son   would give

gledum forgrunden   him ðæs guðkyning (2335)
with flames destroyed   him for this the war-king

gledum forgrunden   þa gen guðkyning (2677)
with flames destroyed   still the war-king

ofer sæ sohtan   suna Ohteres (2380)
over the sea sought   the sons of Ohtere

ofer sæ side   sunu Ohteres (2394)
over the wide sea   the son of Ohtere

Wiglaf maðelode   Weohstanes sunu (2862 = 3076)
Wiglaf spoke   Weohstan's son

                    wæs þæt gewin to strang
lað ond longsum   (133b–134a = 191b–192a)
                    that struggle was too strong
grievous and long-lasting

                    sidfæþmed scip
on ancre fæst   (302b–303a)
                    broad-bosomed ship
on anchor fast

                    sidfæþme scip
oncerbendum fæst   (1917b–1918a)
                    broad-bosomed ship
with anchor-ropes fast

                    ende gebidan
worolde lifes   (1386b–1387a = 2342b–2343a)
                    the end await
of the world's life

                    him ðæs guðkyning
Wedere þioden   (2335b–2336a = 3036b–3037a)
                    him for this the war-king
prince of the Weders

	bugan sceolde
feoll on feðan	(2918b–2919a)
	had to bend
fall in the ranks	

	bugan sceolde
feoll on foldan	(2974b–2975a)
	had to bend
fall on the earth	

(All but five of these are given on pp. 386–389 of the valuable 1956 Harvard dissertation by Robert Payson Creed. Several other lines from the epic go some way towards being identical; among these are 1684b–1686 & 2382–2383, 51 & 1346, 214 & 896, 268 & 645, 289 & 1833, 382 & 458, 460 & 1330, 470 & 1380, 504 & 2996, 698 & 1273, 732 & 784, 762 & 797, 848 & 1593, 1245 & 2153 & 2615, 1258 & 1538 & 2139, 1338 & 2061, 1474 & 2011, 1492 & 2551, 1496 & 2588, 1574 & 2977, 1587 & 3003, 1700 & 2864, 1712 & 2125, 1779 & 2330, 1832 & 2644, 1847 & 2358, 1849 & 2981, 1867 & 2143, 1915 & 1994 & 3108, 1963 & 2949, 2027 & 3080, 2080 & 2127, 2209 & 2733, 2303 & 2934, 2483 & 2991, 2560 & 2576, 2602 & 2862, 200b–201a & 1597b–1598a, 416b–417a & 1591b–1592a, 672b–673a & 1696b–1697a, 796b–797a & 2655b–2656a, 858b–859a & 1956b–1957a, 946b–947a & 1758b–1759a, 1046b–1047a & 3141b–3142a, 1484b–1485a & 2991b–2992a, 2350b–2351a & 2543b–2544a. But they cannot be added to the list unless the rules are relaxed so as to admit a great number of further examples from the *Iliad*.)

Since we have regarded lines from *Beowulf* as identical even when they are no more than ninety percent alike but have regarded lines from the *Iliad* as identical only when they are entirely alike, and since we have included from *Beowulf*

4

but not from the *Iliad* such elements as consist of the latter part of one line with the former part of the next, and since the lines from *Beowulf* are not so long as those from the *Iliad*, our procedure cannot be said to obscure the formular character of *Beowulf* while highlighting the formular character of the *Iliad*. We have a maximum number of thirty-three different lines that recur within the 3182 lines of *Beowulf* (two of these combining into a formulaic passage) to compare with a minimum number of one hundred fifteen different lines that recur within the first 3182 lines of the *Iliad*. On this basis the one poem is less than a third as formulaic as (the first part of) the other.

(And if we insist upon perfect congruence, disregarding the spelling variations in *Beowulf* and the *nu* movable at the end of the line in the *Iliad*, but taking account of every word and inflection, we find fourteen consecutive syllables that recur without change—where? Nowhere in *Beowulf*, but in each of the one hundred fifteen lines that we have listed from the opening books of the *Iliad*.)

Some half-lines from *Beowulf* (owing to their full alliteration) must always be *a* half-lines; others (owing to their partial alliteration) may be either *a* or *b* half-lines. So we might not have been able to predict that the first part of the line would appear scarcely more highly formulaic than the second part—Kistenmacher (pp. 33–39) lists 458 repeated *a* and 438 repeated *b* half-lines. From this even distribution we could, however, have deduced that *a* and *b* half-lines would often combine into longer formulas, such as *æfter hæleþa hryre/hwate Scyldungas* "after the fall of heroes/valiant Scyldings" (2052 = 3005). And from the likelihood that alliteration would be a strong cohesive we could have deduced that an *a* half-line would combine more firmly with a following than with a preceding *b* half-line, so that recurring elements like *ende gebidan/worolde lifes* "the end await/of the world's life" (1386b–1387a = 2342b–2343a) would be uncommon. The results are therefore in order and require no further comment. *But the fact remains that neither alliteration nor any other force caused full lines to recur with Homeric frequency. Beowulf* and the *Iliad*, as formulaic poems, may be alike in kind, but they are very different in degree. This conclusion was announced long ago by Walter Morris Hart, *Ballad and Epic* (Boston 1907) 195–198, but has been generally disregarded by analysts of Old English, perhaps because he gave nothing that could rightly be regarded as evidence.

The eighteen sounds of alliteration (and the measured beat) in *Beowulf* answer to the twenty-three kinds of assonance (and the isosyllabism) in the *Song of Roland*. Synonyms in Old English differ in alliteration: *goldweard* "gold warden" (line 3081) and *hordweard* "hoard warden" (2293), *flota famiheals* "floater foamy-necked" (218) and *wudu wundenhals* "wood wound-necked" (298), *ofer hronrade* "over the whale road" (10) and *ofer swanrade* "over the swan road" (200). Those in Old French differ in assonance: *Respondent Franc, Sire vos dites bien* (line 2487), *Respondent Franc, Sire vos dites veir* (3414); *Ed Oliviers li proz e li gentilz* (176), *Ed Oliviers li proz e li corteis* (576), *Ed Oliviers li proz e li vaillanz* (3186); *La bataille est merveillose e comune* (1320), *La bataille est merveillose e pesant* (1412), *La bataille est merveillose e hastive* (1661), *La bataille est de merveillos destreit* (3420), *La bataille est molt dure ed afichiede* (3393), *La bataille est adurede endementres* (1396). Sometimes the demands of alliteration or assonance are met merely by changes in word order: *Geata dryhten* "lord of the Geats" (line 1484) and *dryhten Geata* (2402), *feond mancynnes* "enemy of mankind" (164) and *mancynnes feond* (1276), *sunu Wihstanes* "son of Weohstan" (2752) and *Weoxstanes sunu* (2602); *De son osberc li at romput les pans* "Of his coat of mail he has broken the sections" (line 1300) and *De son osberc li at les pans rompuz* (1601), *Li emperedre molt fierement chevalchet* "The emperor most proudly rides" (739) and *Molt fierement chevalchet l'emperedre* (3316), *E Peitevins e Normanz e Bretons* (3702) and *E Peitevin e Breton e Norman* (3961).

In their half-lines and full lines the two traditions do not correspond so directly. With regard to alliteration, the half-line of *Beowulf* is to the full line as, with regard to assonance, the full line of the *Roland* is to the laisse. A half-line in Old English can occur only when its alliteration is satisfactory, whereas a phrase of similar length in Old French, except at the end of the line, does not participate in assonance and can therefore occur with great freedom. Here we see why such brief elements in *Beowulf* are repeated so much less often than are their analogues in the *Roland* (to take the best example, *Li quens Rodlant* occurs thirty-three times, always before the caesura, in the first 2701 lines). On the other hand, a full line in Old English is not restricted by its alliteration and can therefore occur with great freedom, whereas one in Old French can occur only when its assonance is satisfactory. It follows that such longer elements in *Beowulf* should be repeated *far more often* (by a factor of perhaps a dozen) than their analogues in the *Roland*. But is this reasoning borne out by the evidence? A list of the recurring lines from the *Roland* will enable us to compare them as a group with those from *Beowulf*. In determining where equivalence lies, we shall require congruence in assonance, but (for the sake of completeness) disregard trivial differences elsewhere —as between "*Son* cheval brochet des esporons d'or fin" (line 1245) and "*Lo* cheval brochet des esporons d'or fin" (3353), or between "*Son* cheval brochet des esporons d'ormier" (1549) and "*Lo* cheval brochet des esporons d'ormier" (1738).

The list from the *Roland* is as follows, passages preceding single lines: 1071–1072 = 1703–1704, 1227–1229 = 1575–1577, 1285–1287 = 1539–1541, 1452–1453 = 3306–3307, 1460–1461 = 3321–3322, 3018–3019 = 3195–3196, 38 = 471, 99 = 2478, 105 = 2408, 123 = 428 = 676, 125 = 680, 180 = 740, 230 = 774, 232 = 776, 431 = 2620, 560 = 3187, 576 = 3755, 618 = 1563, 825 = 2873, 828 = 3613, 829a = 3712, 880 = 1214, 903 = 2776, 1089 = 3718, 1102 = 1717, 1132 = 2383, 1142 = 3869, 1145 = 1545 = 1671, 1198 = 1584, 1245 = 3353, 1276 = 1354, 1302 = 3468, 1412 = 3381, 1478 = 2606, 1545 = 1671, 1549 = 1738, 1814 = 2908, 1832 = 3118, 1957 = 3929, 2236 = 2565, 2500 = 3142, 2646 = 3345, 2943 = 4001, 3341 = 3430, 3658 = 3991. (Nearly half of these are given by Mildred K. Pope, "Four Chansons de Geste: A Study in Old French Epic Versification," *Modern Language Review* 8 [1913] 358–359. And by making the rules slightly less severe we can include 10 & 2570, 13 & 2578, 22 & 3540, 86 & 3893, 267 & 864, 547 & 2793, 609 & 2653, 717 & 3658, 844 & 1024, 969 & 1734, 1197 & 1582, 1294 & 2249, and many more.) Thirty-three different lines that recur within the first 3182 lines of the *Roland* compare (when to Old French is given no special privilege answering to the inclusion for Old English of the latter part of one line with the former part of the next) with thirty-three different lines that recur within the 3182 lines of *Beowulf*.

It would be a mistake to say only that whole formulaic lines were no more common in the *Roland* than in *Beowulf*; it must be added that lines from the one, being capable of appearing in relatively few laisses each, recur surprisingly often, whereas lines from the other, being restricted in no similar manner, recur less often than might have been estimated. Assonance kept the figure 33 for the *Roland*, though alliteration did not keep the figure 33 for *Beowulf*, from being a dozen times larger. And we have not even taken account of the fact that in Old French the formulas for "so-and-so said" regularly occupy only the first part of the line, though in Old English the *mapelode* formulas, which are the most impressive among the longer repetitions, occupy entire lines as a matter of course. When either the *Roland* or the *Iliad* is taken for comparison, *Beowulf* has a low order of recurrence in its lines and passages. The task before us is to decide why, and the answer will not be found quickly.

II. The kennings for Beowulf do not recur so regularly as do the epithetic phrases for Odysseus.

We owe much to the nineteenth-century German scholars who studied, largely from *Beowulf* but also from all the other poems in all the Old Germanic dialects, the ways used to express every major concept; I would acknowledge a special debt to Wilhelm Bode, *Die Kenningar in der angelsächsischen Dichtung* (Darmstadt and Leipzig 1886) 15–16. As the eccentric Homeric circumlocution, the epithetic phrase, provided for the needs of the exacting meter, the eccentric Old English circumlocution, the kenning, provided for the needs of alliteration. The epithetic phrase and the kenning were handsome (and therefore esteemed by the epic audience), but they were also of enormous practical value (and therefore esteemed by the poet). The one easily identifiable distinction between them is also readily explained: the noun to be denoted in Homeric Greek was usually adaptable to the meter and therefore included within the epithetic phrase, whereas the noun to be denoted in Old English was usually dissonant with the alliteration and therefore completely replaced by the kenning.

The circumlocutions for the Homeric heroes are apt to fill the last $2\frac{1}{2}$ or $3\frac{1}{4}$ feet of the line, but many of the most impressive examples are of other lengths, and we shall not overlook them until we need to. However, the circumlocutions for the Old English heroes are in very large proportion half-lines, so we shall neglect elements of all other lengths and classify our examples solely according to alliteration. We wish to find whether the mathematical precision attributed to the Homeric poems is also characteristic of the Old English epic. In the following lists the epithetic phrases for Odysseus (from the *Iliad* and *Odyssey* together) are compared with the half-line kennings for Beowulf (in the one work where he is mentioned).

Nominative Case		Frequency *Il. Od.* Total		
'Οδυσεύς				
'Οδυσσεύς				
δῖος 'Οδυσσεύς	— ᴗᴗ — ᴗ	18	41	59
ἐσθλὸς 'Οδυσσεύς	— ᴗᴗ — ᴗ	0	3	3
θρασὺς ... 'Οδυσσεύς	ᴗᴗ ᴗ — ᴗ	0	1	1
πολύμητις 'Οδυσσεύς	ᴗᴗ — ᴗᴗ — ᴗ	13	65	78
διογενὴς ... πολύμητις 'Οδυσσεύς	— ᴗᴗ — ᴗᴗ — ᴗᴗ — ᴗ	0	1	1
πολύμητις ... 'Οδυσσεύς	ᴗᴗ — ᴗ ᴗ — ᴗ	1	2	3
πτολίπορθος 'Οδυσσεύς	ᴗᴗ — ᴗᴗ — ᴗ	2	2	4
διογενὴς ... πτολίπορθος 'Οδυσσεύς	— ᴗᴗ — ᴗᴗ — ᴗᴗ — ᴗ	0	1	1
πολύτλας δῖος 'Οδυσσεύς	ᴗ — — — ᴗᴗ — ᴗ	5	36	41
Λαερτιάδης πολύμητις 'Οδυσσεύς	— — ᴗᴗ — ᴗᴗ — ᴗᴗ — ᴗ	1	0	1

		Frequency		
		Il.	*Od.*	Total
υἱὸς Λαέρταο, πολύτλας				
δῖος Ὀδυσσεύς	— — — — —◡◡ — — —◡◡ — ◡̱	0	1	1
Ὀδυσεὺς δουρικλυτός	◡◡ — — —◡◡	4	0	4
Ὀδυσεὺς Ἰθακήσιος	◡◡ — ◡◡ — ◡◡	0	2	2
τλήμων Ὀδυσεύς	— —◡◡ —	2	0	2
διογενὴς Ὀδυσεύς 1)	—◡◡ —◡◡ —	0	2	2
Ὀδυσσεὺς ... Διὶ				
μῆτιν ἀτάλαντος	◡ — — ◡ — — —◡◡ — ◡̱	1	0	1
Ὀδυσσεὺς δῖος	◡ — — — ◡	0	1	1
Ὀδυσεὺς ...				
διίφιλος	◡◡ — ◡ — ◡◡	1	0	1
Ὀδυσεὺς Λαερτιάδης	◡◡ — — — ◡◡ —	0	1	1
Ὀδυσεὺς πολύμητις	◡◡ — ◡◡ — ◡	3	0	3
διογενὴς Ὀδυσεύς 2)	— ◡◡ — ◡◡ —	1	3	4

Nominative and Accusative Cases

		Il.	*Od.*	Total
υἱὸς (-ν) Λαέρτεω	— — — — —	0	3	3

Genitive Case

		Il.	*Od.*	Total
Ὀδυσῆος				
Ὀδυσσῆος				
Ὀδυσεῦς				
Ὀδυσσέος				
θείου Ὀδυσῆος	— —◡◡ — ◡̱	0	2	2
Ὀδυσσῆος θείοιο	◡ — — — — — ◡̱	3	24	27
Ὀδυσῆος ἀμύμονος				
ἀντιθέοιο	◡◡ — ◡◡ — ◡◡ — ◡◡ — ◡̱	0	1	1
Ὀδυσῆος ...				
κυδαλίμοιο	◡◡ — ◡ — ◡◡ — ◡̱	0	1	1
Ὀδυσῆος ... θείοιο	◡◡ — ◡ — — ◡	1	1	2
Ὀδυσῆος ἀμύμονος	◡◡ — ◡◡ — ◡◡	0	8	8

			Frequency *Il.* *Od.* Total
Ὀδυσσῆος ... ἄνακτος	⏑ — — —	⏑ — ⏒	0 1 1
Ὀδυσσῆος ... ἀντιθέοιο	⏑ — — —	— ⏑⏑ — ⏒	0 1 1
Ὀδυσσῆος ... κυδαλίμοιο	⏑ — — —	— ⏑⏑ — ⏒	0 2 2
Ὀδυσσῆος μεγα-θύμου	⏑ — — — ⏑⏑ — —		0 1 1
Ὀδυσσῆος μεγα-λήτορος	⏑ — — — ⏑⏑ — ⏑⏑		0 1 1
Ὀδυσσῆος ταλα-σίφρονος	⏑ — — — ⏑⏑ — ⏑⏑		1 11 12
δίου Ὀδυσσῆος ταλασίφρονος	— ⏑⏑ — — — ⏑⏑ — ⏑⏑		0 1 1

Genitive and Dative Cases

ἀντιθέου (-ωι) Ὀδυσῆος (-ι) 1)	— ⏑⏑ — ⏑⏑ — ⏒	1 3 4
2)	— ⏑⏑ — ⏑⏑ — ⏑	0 4 4

Genitive and Accusative Cases

Λαερτιάδεω (-ην) Ὀδυσῆος (-α)	— — ⏑⏑ — ⏑⏑ — ⏒	0 14 14

Dative Case

Ὀδυσῆι δαίφρονι	⏑⏑ — ⏑⏑ — ⏑⏑	0 3 3

Dative and Accusative Cases

Ὀδυσῆι (-α)
Ὀδυσσῆι (-α)

		Frequency		
		Il.	*Od.*	Total
Ὀδυσσῆι (-α)				
πτολίπορθωι (-ον)	˘ — — — ˘˘ — ˘̄	0	3	3
Ὀδυσσῆι (-α)				
μεγαλήτορι (-α)	˘ — — — ˘˘ — ˘˘	1	6	7

Accusative Case

Ὀδυσσέα				
κλυτὸν ... Ὀδυσῆα	˘˘ ˘˘ — ˘̄	0	1	1
ἀγακλυτὸν ...				
Ὀδυσῆα	˘ — ˘˘ ˘˘ — ˘̄	0	1	1
Ὀδυσῆα Διὶ μῆτιν				
ἀτάλαντον	˘˘ — ˘˘ — — — ˘˘ — ˘̄	3	0	3
Ὀδυσῆα δαίφρονα				
ποικιλομήτην	˘˘ — ˘˘ — ˘˘ — ˘˘ — ˘̄	1	4	5
Ὀδυσῆα διΐφιλον	˘˘ — ˘˘ — ˘˘	2	0	2
Ὀδυσῆα πολύφρονα	˘˘ — ˘˘ — ˘˘	0	5	5
Ὀδυσῆα ἄνακτα				
δαίφρονα ποι-				
κιλομήτην	˘˘ — ˘˘ — ˘˘ — ˘˘ — ˘˘ — ˘̄	0	1	1
υἱὸν Λαέρταο				
δαίφρονα	— — — — — ˘˘ — ˘˘	0	1	1
Ὀδυσῆα πτολι-				
πόρθιον	˘ — — — ˘˘ — ˘˘	0	2	2

Vocative Case

Ὀδυσεῦ				
Ὀδυσσεῦ				
Λαερτιάδη				
φαίδιμ' Ὀδυσσεῦ	— ˘˘ — ˘̄	0	5	5
πολύαιν' Ὀδυσεῦ μέγα				
κῦδος Ἀχαιῶν	˘˘ — ˘˘ — ˘˘ — ˘˘ — ˘̄	2	1	3

	Frequency		
	Il.	*Od.*	Total
ὦ 'Οδυσεῦ πολύαινε δόλων ἆτ' ἠδὲ πόνοιο	— ∪∪ — ∪∪ — ∪∪ — — — ∪∪ — ≤	1	0	1
ὄλβιε Λαέρταο πάι πολυμήχαν' 'Οδυσσεῦ	— ∪∪ — — — ∪∪ — ∪∪ — ∪∪ — ≤	0	1	1
διογενὲς Λαερτιάδη πολυμήχαν' 'Οδυσσεῦ	— ∪∪ — — — ∪∪ — ∪∪ — ∪∪ — ≤	7	15	22

We see at once that brief elements combine easily into longer ones; the table does not count any phrase twice, but it might have done so with fairness. When augmented by no further epithet, δῖος 'Οδυσσεύς "brilliant Odysseus" occurs fifty-nine times; as a part of πολύτλας δῖος 'Οδυσσεύς "much-enduring brilliant Odysseus," it occurs forty-one more times; and both recur within υἱὸς Λαέρταο, πολύτλας δῖος 'Οδυσσεύς "son of Laertes, much-enduring brilliant Odysseus." The whole system is very taut; few of the phrases are metrically interchangeable. 'Οδυσεὺς 'Ιθακήσιος could replace or be replaced by 'Οδυσεὺς δουρικλυτός, and the same is true for 'Οδυσσῆος ταλασίφρονος and 'Οδυσσῆος μεγαλήτορος, for 'Οδυσῆι (-α) πολύφρονι (-α) and 'Οδυσῆι (-α) δαίφρονι (-α), and for 'Οδυσῆα δαίφρονα ποικιλομήτην and 'Οδυσῆα Διὶ μῆτιν ἀτάλαντον; any one of the three lines διογενὲς Λαερτιάδη πολυμήχαν' 'Οδυσσεῦ, ὄλβιε Λαέρταο πάι πολυμήχαν' 'Οδυσσεῦ, and ὦ 'Οδυσεῦ πολύαινε δόλων ἆτ' ἠδὲ πόνοιο could replace the other two. But every other expression has its own particular role. Some are nearly equivalent but dissimilar in one characteristic; initially or terminally, there is an often important difference between a long vowel and a short one, or between a vowel and a consonant, or between a single consonant and a consonant cluster; though slight, the distinction between πολύμητις 'Οδυσσεύς and πτολίπορθος 'Οδυσσεύς is nonetheless crucial. If we changed the case (and therefore, frequently, the scansion) of certain words, we could indeed make further changes, such as πολυμήτιος for ταλασίφρονος; yet even this forbidden ground tends to be barren. The choice among the locutions and circumlocutions for Odysseus was determined, it would seem, not by the meaning but solely by the hexameter beat. The poet spoke of the much-enduring man at one time and of the man of many counsels at another, but only as the prosody directed.

Side-by-side with these terms for the Homeric hero may be placed those for the hero of *Beowulf*. We shall, however, limit the series by admitting only phrases in the nominative case (or in the accusative when it is identical with the nominative) and by omitting such adjectival forms as *god mid Geatum* and such relative clauses as *se eow ða maðmas geaf*. From the comparison will appear clearly an important difference between the two epic languages.

	Frequency		
	twofold alliteration	single alliteration	
B		10	bearn Ecgþeowes
		1	Beowulf Geata
C	1		cuma collenferhð
D		2	dryhten Geata
		1	dædcene mon
F	1		frod folces weard
		1	feþecempa
		1	folces hyrde
		1	freca Scyldinga
		1	fyrdwyrðe man

	Frequency	
	twofold alliteration	single alliteration
G	2		goldwine Geata
	1		god guðcyning
	1		guðrinc goldwlanc
	1		guma guðum cuð
		2	Geata dryhten
		1	Guðgeata leod
		1	Geata cempa
		1	Geatmecga leod
H	2		hæle hildedeor
	1		har hilderinc
	1		hordweard hæleþa
		2	Higelaces þegn
		1	hringa þengel
		1	hringa fengel
L		1	lidmanna helm
		1	lindgestealla
M		5	mæg Higelaces
		1	maga Ecgðeowes
N		1	niðheard cyning
R		1	rices hyrde
		1	reþe cempa
		1	rof oretta
S	2		sigoreadig secg
	1		secg on searwum
		3	sunu Ecgþeowes
þ	1		þioden þristhydig
W	1		wlanc Wedera leod
	1		wælreow wiga
	1		werodes wisa
		3	Wedera þioden

	Frequency		
	twofold	single	
	alliteration	alliteration	
		3	Wedergeata leod
		2	wigendra hleo
		1	wigena strengel
		1	winia bealdor
vowel	1		eald eþelweard
	1		æþeling ærgod
	1		æðeling anhydig
	1		æðeling unfrom
	1		yrre oretta
		1	eorla dryhten
		1	æþele cempa
		1	ealdor þegna

These expressions provide for several kinds of alliteration
and so confirm our initial theory. (Transverse alliteration,
however, has been neglected, since it occurs no more often
than can be credited to chance.) Many of the expressions
are similar in construction, precisely as we expected they
would be: *feþecempa*, *reþe cempa*, and *Geata cempa* "foot-,
fierce, Geats' warrior"; *Guðgeata leod* and *Wedergeata leod*
"Battle-, Weather-Geats' leader"; *Geata dryhten* and *eorla
dryhten* "Geats', earls' lord." Yet the collection in its entirety
does not seem an inventory of parts inserted mechanically.
Though the phrases having twofold alliteration are distinct
from those having single alliteration (since the one set was
desirable for the *a* half-lines as the other was necessary for the
b half-lines), the availability of many phrases for the same
need is still the rule rather than the exception. The only one
of these fifty half-lines that has been successful in withstand-
ing competition (from *beaga fengel*, *beaducempa*, etc.) is not

surprisingly a member of the only full line that recurs with conspicuous frequency, *Beowulf maþelode, bearn Ecgþeowes*—and even here there are variants (lines 405 and 2724). *In referring to Beowulf packs of elements alliterate alike, though in referring to Odysseus very few elements scan alike*; so our problem appears close to solution. The greater choice of phrases in the Old English than in the Homeric tradition tells why fewer lines and passages recur without change. However, the explanation goes too far, as we shall see.

III. The kennings for Beowulf are less distinctive but more variable than the epithets for the major Homeric heroes.

Until now our analysis has lacked breadth. We must consider figures besides Odysseus and Beowulf, and must do so systematically—by anatomizing two formula types. Those that suggest themselves are impressive for the number, the size, and the frequency of recurrence, of their constituents. Each of the Homeric formulas begins with a consonant, fills the last $3\frac{1}{4}$ feet of the line, and is found at least once in the nominative; each contains an epithetic augment occurring at least twice in phrases of this length and combining at least once with the name of a heroic figure such as Agamemnon or Nestor; one of the required instances of the epithet must also be in the *Iliad*. Each of the Old English formulas is a half-line kenning, or name, that occurs at least twice and refers at least once to a heroic figure such as Hrothgar or Wiglaf; here one of the required instances must be in *Beowulf*. Δόλοψ αἰχμῆς εὖ εἰδώς "Dolops skilled in spearmanship" is ruled out because its epithet does not appear twice in the *Iliad* and *Odyssey*; *helm Scylfinga* "helm of the Scylfings" is ruled out because it does not in its entirety appear twice in

Old English poetry. The category of Homeric formulas is
the more restrictive, since it answers to the Old English
formulas that begin with a single specific letter of alliteration; but the larger number of half-lines is needed to make
the compilation substantial.

The Homeric formulas are as follows (the plus signs separate the occurrences in the *Iliad* from those in the *Odyssey*):
Names that begin with a vowel and fill the last foot: μέγας
κορυθαίολος "Εκτωρ "great Hector of the flashing helmet"
(12 + 0 times); μέγας τελαμώνιος Αἴας "great telamonian
Ajax (12 + 0 times). Names that begin with a consonant and
fill the last foot: Γερήνιος ἱππότα Νέστωρ "Gerenian horseman Nestor" (24 + 10 times); γέρων ἱππηλάτα Πηλεύς "old-
man horse-driver Peleus" (3 + 0 times); γέρων ἱππηλάτα
Φοίνιξ "old-man horse-driver Phoenix" (3 + 0 times);
γέρων ἱππηλάτα Οἰνεύς "old-man horse-driver Oeneus"
(1 + 0 time). Names that begin with a vowel and fill the last
1¼ feet: πολύτλας δῖος 'Οδυσσεύς "much-enduring brilliant
Odysseus" (5 + 37 times); ποδάρκης δῖος 'Αχιλλεύς "swift-
footed brilliant Achilles" (21 + 0 times). Names that begin
with a vowel and fill the last 1½ feet: ἄναξ ἀνδρῶν 'Αγαμέμνων
(-άμεμνον) "king of men Agamemnon" (44 + 3 times);
ἄναξ ἀνδρῶν 'Αγχίσης "king of men Anchises" (1 + 0 time);
ἄναξ ἀνδρῶν Αἰνείας "king of men Aeneas" (1 + 0 time);
ἄναξ ἀνδρῶν Αὐγείας "king of men Augeas" (1 + 0 time);
ἄναξ ἀνδρῶν Εὐφήτης "king of men Euphetes" (1 + 0
time); ἄναξ ἀνδρῶν Εὔμηλος "king of men Eumelus"
(1 + 0 time). Names that begin with a consonant and fill
the last 1½ feet: βοὴν ἀγαθὸς (-ν) Μενέλαος (-ν) "good-at-the-
cry Menelaus" (16 + 9 times); βοὴν ἀγαθὸς Διομήδης "good-
at-the-cry Diomedes" (21 + 0 times); μενεπτόλεμος Πολυποίτης "staunch in war Polypoetes" (4 + 0 times); μενεπτόλεμος
Θρασυμήδης "staunch in war Thrasymedes" (1 + 1 times);

μενεπτόλεμος Πολυφόντης "staunch in war Polyphontes" (1 + 0 time). Names that consist of a short followed by a long syllable: Δόλων Εὐμήδεος υἱός "Dolon Eumedes' son" (3 + 0 times); Θόας Ἀνδραίμονος υἱός "Thoas Andraemon's son" (2 + 1 times). Names that begin with a consonant and consist of a short syllable followed by a complete foot: Λεοντεὺς ὄζος Ἄρηος "Leonteus, scion of Ares" (3 + 0 times); Ποδάρκης ὄζος Ἄρηος "Podarces, scion of Ares" (1 + 0 time). Names that combine with a following epithet of 1½ feet: γέρων Πρίαμος θεοειδής "old-man Priam godlike" (7 + 0 times); Θεοκλύμενος θεοειδής "Theoclymenus godlike" (0 + 5 times); Νεοπτόλεμος θεοειδής "Neoptolemus godlike" (1 + 0 time); Πολύξεινος θεοειδής "Polyxenus godlike" (1 + 0 time).

(Although a remark of A. E. Housman about Horace cannot be applied to the poet of the *Iliad*, who was not "as sensitive to iteration as any modern," the formula μέγας τελαμώνιος Αἴας never occurs when it would be preceded by the name Αἴας in the same line, but is then replaced by the formula πελώριος, ἕρκος Ἀχαιῶν "a giant, bulwark of the Achaeans"; for the sake of convenience such ancillary phrases are omitted from the list. Furthermore, no epithet has been accepted unless, in a phrase of the prescribed size, in the *Iliad*, it accompanies, at least once, a name in the nominative case; for to include Μενοιτίου ἄλκιμος υἱός "Menoetius' valiant son," or Πατροκλῆος λάσιον κῆρ "Patroclus' shaggy heart," but not πελώριος, ἕρκος Ἀχαιῶν, would be invidious—without modifying the conclusions at all. The list also does not take account of phrases that include a δ' or τ' or other particle. The men represented by the formulas are few for good reason: the numerous minor figures of the epic seldom become the subjects of their clauses; they are far more often the slain than the slayers.

With two exceptions none of the listed formulas recurs slightly altered in the oblique cases or the vocative; both the names and the epithets tend to change in meter with a change of case. The digamma at the beginning of ἄναξ ἀνδρῶν and Οἰνεύς is not printed but is observed by the scansion.)

The Old English formulas are as follows (from *Beowulf* except as specified otherwise): Beowulf Geata (676a, 1191a), bearn Ecgþeowes (10 times), byre Wihstanes (Wiglaf 2907b, 3110b), beaga bryttan (Scyld 35a, Hrothgar 352a, 1487a), brego Beorhtdena (Hrothgar 427a, 609a), bearn Healfdenes (Heregar 469a, Hrothgar 1020b), cyning(as) on corþre (Finn 1153a; *Exodus* 191a plural, 466a plural), Deniga frean (Hrothgar 271a, 359a, 1680b), dryhten Geata (Beowulf 2402a, 2901a), freo(a)wine folca (Hrothgar 430a, Hygelac 2357a, Hrethel 2429a), feþecempa (Beowulf 1544a, Wiglaf 2853a), folces hyrde (Hrothgar 610a, Hygelac 1832a, 1849a, Beowulf 2644b, Ongentheow 2981a; *Meters of Boethius* 10.49b Cato; *Battle of Finnsburh* 46b Finn), frean Scyldinga (Hrothgar 291a, 351a, 500b, 1166a), frod(an, e) fyrnwita(n) (Aescere 2123a; *Andreas* 784a plural; *Elene* 343a David, 438a Sachaeus), goldwine Geata (Beowulf 2419a, 2584a), goldwine gumena (Hrothgar 1171a, 1476a, 1602a; *Elene* 201a Constantine; *Judith* 22a Holofernes), gumena dryhten (Hrothgar 1824a; *Genesis* 515a God; *Daniel* 612b Nebuchadnezzar), Geata dryhten (-ne) (Hygelac 1484b, 1831a, 2991b, Haethcyn 2483a, Beowulf 2560b, 2576a), geongum garwigan (Wiglaf 2674a, 2811a), gomela Scylfing (Ongentheow 2487b, 2968a), gamela Scylding (Hrothgar 1792a, 2105b), geongum (-an) cempan (Offa 1948b, indefinite 2044b, Wiglaf 2626a), helm Scyldinga (Hrothgar 371b, 456b, 1321b), hilderinces (-e, -a, -as) (Grendel 986b, Beowulf 1495a, 1576a, plural 3124a; *Dream of the Rood* 61b plural, 72a plural; *Elene* 263a

plural), har hilderinc (Hrothgar 1307a, Beowulf 3136a;
Battle of Maldon 169a Byrhtnoth; *Battle of Brunanburh* 39a
Constantine; *Exhortation to Christian Living* 57a indefinite),
hæle hildedeor (Beowulf 1646a, 1816a, Wiglaf 3111a;
Andreas 1002a Andrew; *Elene* 935a Judas), hordweard
hæleþa (Hrothgar 1047a, Beowulf later 1852a), Higelaces
þegn (Beowulf 194b, 1574b, Eofor 2977b), Hemminges mæg
(Offa 1944b, 1961b), Hreþles eaferan (-a) (Hygelac 1847b,
2358a, 2992a), leofes (-um, -ne, -ra, -ost) mannes (-um, -an,
-a) (Beowulf 297b, 1994a, 2897a, 3108a, plural 1915b, indefinite 1943b, Hondscio 2080a, Aescere 2127a; *Genesis*
1656b plural, 2589a Abraham; *Soul and Body I* 152b the body;
Christ 913b plural; *Guthlac* 1173a Guthlac's servant, 1257a
Guthlac's servant), leofne þeoden (Scyld 34b, Beowulf
3079b), leod Scyldinga (Hrothgar 1653a, Heregar 2159a),
lindgestealla(n) (Beowulf 1973a; *Andreas* 1344a plural),
mære (-es, -um, -ne, -an) þeoden (-nes, -ne) (Hrothgar 129b,
201a, 345a, 1046b, 1598a, 1992a, Beowulf 797a, 2572a,
2788b, 3141b, Heremod 1715a, Onela 2384a; *Genesis* 853b
God; *Andreas* 94a God; *Dream of the Rood* 69a Christ; *Judith*
3a God; *Menologium* 2b Christ), maga (-o) Healfdenes
(Hrothgar 5 times), mæg Higelaces (Beowulf 5 times), mærne
(-um) maguþegn (-e) (Hondscio 2079a; *Andreas* 366a an
angel), magoþegn modig, modige magoþegnas (Wiglaf
2757a; *Andreas* 1140a plural, 1515a plural; *Wanderer* 62a
plural; *Menologium* 82a plural), modiges (-um) mannes
(-um) (Wiglaf 2698a; *Solomon and Saturn* 327a plural),
niðheard cyning (Beowulf 2417b; *Elene* 195a Constantine),
rices hyrde (-as) (Ingeld 2027a, Beowulf 3080a; *Genesis* 2336b
plural; *Exodus* 256b Moses; *Andreas* 807b God; *Juliana* 66b
Elisaeus; *Meters of Boethius* 26.8b Ulysses, 26.41b Apollo;
Seasons for Fasting 93b Pope Gregory), rice (-an) þeoden (-ne),
rices þeoden (Hygelac 1209a; *Genesis* 864b God, 2674b

Abimelech; *Daniel* 33b God, 109b Nebuchadnezzar; *Andreas* 364b God, 415b God; *Judith* 11b Holofernes), rofne randwigan, rofe rondwiggende (Beowulf 1793a; *Judith* 20a plural), sigoreadig secg (Beowulf 1311a, Beowulf earlier 2352a), sunu Ecgþeowes (Beowulf 1550b, 2367b, 2398b), snottra fengel (Hrothgar 1475a, 2156a), secg(as) on searwum (Beowulf 249a, plural 2530a, Wiglaf 2700a), sunu Healfdenes (Hrothgar 7 times), sunu (-a) Ohteres (Eadgils and Eanmund 2380b, Eadgils 2394b, Eanmund 2612a), sunu Ecglafes (Unferth 590b, 980b, 1808a), sinces brytta(n) (Hrothgar 607b, 1170a, Hygelac 1922b, 2071a; *Genesis* 1857b Pharaoh, 2642a Abimelech, 2728b Abimelech; *Elene* 194b Constantine; *Wanderer* 25b indefinite; *Judith* 30a Holofernes; *Preface to Gregory's Dialogues* 24b King Alfred), sunu Wihstanes (Wiglaf 2752b, 3120b), sigerof kyning (Hrothgar 619b; *Elene* 158a Constantine), þeodcyninges (-a, -as) (plural 2a, Beowulf 2694b; *Genesis* 1965a plural; *Fates of the Apostles* 18b indefinite), þeoden (-ne, -nas) mærne (-e, -a -um) (Hrothgar 353a, Beowulf 2721a, plural 3070a; *Genesis* 2145a King of Sodom, 2709b Abimelech; *Christ and Satan* 597b God; *Phoenix* 165b the phoenix; *Juliana* 86a Elisaeus; *Meters of Boethius* 29.96b the Creator), þeoden Scyldinga (Hrothgar 1675a, 1871a), Wedra þeoden (-nes) (Beowulf 2336a, 2656a, 2786b, 3037a), Wedergeata leod (Beowulf 1492b, 1612b, 2551a), wigendra hleo (Hrothgar 429b, Sigemund 899b, Beowulf 1972b, 2337b; *Andreas* 506a Andrew, 896b Andrew, 1450b Andrew, 1672b Matthew; *Christ* 409a God; *Capture of the Five Boroughs* 12b Eadmund), wine (-um) Scyldinga (Scyld 30b, Hrothgar 148a, 170b, 1183a, 2101b, plural 1418a, Ingeld 2026b), Weohstanes sunu (Wiglaf 2602b, 2862b, 3076b), wineleas wræcca, wræccan wineleasum (Eanmund 2613a; *Genesis* 1051a Cain; *Wife's Lament* 10a the wife; *Resignation* 91a indefinite), werodes wisa

(*Beowulf* 259a; *Exodus* 258a Moses; *Gifts of Men* 55a in-
definite), weroda ræswa(n) (Healfdene 60b; *Daniel* 486b
Nebuchadnezzar), æþeling ærgod (Hrothgar 130a, Aescere
1329a, Beowulf 2342a), eorla drihten (Hrothgar 1050b,
Beowulf 2338b; *Judith* 21a Holofernes; *Battle of Brunanburh*
1b Aethelstan), eald eþelweard (indefinite 1702a, Beowulf
2210a), eþelwearde (-as) (Hrothgar 616b; *Daniel* 55b plural;
Judith 320a plural; *Meters of Boethius* 1.24b plural), eodor
Scyldinga (Hrothgar 428a, 663a), æþelinges (-a) bearn
(Sigemund 888a, plural 1408b, 2597a, 3170a; *Genesis* 1654a
plural, 1698a plural, 1737a plural, 2002a plural, 2620a
plural), eaxlgestealla(n, na) (Aescere 1326a, plural 1714a;
Elene 64a plural; *Riddle* 80.1b horn), æþele (-ne) ordfruma(n)
(Ecgtheow 263a; *Christ* 402a God), æþele (-um) cempa(n)
(Beowulf 1312b; *Andreas* 230b Andrew), Ecglafes bearn
(Unferth 499b; *Battle of Maldon* 267a Aescferth), ealdhla-
fordes (-um) (Beowulf 2778b; *Meters of Boethius* 1.63b plural),
Eormenrices (1201a; *Widsith* 8b, 111b; *Deor* 21b).

(The list contains only substantives. It does not include
adjectives such as *feorrancumene*, or adjectival phrases such as
heard under helme, or phrases composed of an adjective and a
definite article such as *þone selestan*; nor does it include relative clauses such as *þe us beagas geaf*. The list also omits
phrases like *leofa Beowulf* that occur only in the vocative.
Sameness in the roots is held to be a reasonable requirement:
eorl ellenrof [*Beowulf* 3063] is not regarded as identical with
eorl ellenheard [*Andreas* 254], nor *leod landfruma* [*Beowulf* 31]
as identical with *leof leodfruma* [*Exodus* 354]. Furthermore,
the order in which the elements occur is not permitted to
vary, unless for the sake of rhythm rather than alliteration:
wineleas wræcca is grouped with *wræccan wineleasum*, but not
hlaford leofne [*Beowulf* 3142] with *leofne hlaford* [*Meters of
Boethius* 26.72]. Parts of hypermetric half-lines are admitted

so long as they comprise full half-lines elsewhere, and differences in case or number are thought insignificant so long as
the standard length is preserved.)

The epithets and kennings stress many of the same
qualities and are even likely to be rough translations of each
other: ἄναξ ἀνδρῶν "king of men" and *freawine folca* "good
lord of the people," κορυθαίολος "of the flashing helmet"
and *secg on searwum* "man at arms," ποδάρκης "swift-footed"
and *feþecempa* "foot-warrior," γέρων "old man" and *har
hilderinc* "old battle-warrior." The formulas point with exceptional sharpness to the traditions they dominate, for
"much-enduring brilliant Odysseus" does not appear in the
Philoctetes of Sophocles, nor any "hoard warden of heroes"
in the prose of the Anglo-Saxon chronicle. The great difference (and it will be seen to be of importance) is that the
Homeric phrase, in accord with the regulations we imposed,
always contains the name of the man himself; whereas the
Old English phrase does so only in *Beowulf Geata* and
Eormenrices.

The first principle governing the distribution of the epithets is that certain men are distinguished from each other
because their names fail to be identical in metrical shape.
Agamemnon shares ἄναξ ἀνδρῶν with five relatively minor
figures who resemble him chiefly in having names that scan
like his; neither Nestor nor Diomedes, nor Odysseus, nor any
other major figure, can be a further ἄναξ ἀνδρῶν without a
flaw in the dactylic rhythm. A similar conclusion from
similar evidence can be drawn almost at will. The epithet
κρείων "ruling" combines with names to create phrases 2½
feet in length: κρείων Ἀγαμέμνων (29 + 1 times); κρείων
Ἐνοσίχθων i.e. Poseidon (5 + 2 times); κρείων Ἀγαπήνωρ
(1 + 0 time); κρείων Ἑλικάων (1 + 0 time); κρείων Ἐλεφή-
νωρ (1 + 0 time); κρείων Εὔμηλος (1 + 0 time); κρείων

'Ετεωνεύς (0 + 1 time). No man besides Agamemnon is both significant in the *Iliad* and ἄναξ ἀνδρῶν or κρείων, a fact that derives from the tendency of the names to differ in meter.

The second principle governing the distribution of the epithets is that certain men are distinguished from each other *even though* their names are identical in metrical shape. Not only are Odysseus πολύτλας and Achilles ποδάρκης in formulas of $3\frac{1}{4}$ feet, in those of $2\frac{1}{2}$ feet they are πολύμητις 'Οδυσσεύς "Odysseus of many counsels" (14 + 66 times) and πόδας ὠκὺς 'Αχιλλεύς "swift-footed Achilles" (30 + 0 times). The epithets in these phrases are never divided between Odysseus and Achilles, nor do they ever apply to anyone else in the *Iliad* or *Odyssey*, except that the genitive πολυμήτιος is once used for Hephaestus, and the accusative πόδας ὠκύν once for Orsilochus. Even Diomedes and Menelaus, who share βοὴν ἀγαθός in formulas of one length, are distinguished from each other, and from most other men as well, by the formulas of another length: κρατερὸς Διομήδης (19 + 0 times), κρατερὸς Διώρης (1 + 0 time), κρατερὸς Λυκόοργος (1 + 0 time), κρατερὸς Λυκομήδης (1 + 0 time), κρατερὸς Πολυποίτης (1 + 0 time), κρατερὸς Μεγαπένθης (0 + 2 times), κρατερὸς Πολύφημος (0 + 2 times), ξανθὸς Μενέλαος (13 + 5 times), ξανθὸς Μελέαγρος (1 + 0 time). A tendency toward distinctive description can in fact be seen throughout: ποδώκεος (-ι, -α), a genitive-dative-and-accusative synonym for πόδας ὠκύς and ποδάρκης, is used 21 + 2 times for Achilles and restricted to him absolutely. Though ταχύς, used for the lesser Ajax in the phrase 'Οιλῆος ταχὺς Αἴας, is also synonymous with ποδάρκης, πόδας ὠκύς, and the inflected form ποδώκεος (-ι, -α), these chief epithets of Achilles themselves, if not their meaning besides, are still discriminative, or specific.

The first principle governing the distribution of the

kennings is that men are distinguished from each other on the basis of age, rank, nation, and ancestry. A man may be young or old; a warrior or a king; a Geat, a Dane, or a Swede; the son of Weohstan or the son of Ecglaf. Nevertheless, when his life is epitomized in a table of formulas, Beowulf appears to resemble Hrothgar in some respects, Hygelac in others, and Wiglaf in still others. Unlike Odysseus, Achilles, and Hector, he has small claim upon adjectives or common nouns that mark him as unique. Neither tradition describes its heroes without concern for their special qualities, and yet the kennings, when placed beside the epithets, must be thought generic. The usage of the other heroic poems is strong corroboration. In the closing lines of the *Battle of Finnsburh, folces hyrde* "shepherd of the people" refers to Finn rather than to Beowulf, Hrothgar, Hygelac, or Ongentheow; although it cannot describe any man who is not a king, it does describe all kings without discrimination; Healfdene might have been a *folces hyrde* in verse now lost. Whether the homiletic and scriptural poems are also worth attention here is uncertain; for they answer to *Beowulf*, not as the *Odyssey*, but as the *Fall of Troy* by Quintus of Smyrna, answers to the *Iliad*. If the *Exhortation to Christian Living* and *Elene* and *Genesis* are crutches denied us, our analysis of *Beowulf* can stand unsupported; if they are available to us, the generic nature of *har hilderinc, sinces brytta,* and *þeoden mærum*, in contrast with πολύτλας or ποδάρκης, is all the more evident.

The first principle governing the epithets, determined as it is by the prosody, has no analogue for the kennings. Given an epithet like ἄναξ ἀνδρῶν "king of men," μενεπτόλεμος "staunch in war," or θεοειδής "godlike," even if we do not recall the entire squad of those to whom it refers, we can ordinarily say a great deal about what the size of their names

must be. Given a kenning like *eorla dryhten* "earls' lord" or
leod Scyldinga "leader of the Scyldings," unless we recall every
one of those to whom it refers, we can say nothing about the
sound of the names replaced. The second principle governing
the epithets, however, is akin to the first governing the kennings: both have to do with the meaning alone. Homeric
poetry so far has a double weight in its pan, and we need to
right the balance by finding some further, and unshared,
property of Old English poetry; only then will the two
traditions appear to characterize their heroes with the same
degree of precision.

Γερήνιος ἱππότα Νέστωρ "Gerenian horseman Nestor"
appears, from the lack of any alternative, to be used without
respect to time or circumstance; the epithet merely lengthens
its noun in the usual procrustean fashion. Throughout the
Odyssey Menelaus is still βοὴν ἀγαθὸς Μενέλαος, though his
war cry is now of little use, and even as a shade his brother
is addressed as ἄναξ ἀνδρῶν ᾿Αγάμεμνον (*Od.* 11.397 and
24.121). The kenning is seldom so devoid of any remote pertinence to the passages where it occurs: not firmly bound to a
name, it can easily be replaced—*by a phrase of the same size
and alliteration*. When a warrior becomes a king he does not
need to be described as a warrior any longer. If once he was
a *guma guðum cuð* "man known for wars" (*Beowulf* 2178a),
he now becomes a *god guðcyning* "good war-king" (2653a);
if once a *reþe cempa* "fierce warrior" (1585a), he becomes a
rices hyrde "shepherd of the kingdom" (3080a); if once a
Geata cempa "Geats' warrior" (1551b), he becomes a *Geata
dryhten* "Geats' lord" (2576a). When Hrothgar is a *har
hilderinc* "old battle-warrior" (1307a) and *folces hyrde*
"shepherd of the people" (610a), the *hæle hildedeor* "hero
battle-fierce" (1646a) and *feþecempa* "foot-warrior" (1544a)
is Beowulf, who later becomes a *har hilderinc* (3136a) and

folces hyrde (2644b), the *hæle hildedior* (3111a) and *feþecempa* (2853a) now being Wiglaf. The Grendel episodes and the dragon episode are in this manner distinguished by an exact transference of formulas. Though neither the ten years between the two Homeric epics nor the changes in personal situation are indicated by the epithets of the heroes common to both poems, the fifty years between the two main parts of the Old English epic and the change from earl to king are decisively indicated by the kennings for the hero of the entire work. Here is the second principle we hoped to discover: most clearly from pairs of half-lines alliterating on *h . . . h* or *f*, but also from many others, we can see that the kennings vary significantly with the context.

(Here too is evidence that *Beowulf* underlines at least faintly the contrast between Youth [lines 1–2199] and Age [2200–3182]. The arrangement of the formulas bears directly on the dispute between J. R. R. Tolkien, "Beowulf: the Monsters and the Critics," *Proceedings of the British Academy* 22 [1936] 271, and Kenneth Sisam, *The Structure of "Beowulf"* [Oxford 1965] 24.)

The two principles for each tradition could be combined: Homeric heroes have their names accompanied by specific epithets that are irrelevant to context; Old English heroes have their names replaced by generic kennings that are relevant to context. But this summary would obscure two interesting facts. First, the epithets are specific partly for a reason with no analogue in Old English poetry (namely, they are affected by the sound of the names) and partly for a reason with a good analogue in Old English poetry (namely, the poet distinguishes between men even when the sound of their names does not compel him to). Secondly, the kennings are relevant to context partly for a reason with a good analogue in Homeric poetry (namely, they speak appro-

priately of age, rank, nation, or ancestry) and partly for a
reason with no analogue in Homeric poetry (namely, the
poet uses different kennings for the same man in accord with
the meaning important at the moment).

Achilles is always said to be ποδάρκης δῖος Ἀχιλλεύς
"swift-footed brilliant Achilles" if his name is to be expressed in a phrase of that length and case; he is eminently
swift-footed in the epic as a whole but need not be swift-
footed just when he is so described. The term *feþecempa* "foot-
warrior" may refer now to Beowulf and later to Wiglaf if
their names are to be replaced by a half-line of that alliteration; each is significantly a foot-warrior just when he is so
described but need not be a foot-warrior in the epic as a
whole. *Beowulf* would correspond to an *Iliad* in which Odysseus was often πολύτλας δῖος Ὀδυσσεύς "much-enduring
brilliant Odysseus," but when taking up the prize
for the footrace (23.778) was ποδάρκης δῖος Ὀδυσσεύς
"swift-footed brilliant Odysseus" instead. The *Iliad* would
correspond to a *Beowulf* in which the epic hero was always
a *feþecempa* "foot-warrior," never a *folces hyrde* "shepherd
of the people," and was the only *feþecempa* in the poetic
corpus.

An intelligent choice does seem to have been made between the metrically equivalent phrases Ὀδυσεὺς δουρικλυτός
"Odysseus spear-famed" and Ὀδυσεὺς Ἰθακήσιος "Odysseus
of Ithaca," for the one occurs in the *Iliad*, an epic of war, and
the other in the *Odyssey*, an epic of return. But such examples
are uncommon. It is more typical that πολύτλας δῖος
Ὀδυσσεύς "much-enduring brilliant Odysseus" recurs in a
routine and dominant manner, with no competitor. The exception has its analogue in the automatic, inattentive repetition of the phrase *bearn Ecgþeowes* "child of Ecgtheow"; for
it is more typical that *folces hyrde* "shepherd of the people"

is carefully restricted to men who are at the moment rulers
of high degree.

The Homeric will tend to resemble the Old English idiom
if the epithets are divided, according to the sense of the
passage at hand, among men whose names have all the same
length. Let the great heroes be Actor, Haemon, Enops,
Ipheus, Otreus, Ilus (instead of Priam), Atreus (instead of
Agamemnon), Ajax, and Hector. When one of them is conspicuous for his helmet let him be spoken of as μέγας κορυθαίολος Ἄκτωρ (Αἵμων, Ἤνοψ, Ἰφεύς, etc.) "great Actor
(Haemon, Enops, Ipheus, etc.) of the flashing helmet";
when conspicuous for his shield, as μέγας τελαμώνιος Ἄκτωρ
(Αἵμων, etc.); and when swift of foot, as ποδήνεμος ὄβριμος
Ἄκτωρ, etc. The resemblance will be even closer if the
names are completely replaced. Let anyone who marshals his
contingent be spoken of as a μελαμφαρὴς ἀγὸς ἀνδρῶν "black-
robed leader of men"; and on other occasions let him be a
φιλοψευδὴς ἀγορητής "fond-of-lying orator" or a μαχητὴς
ὠκυπέδιλος "warrior swift-sandaled." Similarly, the Old
English will tend to resemble the Homeric idiom if the
kennings are allowed to recur without concern for the particular situation and if they are restricted each to a single man.
Let Hrothgar and no one else be remembered as the *har
hilderinc* "old battle-warrior"; and with the same alliteration
let Beowulf be the *hordweard hæleþa* "hoard warden of heroes"
and Wiglaf the *hæle hildedeor* "hero battle-fierce." The resemblance will be even closer if every phrase is required to
include either the name of the man himself or such an
alternative as cannot possibly be ambiguous. Here we need
only compose *Beorhtdena Hrothgar* "Bright-Danes' Hrothgar"
(as a replacement for *bearn Healfdenes* "child of Healfdene,"
which refers to both Hrothgar and Heregar), *Freaware fæder*
"Freawaru's father" (a replacement for *frea[o]wine folca*,

which refers to Hrothgar, Hygelac, and Hrethel), *Hrothgar hilderinc* (for *har hilderinc*), and the like.

Now it is clear that every one of these changes would mean both a gain and a loss. So long as an epithet or kenning is used for one man alone and as often for him as its meter or alliteration permits, he will appear different from everyone else but will not appear to change throughout all his experiences; whereas if an epithet or kenning is used for several men, though only when its sense is especially apt, they will each be capable of changing but not of seeming unique. The possibly regrettable feature of either style is a necessary consequence of a virtue: the only way for the phrases to be both distinctive and true to context is to cease being formulaic.

We could, however, ask each tradition, in its way, to characterize the heroes more closely. The second principle concerning the distribution of the epithets has not been observed in the phrases βοὴν ἀγαθὸς Μενέλαος "good-at-the-cry Menelaus" and βοὴν ἀγαθὸς Διομήδης "good-at-the-cry Diomedes" (for by describing both major figures the epithet lacks the distinctiveness we find elsewhere). The first principle has not been effectively observed in the line 'Αντίλοχος δ' 'Αχιλῆι πόδας ταχὺς ἄγγελος ἦλθε "Antilochus to Achilles the swift-footed messenger came" (*Il.* 18.2): since Achilles is said to be swift-footed far more often than Antilochus or anyone else is, we expected the form ταχεῖ, or ταχέ', which would refer to him. (Here an epithet has managed to combine, at least indirectly, with names of very different metrical natures.) Likewise, the second principle concerning the distribution of the kennings has not been observed in the phrase *Wedergeata leod* "Weather-Geats' leader" (for by denoting Beowulf equally well at both stages of his career it lacks the contextual relevance we find elsewhere). And the first principle has not been effectively observed in the line where *mære þeoden* "famous prince" refers to Onela (*Beowulf* 2384). (The term may point to so many men that we must make an identification with more than ordinary care.)

From these examples we can also see that the name's being an integral part of the formula is in itself neither an advantage nor a disadvantage. For determining to whom the phrase refers, the Homeric epithet is usually of no value (since the name it accompanies is as clear as can be), whereas the kenning is of crucial value (the name it has replaced being hidden). Consequently, when an epithet lacks distinctiveness, occurring widely with names of one or more metrical sizes, it tends to become meaningless (we are never confused but may be somewhat bored), whereas when a kenning lacks sharpness, being both generic for various men and only vaguely relevant to context, it tends to leave us in serious doubt (we are not bored but our powers of concentration may be overtaxed). The one side of the coin has the same value as the other: there would be no profit either in subtracting the names from the formulas of the *Iliad* or in adding them to those of *Beowulf*.

What matters is that the same epithets or kennings should not be used for the epic figures whose interrelationships are momentous, and here the two traditions are eminently successful. The heroes who face each other in the *Iliad* usually have names dissimilar in meter and are accordingly (by the first principle) all but unable to share the same epithets between them. There was a barrier against the possibility that Achilles, in challenging the superior power of Agamemnon, in the first book, should himself be said to be an ἄναξ ἀνδρῶν "king of men." But even when the names are metrically identical the epithets continue (by the second principle) to be different. In phrases $3\frac{1}{4}$ and $2\frac{1}{2}$ feet in length,

Hector is (μέγας) κορυθαίολος ῞Εκτωρ and Ajax is (μέγας) τελαμώνιος Αἴας, though either κορυθαίολος or τελαμώνιος might have been, just as μέγας is in fact, used for both with perfect scansion. The difference is important in the episode of shield warfare (*Il.* 7.224–287) where κορυθαίολος ῞Εκτωρ occurs three times and τελαμώνιος Αἴας twice. Had Hector and Ajax been described as alike, our interest should have ebbed considerably. Similarly, the one occurrence of *hilde-rinc(es)* for Grendel reminds us that (by the first principle) the monsters do not ordinarily have a claim on the kennings used for men. A sufficient supply of terms alike in alliteration but different in meaning kept an *atol æglæca* "horrible troll" (*Beowulf* 159, 732, 816) or an *eald uhtsceaða* "old dawn scather" (2271) distinct from an *æþeling ærgod* "nobleman good from far back" or an *eald eðelweard* "old home warden"; the *hordes hyrde* "guardian of the hoard" (887) is distinguished from a *hordweard hæleþa* "hoard warden of heroes," and the *gromheort guma* (1682) from a *guma guðum cuð*. And when Hrothgar and Beowulf, or Beowulf and Wiglaf, are parts of the same episode, the one (by the second principle) is a *har hilderinc* "old battle-warrior" and the other a *hæle hildedeor* "hero battle-fierce": had these phrases been arranged in any other order, we should have lost our way.

The occurrence in a given line of κορυθαίολος ῞Εκτωρ "Hector of the flashing helmet," or *har hilderinc* "old battle-warrior," does not cause us to collocate the instances where the phrase occurs elsewhere; we simply do not remember them—though we may recall that Hector is the only man regularly described in this way, or that Hrothgar, like Beowulf, is somehow said, by one term or another, to be old, as Hygelac is said to be young. Even less do we regard κορυθαίολος as often pertinent to the passages where it appears, or *har hilderinc* as a mark of individuality. Still, the

partly formulaic nature of Homeric and Old English epic
does not by any means take the possibilities of criticism from
our reach; it merely encourages us to develop special tech-
niques. The question "What might the poet have said instead?"—more exactly, "What expression did he avoid?"—
may be a useful beginning. In accord with the second principle concerning the distribution of the epithets (that even
men whose names have the same length are apt to be
distinguished from each other), we can decide whether
ἐσθλὸς 'Οδυσσεύς "noble Odysseus" has any merit or not. It
appears that the only comparable epithet of this size belongs
to the phrase ὠκὺς 'Αχιλλεύς "swift Achilles"; to tell the men
apart a difference in epithet is of value, and the greater right
of Achilles to be ὠκύς leaves Odysseus with ἐσθλός. In this
instance the poet was not brilliant, but his choice may well
have been the best available. Similarly, in accord with the
second principle concerning the distribution of the kennings
(that they are used with regard for the situation), we can decide whether *æpeling unfrom* "nobleman spiritless" (*Beowulf*
2188) is a good reproof for Beowulf as a slack youngster.
Here we gather that the usual phrase might be *æpeling ærgod*
"nobleman good from far back," which would strike us as
incongruous.

Monsters in Homeric and Old English poetry sometimes
resemble men, though of course sometimes not, and in
assessing the poet's mastery over his formulaic diction we
ought to glance at what he might have said instead. The
Cyclops is described in the genitive as μεγαλήτορος ἀνδροφάγοιο "great-hearted man-eater" (*Od.* 10.200), terms of
different kinds. μεγαλήτορος "great-hearted" is elsewhere
used (counting the genitive only) twenty-six times in the
twin epics (always in the same part of the line), always for
men of nobility. ἀνδροφάγοιο "man-eater" never occurs ex-

cept this once, when it replaces such terms as ἀνδροφόνοιο
"man-slaying," ἱπποδάμοιο "breaker of horses," and ἀντιθέοιο "equal to the gods." These examples suggest two
generalizations which can be shown with parentheses: to
speak about monsters and men with the same words (with
different words) was an easy course (a hard course) that led
to inappropriateness (appropriateness). But the generalizations may prove unreliable. When Grendel's hate is described as a *healðegnes hete* "hall-thane's hate" (*Beowulf* 142),
our first thoughts are of same words, an easy course, and
inappropriateness. Since in the story the troll is now be-
coming a resident of the house, however, there is merit in
the argument—of James L. Rosier, "The Uses of Association," *PMLA* 78 (1963) 8, and Stanley B. Greenfield, "The
Canons of Old English Criticism," *ELH, A Journal of
English Literary History* 34 (1967) 148—that the term is in a
way very fine. What might the poet have said instead,
though? What were the alternatives? Instead of "hall-
thane's hate" he might have said *helðegnes hete* "hell-thane's
hate," cf. *helle þegna* in *Guthlac* 1069 (perhaps he actually did
say *helðegnes* or *helle þegnes*, but was misunderstood by a copy-
ist, possibly at second or third hand); or he might have said
heorowearges hete "outcast's hate," cf. *heorowearh hetelic* in
Beowulf 1267.

IV. The kennings for Beowulf lack the economy of
the epithetic phrases for Odysseus.

From our study of the formula types let us reassess the
comparison of all the epithetic phrases for Odysseus and all
the half-line kennings for Beowulf. We failed at first to see
that *feðecempa, folces hyrde, har hilderinc, hordweard hæleþa, rices
hyrde, secg on searwum, eald eþelweard, æþeling ærgod,* and *eorla*

5

dryhten, which are used for the epic hero only once each,
were formulaic; now recognizing that every one of them is
used for him and for someone else besides, we see that they
certainly are formulaic. We also failed to see that, for referring to the epic hero, there was need for more than a
single half-line with any given alliteration; now recognizing
that—unlike their Homeric analogues—the old English
circumlocutions for heroes pertain not to distinctive character but to the specific occasion, we see that the need was
great. Nevertheless, the value of many of the kennings remains doubtful.

Epic economy can be defined in two ways: shall we say
that it is, or that it is not, violated by the different epithets
for men whose names have the same size, and by the different
kennings for the same man at various stages of his career?
We shall say here that it is not—no one will be able to accuse
us of thinking that the epic cloth, in its ideal state, ought to
be threadbare. We hold the economy to be violated no more
often, by the phrases for Odysseus, than when they are alike
in meter, and no more often by the phrases for Beowulf than
when they are alike in both alliteration and sense. At the
very most, we found six examples in the one group: the
metrical equivalents are Ὀδυσεὺς Ἰθακήσιος and Ὀδυσεὺς
δουρικλυτός, Ὀδυσῆος ταλασίφρονος and Ὀδυσῆος μεγαλήτορος, Ὀδυσῆι (-α) πολύφρονι (-α) and Ὀδυσῆι (-α) δαίφρονι
(-α), Ὀδυσῆα δαίφρονα ποικιλομήτην and Ὀδυσῆα Διὶ μῆτιν
ἀτάλαντον, and, finally, διογενὲς Λαερτιάδη πολυμήχαν'
Ὀδυσσεῦ and ὄλβιε Λαέρταο πάι πολυμήχαν' Ὀδυσσεῦ
and ὦ Ὀδυσεῦ πολύαινε δόλων ἆτ' ἠδὲ πόνοιο—the first
four of these sets contributing one surplus phrase each,
the last contributing two. How many violations of economy
do we find in the other group? On the assumptions that the
replacements ought to be used for Beowulf elsewhere, that

twofold and single alliteration ought to be preserved, that
transverse alliteration ought to be preserved as well (whether
or not the poet was aware of it), and that iteration should
never be introduced—twelve terms may be deleted, entirely,
with no appreciable effect. For *freca Scyldinga* "soldier of the
Scyldings" (1563) read *feþecempa* "foot-warrior," for *guma
guðum cuð* "man known for wars" (2178) read *guðrinc
goldwlanc* "warman gold-proud," and for both *Guðgeata leod*
"War-Geats' leader" (1538) and *Geata cempa* "Geats'
warrior" (1551) read *Geatmecga leod* "leader of the Geat-
men"; for *hringa þengel* "prince of rings" (1507) read
Higelaces þegn "Higelac's thane," for *rof oretta* "famed warrior" (2538) read *rices hyrde* "shepherd of the kingdom," and
for both *werodes wisa* "master of the contingent" (259) and
wælreow wiga "battle-fierce man" (629) read *wlanc Wedera
leod* "proud leader of the Weders"; for *Wedergeata leod*
"Weather-Geats' leader" in its three occurrences (1492,
1612, and 2551), read *Wedera þeoden* "Weders' chief"; replace *wigena strengel* "captain of warriors" (3115) with
wigendra hleo "warriors' protector," *æþeling anhydig* "nobleman resolute" (2667) with *æþeling ærgod* "nobleman good
from far back," and *æðele cempa* "noble warrior" (1312) with
ealdor þegna "marshal of thanes." Very seldom—though *wlanc
Wedera leod* (in 629) is one instance, and *ealdor þegna* (in 1312)
another—are the substitutions an improvement; they are
merely no deterioration; we lose some estimable nuances
but gain others. The surplus is *twice* as large among the half-
lines for Beowulf as among the epithetic phrases for Odysseus.
An impartial judge might say the ratio was even greater; he
would not say it was any less.

(Are we concerned here with variation? Not if that word
refers to the occurrence of synonyms in the same brief passage. For our substitutions, improving the economy, have

kept the variation without fail. If we said there was a violation of economy when synonyms alike in alliteration occurred in the same brief passage, we should indeed be at fault; but we have not said anything of the kind. Our ratio of two to one, for the violations of economy among the half-lines for Beowulf and the epithetic phrases for Odysseus, is simply fair and accurate.)

Now I should not regard a ratio of such a low order as having much importance if it were not associated with a further one. The terms for Odysseus occur in the aggregate almost *five times* as often as do the kennings for Beowulf with which we compared them; there was almost five times as great an opportunity for a violation of economy to be perpetrated. If multiplied, the numbers indicate that the Homeric diction is nearly ten times as stereotyped as the Old English; perhaps we ought to add instead, or raise one of the numbers to the power of the other; but in any event the conclusion cannot be disputed. *After having allowed for the unforeseen fact that the kennings vary appropriately with the context we still find that they lack the economy of the Homeric epithets.* Unless our analysis of the formula types has led to results that are atypical and unreliable (and I would assert that it has not led to results of this kind), we can conclude that the Old English diction ranks low in economy as a general rule. Here is a dependable reason why *Beowulf* does not contain so many recurring lines as do the first few books of the *Iliad*.

Four / The poetic diction of *Beowulf* has been reformed but not converted.

The first agent in the religious conversion of the Anglo-Saxons was the sixth-century Irishman Columba, who founded the monastery at Iona from which a later generation carried Christianity to the Thames. The second agent was Augustine, whom at the close of the sixth century Pope Gregory directed to Kent, where a mission prospered while the missionary lived, but afterwards declined, perhaps owing to the failure of his successors to learn the language of the island. A third agent was Aldhelm, in whose training—under Maeldubh at Malmesbury, and then under Theodore and Hadrian, who had been sent as reinforcements to Canterbury by Pope Vitalian—the Celtic and Roman strands of Christianity were fused. Aldhelm was the greatest apostle in Wessex during the latter part of the seventh century, and *Beowulf*, because of its being written in West Saxon, seems likely to have been washed in the currents he created. What cannot be accepted is the prevailing opinion that the epic shows signs of thoroughgoing indebtedness to Scripture and liturgy; for the religious elements are actually those of a barely reformed Germanic heathenism. The influential papers by Fr. Klaeber, "Die christlichen elemente im Beowulf," *Anglia* 35 (1911) 111–136, 249–270, and 453–483, and 36 (1912) 169–199, are my target, and my weapon is the premise that, in its formulaic structure, the poetic diction looked towards the past rather than the future.

I. The words for providence

James A. Notopoulos, "Homer, Hesiod and the Achaean Heritage of Oral Poetry," *Hesperia* 29 (1960) 177–197, defended the attractive thesis that the Homeric and Hesiodic epic languages, which are occasionally dissimilar but often identical, separated from each other quite late in their evolution, and it may be assumed that the Old English and Old Norse poetic languages are similarly related, though the Achaean diction had matured longer than its Germanic counterpart before each divided into branches. Every word in *Beowulf* that has a cognate in the poetic *Edda* is likely to have been a part of verse from a very early time, and that the number of such words is considerable has been shown by the monumental lexica to either dialect. Many of the most common Old English names for god—it is admittedly tendentious to use a lower-case *g*, but equally tendentious to use the capital letter—refer to similar forces in Old Norse legend, and the sense of these names in seventh-century England was conceivably much the same as in tenth-century Norway or Iceland. During the development of the Old English and Old Norse corpora in isolation from each other, the vocabulary of each acquired distinctive nuances of meaning; yet the stereotyped diction must have been a conservative, even a reactionary, influence on popular thought. So I would claim that no word in the following list differs from its cognate more than do the present-day Norwegian *time* "hour" and *sky* "cloud." Let it be mentioned once and for all that many of my citations are to be found in such standard compilations as the Cleasby-Vigfusson Icelandic-English dictionary.

As *god* is common in *Beowulf*, *goð* is common in the *Edda*. The Cleasby-Vigfusson dictionary remarks that the Old Norse word is often used without the definite article and seems, like the Hebrew *ʾelōhîm* (the word that is nearly always behind the translation "God" in the Old Testament), to be singular in meaning though plural in form. The Old English word is held to be Christian or heathen according to whether it is singular or plural, but we have no evidence that the singular form was not used from the first: in the *Iliad* the gods are referred to as *theoi*, and one specific god or another as a *theos*; but often enough (for example, 7.288, 13.727, and 19.90) *theos* has the vaguer sense of "providence" or "fate," much as it does in the Septuagint and New Testament. So the phrase *halig god* "holy god" of *Beowulf* 381 and 1553 answers almost exactly to the *ginnheilog goð* of *Vǫlospá* 6, 9, 23, and 25, and *Locasenna* 11. The words *metod* and *wyrd* are also common in *Beowulf*; *mjǫtuðr* "fate" occurs in *Vǫlospá* 46, *Sigurðarqviða in scamma* 71, and *Oddrúnargrátr* 16; and *Urðr*, one of the Norns, is mentioned in *Vǫlospá* 19. Like the Greek *kurios* and the Latin *dominus*, the Old English *frea* and the Gothic *frauja* are common nouns, while the Old Norse *Freyr* has become a personal name. As the Old English *dryhten* often means the same as *god* but equally often refers to an earthly prince, the Old Norse *dróttinn* refers to Freyr in *For Scírnis* 3 but retains its ordinary meaning in *hafra dróttinn* "master of goats," *Hymisqviða* 31, and *þursa dróttinn* "lord of giants," *Þrymsqviða* 6. The Old English *fæder* is an alternative for *god* in *Beowulf* 188 and 1609, as *fæder alwalda* is in line 316.

Similarly, *sigfǫðr* in *Vǫlospá* 55, *Grímnismál* 48, and *Locasenna* 58; *valfǫðr* in *Vǫlospá* 1, 27, and 28; *heriafǫðr* in *Vǫlospá* 43, *Vafðrúðnismál* 2, *Grímnismál* 19, and *Hyndlolióð* 2; *herfǫðr* in *Vǫlospá* 29; *aldafǫðr* in *Vafðrúðnismál* 4 and 53; and *alfǫðr* in *Grímnismál* 48 and *Helgaqviða Hundingsbana in fyrri* 38—all refer to Othin.

Like *frea*, *dryhten*, and *fæder*, but unlike *metod* and *wyrd*, the Old English *waldend* and *alwalda* were probably used for men before they became names of god. Likewise *allvaldr* in *Helgaqviða Hundingsbana in fyrri* 21 refers to Helgi, and *fólcvaldi goða* in *For Scírnis* 3 to Freyr. Halfway through the longest passage of verse in the saga of Harald the Fairhaired —*Heimskringla*, ed. Finnur Jónsson (Copenhagen 1893–1901) 1.124—*allvalds* refers to Harald, and in a poem by Kormákr that is quoted near the beginning of Skáldskaparmál—*Edda Snorra Sturlusonar*, ed. Finnur Jónsson (Reykjavik 1907) 123— *allvald* apparently refers to Othin. The phrase *waltant got* in line 49 of the Old High German *Hildebrandslied*, furthermore, resembles the *god . . . waldend* of *Beowulf* 1751–1752 and 2874–2875. Thus the Gothic *allwaldands* may have existed in the Germanic poetic tradition before it was used in 2 Corinthians 6:18 as a translation of the Greek *pantokratōr*, a word that had been adapted for the New Testament by its use in the Septuagint as a translation of the Hebrew *šadday*. The Vulgate regularly renders both *šadday* and *pantokratōr* as *omnipotens*, a common synonym or epithet for Jupiter throughout the *Aeneid*, the phrase *pater omnipotens* alone occurring in 1.60, 3.251, 4.25, 6.592, 7.141, 7.770, 8.398, 10.100, and 12.178. One who believes with Klaeber that *Beowulf* was influenced by both Latin Christianity and Virgilian epic cannot accordingly be sure whether *Credo in Deum, Patrem omnipotentem* from the Creed, or the epithetic phrase for the Roman god, was responsible for *fæder alwalda*. But the dilemma contains its own resolution: for if *omnipotens* was merely an old word later given a special sense, *alwalda* may have been an old word too, and the search for a foreign source is unwarranted.

The correspondence of the Germanic vocabularies is far from complete, since certain Old English kennings for *god*—such as *heofena helm* and *rodera rædend*—have no exact cognates recorded in Old Norse, and since a number of words in the *Edda*—such as *regin*, *æsir*, *vanir*, and *tívar*—have no cognates in *Beowulf*. This circumstance is a counterweight against the general identity of the two dialects, but the differences are more readily understandable as the result of regional preference than as clues to religious instruction, just as no worthwhile conclusion can be drawn from the fact that the words for boy and girl in present-day Norwegian, *gutt* and *pike*, are not the same as those in Swedish, *pojke* and *flicka*. What may be significant is the absence from *Beowulf* of the northern divinities known in Old English as Woden, Tiw, and Thunor—who probably answer to both the Mercury, Hercules, and Mars mentioned by Tacitus as the gods to whom the Germanic tribes made sacrifice (*Germania* 9) and the daemones in England to whom were made the sacrifices condemned by Bede (*Ecclesiastical History* 1.30). Since followers of the religious movement of the seventh century sometimes reverted to these rites—as is manifest from passages in Bede (*Eccles. Hist.* 2.5 and 3.30) and *Beowulf* itself (lines 175–188)—the gods lacking in Old English poetry but familiar from the *Edda* may be thought the chief element of the native belief that could not be accommodated by the monotheism of the coming time. Woden, Tiw, and Thunor, powers differing in character and cult, were condemned with a corollary emphasis upon *god*, *wyrd*, and *metod*, abstractions similar conceptually and related in no clear fashion—

though god may avert wyrd (*Beowulf* 1056), wyrd is every
man's metod (2526–2527). The change was from within the
language rather than from without, it subtracted rather than
added, and to a contemporary it must have been less a revo-
lution, or a conversion, than a reformation. The phrase
fæder alwalda continued to seem as biblical as *pater omnipotens*
does in the *Aeneid*, and *Beowulf* is to this extent neither Christian nor unchristian but pre-Christian.

II. The idea of the Son

Let us inspect for contrast one of the Old Saxon versions—
Die kleineren althochdeutschen Sprachdenkmäler, ed. Elias von
Steinmeyer, 2nd ed. (Berlin 1963) 20—of a renunciation
dating from at least the fourth century (Cyril of Jerusalem in
the *Patrologia Graeca*, ed. J. P. Migne, 33:1068–1073) and
still in use today:

Do you forsake the devil? (Et respondet:) *I forsake the devil.*
And all the devil's display? (Respondet:) *And I forsake all the
devil's display.* And all the devil's works? (Respondet:) *And I
forsake all the devil's works and words, Thunor and Woden and
Seaxnet and all those unholy ones who are their companions.* Do you
believe in God the Father Almighty? *I believe in God the
Father Almighty.* Do you believe in Christ, the Son of God?
I believe in Christ, the Son of God. Do you believe in the Holy
Ghost? *I believe in the Holy Ghost.*

Forsachistu diobolae? et respondet: ec forsacho diabolae.
end allum diobolgelde? respondet: end ec forsacho allum
diobolgeldae. end allum dioboles uuercum? respondet: end
ec forsacho allum dioboles uuercum and uuordum, Thunaer
ende Uuoden ende Saxnote ende allum them unholdum,
the hira genotas sint. gelobistu in got alamehtigan fadaer?
ec gelobo in got alamehtigan fadaer. gelobistu in Crist, godes

suno? ec gelobo in Crist, gotes suno. gelobistu in halogan
gast? ec gelobo in halogan gast.

(Seaxnet may well be a byname of Tiw: see Bruce Dickins,
"English Names and Old English Heathenism," *Essays and
Studies by Members of the English Association* 19 [1934] 154.)

Once again, the change from old to new was largely a
matter of deletion; yet certain conceptions, absent from
Beowulf, have here been brought forward for the first time.
No way had been prepared for the Holy Ghost, nor was
there previously, though Othin the father has a son mentioned in *Vǫlospá* 55, any idea that the Father and the Son
were aspects of one Being.

In several Old English poems we find them to be not
merely One but one and the same. *Christ* (727–728, 1216–
1218) tells that the Father ascended to the cross, and that
"Christ sits on his throne, on his high seat, the God of
heavenly hosts, the Father Almighty." Such lines are sometimes said to show muddled thought, but they are perhaps
fairly representative of monophysitism (see the *Dictionnaire de
théologie catholique* s.v. *Eutychès*), which itself is more likely
than not to have been brought from the East to Canterbury
by Archbishop Theodore. The lines even have some scriptural authority, at least for those who believe that Jesus
Christ fulfils Isaiah 9:6, "For unto us a child is born, unto
us a son is given: and the government shall be upon his
shoulder: and his name shall be called Wonderful, Coun-
sellor, The mighty God, The everlasting Father, The Prince
of Peace." In addition, there was in Old English poetry a
special reason for the distinctions among the three Persons
to become blurred, since every concept demanded a series of
expressions differing in sound but capable of being used as if
exactly alike in meaning. Consider whether we can or cannot

find a reference to the Trinity in the following passage (*Daniel* 399–403):

We bless Thee, Lord of all peoples, Father Almighty, True Son of Providence, Savior of souls, Helper of heroes, and Thee, Holy Ghost, we honor in glory, WiseMaster.

	We þec bletsiað,
frea folca gehwæs,	fæder ælmihtig,
soð sunu metodes,	sawla nergend,
hæleða helpend,	and þec, halig gast,
wurðiað in wuldre,	witig drihten.

Yes, we can indeed find such a reference; still, the passage is trinitarian in a Germanic fashion, not merely because *metod* and *fæder* have roots deep in heathenism, but also because *soð sunu metodes* stands in apposition to (i.e. as a variation of!) *fæder ælmihtig*. Certain Old English poets may therefore be held to have pronounced phrases of the Creed like those in the Old Saxon renunciation, to have been converted on the basis of monophysite doctrines, and to have made verse the more readily by regarding the kennings for the Father as synonymous with those for the Son; but none of these conclusions can be applied to the poet of *Beowulf*.

Even the most technical arguments we can devise from an analysis of the formulaic diction will lead to the same decision: conversion is manifest elsewhere, but not in the epic. The phrases *soð sunu metodes* "True Son of Providence" (*Daniel* 401 = *Elene* 461, *Elene* 564) and *sigora soðcyning* "victories' true-king" (*Beowulf* 3055, *Christ* 1228, *Phoenix* 329, *Order of the World* 67) are *a* half-lines of similar alliteration. No mechanical factor prevents either from replacing or being replaced by the other. But the former is Christian, by sometimes referring to the Son as being tantamount to the

Father, whereas the latter is monotheistic, whether Christian or heathen. Likewise, *wealdenes bearn* "Ruler's Child" (*Andreas* 576) and *waldend fira* "ruler of men" (*Beowulf* 2741) are *b* half-lines of similar alliteration, and are on this account interchangeable, the former testifying to Christianity, the latter to monotheism. In spite of providing for the same prosodic needs, the formulas cannot be dated with respect to each other, except that "True Son of Providence" and "Ruler's Child" must be late, whereas "victories' true-king" and "ruler of men" may be late or early. From their use of *soð sunu metodes* and *wealdenes bearn* we can conclude that the poets of *Daniel* and *Andreas* had some awareness of Christ. From his use of *sigora soðcyning* and *waldend fira* instead we are unable to say whether the poet of *Beowulf* had such an awareness or not; it is only from our failure to find in his work a single explicit reference to New Testament materials that we decide he knew nothing of them. The convention of capitalizing the words for the God of the Bible but not those for the god of Germanic thought leads us to translate *fæder ælmihtig* from *Daniel* as "Father Almighty" but *fæder alwalda* from *Beowulf* as "father almighty." The distinction is juridical; it has chiefly the advantage of marking where teachings about the Son augmented the native belief in the father, a belief that at first had needed to be strengthened by the elimination of Woden, Tiw, and Thunor. *Daniel* is Christian in a way that *Beowulf* is not, though the religious elements of *Beowulf* have been reformed in a way that those of the *Edda* have not.

III. The idea of heaven and hell

The epic conception of the world is entirely Germanic. *Tiw father* would be an exact cognate of *Jupiter*, *Zeus pater*, and *Dyaus pitar*, and since the name in Sanskrit is a common

noun with the sense "brightness," Tiw was from the beginning a god of the sky—as was Thunor, the thunder. Modern
English distinguishes between "heaven" (a theological term)
and "the heavens, the sky"; but Old English does not:
before Christianity as well as afterwards *heofon* was the locale
from which the forces governing man held their hand upon
him. The earth was a *middangeard* "mid-yard, middle
ground." Below was *hel*, probably "that which hides"; the
word itself answers closely to *hades*, probably "the unseen,"
both of them referring to the place of the dead and to the
numen as well (*Beowulf* 852). That hell was always abhorrent
to the Anglo-Saxon mind cannot perhaps be demonstrated,
but it can, and ought to, be inferred from the everyday
Homeric phrase "hateful to me as the gates of Hades" (*Il.*
9.312 = *Od.* 14.156). Long before our own time, *Easter* became Christian and *Tuesday* ceased to be heathen; we are
unable to assert anything of the kind about hell or heaven in
Beowulf.

There are references to the survival of the spirit when it
departs from the body, and even to a judgment upon the
kind of life a man has lived (*Beowulf* 2741–2742, cf. 977–979,
1002–1008); and there is in variation with *metod* the kenning
dæda demend "judge of deeds" (181). These matters we cannot declare to be pre-Christian. Yet we cannot declare them
not to be pre-Christian, either. Partly from folklore or else
entirely from his imagination, the poet of the *Odyssey* created
torments in the next world for Tityus, Tantalus, and Sisyphus (11.576–600), and to deny that the poet of *Beowulf* had
similar resources available, from his own culture and his own
mind, is unwarranted. The idea of a final reckoning, possibly followed by punishment, is as apt in the one tradition
as in the other. No one will compel us to say that the idea in
Old English poetry derived from an Irish or Roman mission;

even less will anyone convince us that the idea could have altered much the Germanic formulations of heaven and hell.

Expecting the dead to be raised incorruptible from their graves, or aware of the implications latent in heathen ceremonies, the Christian church has ordinarily favored burial in the earth. Yet the cremation of Beowulf (3137–3168) and the ship burial of Scyld (26–52), treasure being laid down with the body in both instances, are described with energy and favor. Several explanations can be given: the epic is a composite of fragments from different times, the poet archaized for the sake of realism, a desire for consistency was not prominent among his motives, or the poetic diction was adapted best to a funeral by fire or sea. Now there may be truth in one or more of these solutions, yet none of them is necessary here. Towards the end of the eighth century Charlemagne banned cremation in Saxony—*Monumenta Germaniae Historica*, Legum Sectio II, Tomus I (Hanover 1882) 69—but for the years and the land with which we are concerned such a prohibition is unknown (and Charlemagne was a bloodier guardian of the faith than any English prince or bishop has been). And the Sutton Hoo find (though the cenotaph may indicate the inhumation of the body) shows that in real life, not in song or fable only, a prince was honored by a ship burial with a laying down of treasure; whether or not there is evidence of conversion in spoons lettered *Saulos* and *Paulos*—R. E. Kaske, "The Silver Spoons of Sutton Hoo," *Speculum* 42 (1967) 670–672, leads me to say not—the influence of the East on the West failed to obliterate the indigenous ways of thinking and doing. So the funerals of the epic are typical of its day, and in discussing them we need not speak of a patchwork, or archaism, or inconsistency, or the bondage of a traditional style.

The Germanic and biblical views of the world are nowhere

more similar than in taking heaven to be the place of god.
If Caedmon's hymn had not survived we might still have
said that the Creation was the first lesson taught for the conversion of the Anglo-Saxon nation. There is on balance less
reason to deny than to assume that the scop's song in Heorot
summed up the larger part of the *Beowulf* poet's own com-
mitment to the religious movement of his time. If old, the
kenning *scyppend* "maker" gained additional meaning; if
new, it introduced Scripture without implying the presence
of Christ. Since the epic never refers to the Son, *Woden*, *Tiw*,
and *Thunor* had been, not renounced in a preface to the
Creed, but taken from the sky in accord with a change,
quite possibly a return, to a religion of simpler lines.

IV. The words for the monsters

The poet accounts for the handsome things in this life on
the basis of the Creation; for the misshapen and menacing
things, otherwise. *As descendants of Cain or as a consequence of
his crime* (the text has both meanings, though chiefly the
former), *eotens, elves, orcs, and giants came upon the earth* (111–
113a, cf. 1265b–1266a); *the giants warred with god* (113b, cf.
1689a) *and were destroyed by the Flood* (1689b–1690, cf. 114b).
Grendel was proscribed among (106–107a)—*i.e. belongs to* (1266b)
—*the race*; *specifically, he is an eoten* (761a). These matters are
closely related and form a single myth. (Why was not
Grendel destroyed by the Flood? The poet was simply inconsistent, or he regarded Grendel as an exception, or he
believed that the Flood destroyed the giants but not the
eotens.) Many of the details are native; only a few are im-
migrants. The oppobrium attached to fratricide—elsewhere
emphasized in the ignominy of Unferth (587–589) and
Haethcyn (2435–2440) and in the satisfaction taken by

Beowulf from the thought that he cannot be charged with
the life of a kinsman (2741–2742a)—is an aspect of the
Germanic regard for blood ties (cf. Tacitus, *Germania* 20; the
Hildebrandslied; and *Vǫlospá* 45). The eotens and elves, and
probably the orcs (cf. Old Norse *örkn*), belong not to the
South but to the North; and the idea that giants or eotens
warred with god (or the gods) is less, and the idea of the
Flood perhaps no more, scriptural than indigenous (see
Vǫlospá 24–25, and Snorri, *Gylfaginning* 7). Finally, Grendel
and his mother resemble the trolls of the sagas—just as the
wyrm, or serpentine dragon, is like the world-encircling *ormr*
and the Fafnir-*ormr* of the *Edda*. The myth was biblical, but
not entirely so, and not exclusively so; an English mind was
prepared to regard it as English.

We must credit a missionary for having introduced the
name of Cain (which was originally Semitic), for having im-
ported the word *gigantas* (evidently from a Greek or Latin
version of the text about the "giants in the earth in those
days"), and for having coined the learned word *forscrifan*
(evidently by analogy from *proscribere*). We may credit either
a missionary or the poet for having brought together the
details about Cain, the giants, and the Flood, from the fourth,
sixth, and seventh chapters of Genesis. But we must credit
the poet, and not a missionary, for having given a Germanic
stamp—by adding the eotens and elves and the *battle* of the
giants—to this second, and last, of the Bible stories the epic
refers to. Its (negative) answer to the question "Were the
ogres of the march also a part of the Creation?" is unlikely
to have had any analogue in the legends of the people before-
hand, but to the poet and his audience Cain was an Anglo-
Saxon, no more remote than Weland the smith.

We began by acknowledging that *Beowulf* might have been
washed in the currents created by Aldhelm—which are

perhaps best fathomed from a pleasing and often cited anecdote given by William of Malmesbury, *De gestis pontificum Anglorum*, ed. N. E. S. A. Hamilton (London 1870) 336. *Aldhelm would take a position on a bridge connecting town and country, as if he were a bard by profession, and would compose poetry in which words from the Scriptures were combined with more popular matters. By this method he led the people to morality more surely than he could have done with bans of excommunication.* So reads the story, and it may be true; but what was the poetry like? It was like *Beowulf* itself—though the epic poet (so far as we can tell) had less of a motive than Aldhelm to omit the Incarnation from his moralizing. Cain had come within his perspective; Judas evidently had not.

Some scholars will argue against us that Revelation 20:2, "the dragon, the old serpent, which is the Devil, and Satan," comments upon a conception behind the *Altus prosator*, where Satan is described as the

> Draco magnus taeterrimus
> terribilis et antiquus,
> qui fuit serpens lubricus.

"Since the poem is attributed to Columba, *draca* may, owing to its derivation from Latin or Greek, be a Columban element in Old English; and, since the word is imbedded near the core of the formulaic style, *Beowulf* is richly imbued with ecclesiastical color, after all." This is the objection of our opponents, and we meet it directly. The effect of the second sound-shift upon the Old High German *trahho* indicates that a form of *draca* already existed in West Germanic when the Celtic monks began to break their path through Northumbria, and the occurrence of *dreki* in *Vǫlospá* 66 suggests that the word was known in all the Germanic dialects even before the conversion of the Goths. Because the dragon was an ancient military emblem (see the Pauly-Wissowa *Real-encyclopädie* s.v. *draco*) over a domain that finally extended to Scandinavia—for the Cleasby-Vigfusson dictionary observes that *dreki* in the *Heimskringla* generally denotes a warship with a dragon beak—the word and the sign are likely to have been taken together from the heraldry of southern Europe. The originally foreign *draca* was useful in Old English, on account of its alliteration, as an alternative to *wyrm*, just as the originally foreign *draco* was useful in Latin, on account of its meter, as an alternative to *serpens* (see also *Aeneid* 2.214–225): neither here nor there is the word necessarily connected in any way directly with the Bible.

Two other allegedly biblical terms we explain in much the same way. Quite certainly borrowed ultimately from the Greek *diabolos*, after the bilabial voiced stop had become a labio-dental continuant, *deofol* more probably reached Old English from Gothic than from Latin, since the second sound-shift had affected the Old High German *tiufal* as it had *trahho*: that *deofol* preceded baptism in England is accordingly a tenable assumption. Obscure in origin but apparently similar in meaning to the Latin *paganus*, *hæþen* is akin to the Gothic *haiþno* used to render the Greek feminine *Hellēnis* in Mark 7:26. Wulfila was formerly held to have coined the word from the Greek *ethnos*, aspirating the initial vowel to emphasize a connection with the heath, but this etymology is unconvincing if not astounding, and the connection with the heath must be native and authentic instead. Unlike the dragon and the devil in the Apocalypse, *draca*, *deofol*, and *hæþen* cannot be regarded as synonyms or kennings for each other. Yet they do hold certain senses in common (and as a consequence the catalogue of eotens, elves, and orcs seems to have been intended as indicative rather than exhaustive; that the dragon belongs to the race of Cain is nowhere said explicitly, but also nowhere denied). The glove of Grendel in *Beowulf* 2088 was made from dragon hides and by devil powers; he seeks out the tribe of devils in line 756; he has a heathen soul in 852 and leaves a heathen hand-spur in 986, just as the dragon's treasure is a heathen hoard in 2216 and heathen gold in 2276. If *draca*, *deofol*, and *hæpen* were elements of Old English song throughout the seventh century, these lines owe no identifiable debt to the preaching of the early church, and cannot have impressed an audience as an innovation from Rome or Iona. The new religious movement did indeed cause *hæpen* to describe not only Grendel and the firedrake but also those who practiced the older ceremonies: oppressed by a *gast* "ghost, demon" (102, 133), the Danes pray to a *gastbona* (not "destroyer of the soul" but) "ghost-bane, demon-slayer" (177)—presumably Woden, Tiw, or Thunor—and are censured as *heathens* for doing so (179). That this bold extension of the word implies an awareness of Christ, however, is an unwarranted assumption in need of excision by Occam's razor. The Old Saxon *Heliand* and the *Song of Roland* indicate the readiness with which Christianity could put on the armor of the heroic age, but the Old English epic is not Christian in any important manner at all.

V. The case against allegory

We may distinguish initially between the kinds of allegorizing developed by the contemporaries Philo Judaeus and St. Paul. Philo ransacked the Pentateuch for its philosophical implications; Paul looked upon the Old Testament as a prefiguration of the New, or at least as the foreshadowing of a truth to be revealed later. To Philo (*Allegorical Interpretation*

2.12), Adam recognizing Eve as bone of his bones is Mind recognizing Sense-perception. To Paul (Romans 5:14–20), Adam and Christ are type and antitype: by the offense of the one came the judgment, by the righteousness of the other came grace abounding. To Philo (*Preliminary Studies* 4), Sarah is Wisdom, and Hagar the instruction of the schools— grammar, music, geometry, rhetoric, and dialectic. To Paul (Galatians 4:24–26), Sarah and Hagar are an allegory for the two covenants, or for the earthly and heavenly Jerusalems. Both styles of interpretation were adopted by the Church Fathers and influenced Christian theology almost to the present day. The approach of Philo has now passed from fashion, owing partly to Pope Pius XII's encyclical *Divino Afflante Spiritu*, delivered 30 September 1943, which warns that the faithful "wish to know what God has told us in the Sacred Letters rather than what an ingenious orator or writer may suggest by a clever use of the words of Scripture." The approach of Paul, on the other hand, still seems rewarding: we realize more and more that the Old Testament ought to prefigure the New in certain ways since the gospels were written with the belief that they recorded the fulfilment of what had been promised before.

The vogue in the criticism of secular literature has changed similarly. No one agrees with the folklorists of an earlier generation in their Philonic interpretation of the monsters in *Beowulf* as being the elements or the North Sea. But several scholars do propose Pauline interpretations of the epic hero as being a type of Christ. Our attack is upon this latter school, and we begin by citing the well known letter of Alcuin to the abbot at Lindisfarne: *Bibliotheca rerum Germanicarum*, ed. Philipp Jaffé, 6: *Monumenta Alcuiniana* (Berlin 1873) 357: "Let the words of God be read when the monks are at table. That is the place to hear a reader, not a harpist; the sermons of the Fathers, not the songs of the heathen. What has Ingeld to do with Christ? Your house is narrow; it will not be able to hold both of them. The heavenly King does not wish to have communion with the lost pagans who are kings in name only; for He reigns in the heavens as King everlasting, while the lost pagan tears his hair in hell. Hear the voices of readers in your houses, not the hubbub of laughing men in your streets." It is clear that Ingeld and Beowulf never had anything to do with Christ until recently.

Nevertheless, there are two details that must be explained before our position can be firmed down; both have to do with numbers. The first is this: at *non* "the ninth hour" Beowulf is hidden in the mere, and his friends do not expect to see him again (1600). Now have we here an allusion to the ninth hour of the crucifixion, when the heavens grew dark? Perhaps we do, since its vowel shows that the word derived from the Latin *nona*. But then perhaps not, since *noon* is for us a more ordinary region of time than tierce or sext. Why may not *non* have had the modern, secular sense from the first? The Old English poet is likely to have meant neither the canonical office nor the hour on the cross but merely "midday."

The second detail is more impressive and will require a lengthier comment. As the twelfth in a company of warriors, Beowulf goes to fight the dragon; the man whose theft of the cup had brought on the devastation is the thirteenth (2401–2407). Is the enumeration an allusion to Christ, the eleven loyal disciples, and Judas? We grant without comment that the number of the Twelve Peers about Charlemagne in the *Song of Roland* (though the traitor Ganelon is not among them: see lines 2402–2410) may have been determined from the New Testament, but certain other groups of this size cannot so easily have had anything to do with each other historically and must be similar only by coincidence. Are twelve men cremated with Mul in the *Anglo-Saxon Chronicle* for the year 687 because twelve Trojans are cremated with Patroclus in *Iliad* 23.181–182, and does either dozen-plus-one pertain in any way to Christianity? What of the twelve companions of Guntharius in Ekkehard 1 of St. Gall's *Waltharius*, and the twelve companions of Hǫrðr in *Harðar Saga ok Hólmverjar*? (See George Philip Krapp and Elliott V. K. Dobbie, ed. *The Anglo-Saxon Poetic Records* [New York 1931–1953] 6 xxi, and G. V. Smithers, *The Making of "Beowulf"* [Durham, Eng. 1961] 8.) Unless we are prepared to find spiritual significance in the size of these bands too, the number of the companions of Beowulf will no longer strike us forcibly.

Even the double emphasis, on twelve and then on thirteen, is only a sign, confirmed later on, that the poet kept count. For the moral does not concern Beowulf or the thief of the cup, but the eleven thanes who accompanied them: it is made explicit that, of these, Wiglaf stood by his prince whereas the other ten did not (2847). What allegorical sense lies behind the double emphasis on numbers when Wiglaf chooses out seven men, and goes himself as the eighth (3122–3123), to bear away the treasure? Can we possibly agree that twelve and thirteen, in one instance, are allegorical, but the other numbers of the poem not?

There are two seas (858, 1297, 1685, 1956), a treaty is made on two sides (1095), Wealtheow goes to where two kinsmen are sitting (1163), Beowulf sits by two brothers (1191), two bracelets are shown to him (1194), the Danes have seen two march-steppers (1347), and Beowulf faces the dragon in a contest of two (2532). Beowulf gives three horses (2174), and the dragon is angry for a third time (2688). Four children were born to Healfdene (59), four treasures are given to Beowulf (1027), four men carry Grendel's head (1637), and four horses follow other gifts (2163). Beowulf bound five eotens (420), and was in the sea with Breca five nights (545). He swam with Breca seven nights (517), he was seven years old when Hrethel adopted him (2428), and Wiglaf calls forth seven thanes (3122). Hrothgar orders that eight horses be brought in (1035), and Wiglaf is the eighth in a band (3123). Beowulf slew nine nickers (575). Ten warriors fail Beowulf (2847), and the Geats build his monument in ten days (3159). Grendel's onslaughts lasted twelve winters (147), Hrothgar gives twelve treasures (1867), Beowulf is the twelfth in a band (2401), and twelve men ride about his pyre (3170). The man who found the cup is the thirteenth in a band (2406). Beowulf is the fifteenth in a band (207), and Grendel devoured fifteen men (1582). Grendel seizes thirty men (123), Beowulf has the strength of thirty men in his grip (379), and he has on his arm thirty sets of armor (2361). He rules the kingdom fifty winters (2209, 2733), and the dragon is fifty feet long (3042). Grendel's mother ruled the flood, and Hrothgar the Danes, for a hundred half-years (1498, 1769). The dragon guarded the hoard for three hundred winters (2278). Beowulf promises help with thousands of warriors (1829), and the dragon's treasure had lain in the earth for a thousand years (3050). Hygelac gives seven thousand acres (?) to Beowulf (2195) and a hundred thousand roods (?) each to Eofor and Wulf (2994).

If the poet had intended a few numbers to have a higher meaning would he have littered his work with so many more? Was he acute enough to create an allegory that he was then callous enough to destroy? The numerological arguments fail to show Christ behind *Beowulf*, and yet they

were the chief reason for thinking that the poem said more
than it seemed to.

The kennings for heroes, unlike the epithetic phrases that
are their Homeric counterparts, do not include the names of
the men being referred to, and therefore do not denote
particular individuals with absolute clarity. It would be a
fair résumé to say that the typical kenning of this kind was
generic, and that it was relevant to (or intelligible from) its
contexts. When Hrothgar has the age and rank of a *har
hilderinc* "old battle-warrior" (1307) and *folces hyrde* "shepherd of the people" (610), the *hæle hildedeor* "hero battle-
fierce" (1646) and *feþecempa* "foot-warrior" (1544) is
Beowulf; when Beowulf has the age and rank of a *har
hilderinc* (3136) and *folces hyrde* (2644), the *hæle hildedeor* (3111)
and *feþecempa* (2853) is Wiglaf. The same is true when the
kennings for heroes have a religious sense: *mære þeoden*
"famous prince"—which is used for Hrothgar (129), Beowulf (797), Heremod (1715), and Onela (2384) in the epic
—is sufficiently generic, and sufficiently relevant to (or intelligible from) its contexts, to be used for God the Father in
Genesis (853), *Andreas* (94), and *Judith* (3), and for Christ in
the *Dream of the Rood* (69) and the *Menologium* (2); and so for
gumena dryhten, *rices hyrde*, and *wigendra hleo*, which all refer
sometimes to men, sometimes to God. Here again Old
English resembles Old Norse: in discussing the kennings used
for Christ, Snorri (*Skáldskaparmál* 51–52) noted that *konungr
manna* "king of men" might apply to other rulers just as
well, but could always be rightly understood from the passages where it occurred. Nevertheless, when *mære þeoden*,
gumena dryhten, *rices hyrde*, *wigendra hleo*, and *konungr manna* are
used for God or Christ, they continue to seem heroic.

Many words for the Germanic gods, or for the pre-Christian idea of god, could also be used for God—even more easily than the kennings for heroes could. These words were generic for slightly different conceptions, and intelligible from contexts where those conceptions were expressed; but they must always have given the impression of being conventional. The earlier meaning was the basis for the later one and could not be expunged. In the homiletic and scriptural poems, when the kennings for heroes are used for God or Christ they continue to seem heroic, and when the old words for providence are used for God they continue to seem Germanic or pre-Christian. And in *Beowulf*, which is neither homiletic nor scriptural to any wide degree, the old words for providence seem pre-Christian altogether.

Scholars would never have regarded *alwalda* as Christian if the allusions to Genesis and the description of the Danish apostasy had been lacking and if *non* and the numbers twelve and thirteen had not at first brought the New Testament to mind. But was the evidence really adequate and reliable? If the stories of the Creation and Cain did not greatly alter the Germanic perspective, if the condemnation of Woden was accepted as a reformation of the native religion, and if poets had not acquired a use for allegory, *alwalda*, *metod*, and *wyrd* could not have been much affected by any missionary in England. A cleric in the epic audience, or monastic library, might here and there have found hints of orthodox doctrine (or heterodox doctrine), but the true-born Englishman in the audience must have understood *halig god* in the same manner as *ginnheilog goð* was understood by the audience of the *Vǫlospá*. For the old simplices, compounds, phrases, *formulas*, gave the poetic tradition a religious continuity not easily broken.

Five / No element of Old Testament poetry is more likely than not to have been created for the passage in which it now appears.

Many present-day Old Testament scholars use the term *oral tradition* to mean the sort of oral *transmission* that is defined in these widely respected assertions by H. S. Nyberg, "Studien zum Hoseabuche," *Uppsala Universitets Årsskrift* 1935, 8 (here condensed): "In its present form the Old Testament was created by the Jewish community after the exile. What existed before then had in only small part been put into writing. The prophets did not write, but left their work to circles, and centers, of tradition, which handed it down. During the course of transmission certain changes occurred, but as a result of retelling, not of re-editing." According to this hypothesis Isaiah stood to Isaianidae as Homer stood to the Homeridae—an engaging idea that I wish to declare at the outset as remote from our subject here. We are concerned with the poetry alone, not with the prose as well, and our special problem is not "How was it transmitted?" but "How was it composed in the first place?" The term *tradition* will for us refer to the customs and conventions behind the making of the poetry, *traditional* will have much the same sense as "customary, conventional," and *oral tradition* will sum up our deduction that, because they are often repeated, elements of two types were developed, at least in part, without the aid of writing. In discussing these types we shall from time to time oppose Lowth and Gunkel, eminent names in (different kinds of) form criticism; with small adjustments one argument of formula criticism will tell against them both.

I. Word pairs

a. They determine the kinds of parallelism.

In lecture 19 of his *De Sacra Poesi Hebraeorum* (Oxford 1753), Robert Lowth established the principle that Hebrew poetry was marked by a parallelism in meaning between the members (here called hemistichs) of longer units (or distichs). As a primary requirement this semantic balance is analogous to the meter of Homeric poetry, the alliteration of Old English poetry, and the assonance of Old French poetry. All four corpora had secondary requirements as well—a regular number of accents though not of syllables in the Old Testament, hidden laws of word division in the *Iliad* (a single word seldom or never fills the third foot exactly: see Eugene G. O'Neill, Jr., "The Localization of Metrical Word-Types," *Yale Classical Studies* 8 [1942] 109), a regular number of accents though not of syllables in *Beowulf*, and a regular number of syllables in the *Song of Roland*—but for the sake of simplicity we shall take only the primary, and not the secondary, requirements into account. Lowth distinguished among three main kinds of parallelism: synonymous (the hemistichs mean the same), antithetical (the hemistichs are somehow opposed), and synthetic (the hemistichs are related in no clear fashion); the following list gives two examples of each kind:

And did eat up all the herbs in their land,
and devoured the fruit of their ground (Ps. 105:35)

He hath filled me with bitterness,
he hath made me drunken with wormwood (Lam. 3:15)

The poor useth intreaties;
but the rich answereth roughly (Prov. 18:23)

A wise man's heart is at his right hand;
but a fool's heart at his left (Eccl. 10:2)

Yet man is born unto trouble,
as the sparks fly upward (Job 5:7)

The watchmen that go about the city found me:
to whom I said, Saw ye him whom my soul loveth?
   (S. of Sol. 3:3)

A general advantage of classifying the kinds of parallelism, or meter, or alliteration, or assonance, is that we become acutely conscious of rarities. One example belongs to the subcategory of *staircase* synonymous parallelism: "The mountains skipped like rams, and the little hills like lambs" (Ps. 114:4). Another is the entirely spondaic line ψυχὴν κικλήσκων Πατροκλῆος δειλοῖο "calling the soul of wretched Patroclus" (*Il.* 23.221); a third is the single line from *Beowulf* alliterating on *sp-* (873); and a fourth is the single laisse from the *Song of Roland* assonating on a feminine *-ei-* (975–993). A general disadvantage of classifying is that we are stunned into regarding as regular what is in fact irregular. Synthetic parallelism should perhaps not be regarded as parallelism at all; the sense-rhyme dominating the synonymous and antithetical verses is less evident in the synthetic verses, which

are accordingly by no means so easy to recognize as being
poetry. Only the very great number of similar examples
causes us to hesitate before saying that "Yet man is born unto
trouble, as the sparks fly upward" (Job. 5:7) is a flaw—
comparable to the faulty meter of *Iliad* 18.105 (where the
first syllable of οἶος is short), the faulty alliteration of *Beowulf*
2888 (where the alliteration in the *b* half-line falls on the
second, not the first, of the accented syllables), and the faulty
assonance of *Roland* 2300 (where *une piedre byse* sounds with a
feminine *u-*; cf. *une piedre bise* sounding with a feminine *i-* in
2338).

We also encounter in the Old Testament a difficulty without analogue. Since the kinds of parallelism are determined
from meaning, rather than sound, their number is highly
questionable. The terms *synonymous*, *antithetical*, and *synthetic*
are sometimes augmented with *comparative*, *parabolic*, and
emblematical, but even these will not suffice. For the balance of
"A wise man's heart is at his right hand; but a fool's heart
at his left" (Eccl. 10:2) is not quite to be found in "A wise
son maketh a glad father: but a foolish man despiseth his
mother" (Prov. 15:20). Both are antithetical in the main:
but is "father" antithetical to "mother"? If the categories
are to have precision, the two verses ought not be grouped
together, and yet they cannot be kept far apart. This is the
first of the three vitiating limitations in the Lowth technique:

1. There are no objective criteria that once and for all define
   with respect to each other a usefully small number of
   different kinds of parallelism.
2. The classification does not observe that certain distichs,
   though different in the kinds of parallelism they exhibit,
   are nevertheless very much alike in their word pairs.

3. There is no road from the classification to any further
   theory concerning the origin of the poetry.

The second and third of these are now our long concern, and
we turn from the large composites to the small components.
    It is already clear that the parallelism of a distich derives
from the balance of the word pairs. In Psalms 105:35 ("And
did eat up all the herbs in their land, and devoured the fruit
of their ground"), "did eat up" corresponds to "devoured,"
"herbs" to "fruit," and "land" to "ground"; in Lamenta-
tions 3:15 ("He hath filled me with bitterness, he hath made
me drunken with wormwood"), "hath filled me" corresponds to "hath made me drunken," and "bitterness" to
"wormwood"; in either distich the synonymy of the hemistichs hangs on the synonymy of the word pairs. In Proverbs
18:23 ("The poor useth intreaties; but the rich answereth
roughly"), "poor" is balanced by "rich," and "useth intreaties" by "answereth roughly"; in Ecclesiastes 10:2 ("A
wise man's heart is at his right hand; but a fool's heart at his
left"), "wise man" is balanced by "fool," and "right" by
"left"; the antithesis of the hemistichs is an aftermath of the
antithesis of the word pairs. In Proverbs 15:20 ("A wise son
maketh a glad father: but a foolish man despiseth his
mother"), the parallelism is mostly antithetical, but not
entirely, since "father" is not quite antithetical to "mother."
In Job 5:7 ("Yet man is born unto trouble, as the sparks fly
upward") and Song of Solomon 3:3 ("The watchmen that
go about the city found me: to whom I said, Saw ye him
whom my soul loveth?") the parallelism is obscure precisely
because there are no word pairs—such as "eat/devour,"
"herb/fruit," "land/ground," "fill/make drunken," "bitter-
ness/wormwood," "poor/rich," "use intreaty/answer
roughly," "wise man/fool," or "right/left"—to discipline

the longer clauses or phrases into alignment. If we are to penetrate very far into the structure of the poetry, we must turn our attention from the end products towards the basic materials, the word pairs themselves.

b. The word pairs assisted composition rather than memory.

It is a crucial and intriguing fact that several word pairs recur with noticeable regularity. Let us consider the verses—all cited by the *Lexicon in Veteris Testamenti Libros*, ed. Ludwig Koehler and Walter Baumgartner (Leiden and Grand Rapids 1951–1953) 508 and 935—that contain *māwet* "death" and *šeʾôl* "grave" or "hell":

The sorrows of hell compassed me about;
the snares of death prevented me (2 Sam. 22:6)

For in death there is no remembrance of thee:
in the grave who shall give thee thanks? (Ps. 6:5)

Her feet go down to death;
her steps take hold on hell (Prov. 5:5)

for love is strong as death;
jealousy is cruel as the grave (S. of Sol. 8:6)

We have made a covenant with death,
and with hell are we at agreement (Isa. 28:15)

I will ransom them from the power of the grave;
I will redeem them from death (Hos. 13:14)

who enlargeth his desire as hell,
and is as death (Hab. 2:5)

(See also Ps. 18:5, 49:14, 89:48, Prov. 7:27, and Isa. 28:18 and 38:18.)

The regularity of the linkage of the parallel terms here is not in the least unusual and our specific comment will apply widely. We conclude that the word pair "death/grave," not just the single words "death" and "grave," must have belonged to a fund of formulas that were a national property. It will be argued against us that the two nouns, because of their everyday character and natural association with each other, might still have been combined, again and again, by poets who created the word pair independently and spontaneously. We reply that *tannîm* "dragons" and *bᵉnôt yaᶜᵃnāh* "owls" are so rare, and so unlikely each to have repeatedly suggested the other, that the word pair "dragons/owls" can have recurred only from the influence of habit, or common practice:

I am a brother to dragons,
and a companion to owls (Job 30:29)

and it shall be an habitation of dragons,
and a court for owls (Isa. 34:13)

I will make a wailing like the dragons,
and mourning as the owls (Mic. 1:18)

H. L. Ginsberg, "The Rebellion and Death of Baᶜlu," *Orientalia* N. S. 5 (1936) 172, has shown that the word pairs in the texts from Ugarit are the same as those in the Old Testament. Was the poetry in the one dialect a source for the poetry in the other? No, the likeliest explanation is that the tradition was neither specifically Ugaritic nor specifically Hebrew, but common to both cultures and more ancient than the differences between them. So a search for hidden traces of the stereotyped poetic idiom is unusually inviting. Verses have long been emended to improve their parallelism: G. R. Driver—"Notes on Isaiah," in *Von Ugarit nach*

6

Qumran, Eissfeldt Festschrift, ed. Johannes Hempel and Leonhard Rost (Berlin 1958) 45—reads "They also that erred in spirit shall come to understanding, and they that murmured shall learn doctrine" (Isa. 29:24) as "They also that erred in spirit shall come to understanding, and *they of muddled sense* shall learn doctrine." But emendation on the basis of the word pairs is a new and still more powerful technique, devised by Stanley Gevirtz—*Patterns in the Early Poetry of Israel*, Studies in Ancient Oriental Civilization 32 (Chicago 1963) 89–90—who reads "From the blood of the slain [$h^a l\bar{a}l\hat{\imath}m$], from the fat of the mighty" (2 Sam. 1:22) as "From the blood of the *valiant* [$hay\bar{a}l\hat{\imath}m$], from the fat of the mighty," owing to the parallelism of "valiant" and "mighty" in 2 Samuel 17:10, Isaiah 5:22, Jeremiah 48:14, and Nahum 2:3.

The word pairs also point up sometimes the similarity between verses that differ in their kinds of parallelism; consider these examples of (1) $s^e p\bar{a}tayim$ "lips"/*peh* "mouth" and (2) $s\hat{\imath}r$ "ambassador"/$mal^{e\jmath}\bar{a}k$ "messenger":

1. The lips of the righteous know what is acceptable:
    but the mouth of the wicked speaketh frowardness
        (Prov. 10:32)

    For the priests's lips should keep knowledge,
    and they should seek the law at his mouth (Mal. 2:7)

2. A wicked messenger falleth into mischief:
    but a faithful ambassador is health (Prov. 13:17)

    That sendeth ambassadors by the sea,
        even in vessels of bulrushes upon the waters,
    Saying, Go, ye swift messengers,
        to a nation scattered and peeled (Isa. 18:2)

Our arrangement of these four verses is surely the best: to set the two from Proverbs (which are antithetical) against the two from the prophets (which are not) would be to emphasize the trait of less significance. This is one of the reasons why we are interested not in the innumerable kinds of parallelism but in the word pairs which satisfied this primary requirement.

Now why should parallelism have been established as a requirement for poetry in the first place? Ezra 3:10–11 (cf. Neh. 12:24–40) tells that priests with trumpets and Levites with cymbals "sang together by course in praising and giving thanks unto the Lord; because he is good, for his mercy endureth for ever toward Israel"—and we gather that the work they performed was either the same as or similar to Psalm 136, which begins with just these words. So it may have been for the sake of such singing in course, by alternating choirs, that hymns and prophecies were originally created. Yet Psalm 136 is exceptional for the simplicity of its construction; "for his mercy endureth for ever" is the latter part not only of the first but also of every other verse. We may speak of a responsory here but cannot with equal confidence do so anywhere else.

A second explanation of parallelism—that it was an aid to the memory of the audience—is even less commendable. When we learn biblical poetry by heart our difficulty lies, precisely where an awareness of parallelism is of no value to us, in recalling how the several distichs are arranged. The twofold nature of these verses—"Thou makest us a byword among the heathen, a shaking of the head among the people" (Ps. 44:14), "My confusion is continually before me, and the shame of my face hath covered me" (Ps. 44:15), and "For the voice of him that reproacheth and blasphemeth; by reason of the enemy and the avenger" (Ps. 44:16)

—does not in any way help us to keep the three in mind as being consecutive. Nor is it clear that the latter hemistich, completing the distich, ensures the survival of the former; we are not certain to recollect the whole more easily than either half alone; "Thou makest us a byword among the heathen" is not forgotten sooner than the verse in its entirety. So neither for marshalling the distichs of a passage, nor for saving any hemistich from oblivion, is the technique of re-statement particularly worth while. The other merits of parallelism are all subordinate to what we may take as its true cause: "Thou makest us a byword among the heathen, a shaking of the head among the people" is satisfying to a degree that its half alone would not match; and parallelism was created to satisfy a desire for *high style*.

How then did the word pairs become established? In the parts of the Old Testament that are not marked by parallel-ism and are therefore conventionally referred to as prose, certain elements recur in series, and in the poetry these same elements, though occasionally occurring in series, are more regularly the word pairs joining together successive hemi-stichs. Here is perhaps the strongest evidence that the prose (where the key terms of this special kind are adjacent to each other) and the poetry (where they stand as a rule at an even distance from each other) are closely related. In the prose *yayin* "wine" is apt to be followed immediately by *šēkār* "strong drink," whereas in the poetry "wine" is apt to have "strong drink" as its counterpart, or echo. We notice eight instances of each sort:

Do not drink wine nor strong drink (Lev. 10:9)

He shall separate himself from wine and strong drink
  (Num. 6:3)

or for wine, or for strong drink (Deut. 14:26)

neither have ye drunk wine or strong drink (Deut. 29:6)

and drink not wine nor strong drink (Jud. 13:4)

and now drink no wine nor strong drink (Jud. 13:7)

neither let her drink wine or strong drink (Jud. 13:14)

I have drunk neither wine nor strong drink (1 Sam. 1:15)

Wine is a mocker,
strong drink is raging (Prov. 20:1)

it is not for kings to drink wine;
nor for princes strong drink:
Lest they drink, and forget the law,
and pervert the judgment of any of the afflicted.
Give strong drink unto him that is ready to perish,
and wine unto those that be of heavy hearts (Prov. 31:4-6)

Woe unto them that rise up early in the morning,
that they may follow strong drink;
that continue until night,
till wine inflame them! (Isa. 5:11)

Woe unto them that are mighty to drink wine,
and men of strength to mingle strong drink (Isa. 5:22)

They shall not drink wine with a song;
strong drink shall be bitter to them that drink it (Isa. 24:9)

But they also have erred through wine,
and through strong drink are out of the way;
the priest and the prophet have erred through strong drink,
they are swallowed up of wine (Isa. 28:7)

they are drunken, but not with wine;
they stagger, but not with strong drink (Isa. 29:9)

Come ye, say they, I will fetch wine,
and we will fill ourselves with strong drink (Isa. 56:12)

Similarly, ʿānî "poor" and ʾebᵉyôn "needy" are a series in
prose (Deut. 15:11, 24:14) and a word pair in poetry (Job
24:4, Ps. 9:18, 12:5, 72:4, 72:12, Prov. 30:14, 31:20, Isa.
32:7, Amos 8:4); and so for many other examples.

(When the group contains three elements, they are sometimes of the same weight, and sometimes not. ḥaṭṭāʾt "sin,"
ʿāwōn "iniquity," and pešaʿ "transgression"—all three [Ex.
34:7, cf. Lev. 16:21] or any two [Ex. 34:9, Deut. 19:15, cf.
Neh. 9:2; Jos. 24:19, cf. Lev. 16:16; Num. 14:18]—may be
a series in prose; and in poetry all three [Eze. 21:24, Dan.
9:24, cf. Job 14:16–17, Ps. 32:1–2, 32:5, 51:2–3, Isa. 43:24–
25, 59:12] or any two [1 Sam. 15:23, Job 10:6, 10:14,
Ps. 51:5, 51:9, 85:2, 103:10, 109:14, Prov. 5:22, Isa. 5:18,
6:7, 59:2, Jer. 5:25, 30:14, 31:34, 50:20, Lam. 4:6, 4:13,
4:22, Dan. 4:27, Hos. 4:8, 9:9, 13:12; Isa. 44:22, 58:1,
Amos 5:12, Mic. 1:5, 1:13, 3:8, 6:7; Job 31:33, 33:9, Ps.
65:3, 89:32, Isa. 50:1, 53:5] may be parallel to each other
in successive hemistichs. gēr "stranger," yātôm "fatherless,"
and ʾalᵉmānāh "widow" may also be a series in prose [Deut.
14:29, 16:11, 24:19, 24:20, 24:21, 26:12, 26:13, 27:19,
Zec. 7:10, cf. Ex. 22:21–22, Deut. 10:18, Mal. 3:5], and in
poetry any two of them, in series, may be balanced by the
third [Ps. 146:9, Eze. 22:7; Ps. 94:6; Deut. 24:17]; but
"fatherless" and "widow," without "stranger," are the
ordinary word pair [Ex. 22:24, Job 22:9, 24:3, Ps. 68:5,
Isa. 1:17, 1:23, 10:2, Jer. 49:11, cf. Job 29:12–13, 31:16–
17], and "stranger" is never to be found with either "fatherless" or "widow" alone.)

Now when two elements are both a series in prose and a
word pair in poetry, there is very good, though not conclu-

sive, reason for believing that the prose convention either influenced, or was influenced by, the poetic convention. Prosateurs either lent to poets, or borrowed from them, the habit of referring to wine and strong drink as if these elements were inseparable. How shall we choose between the alternatives? The question is not "Which species of composition, the prose or the poetry, seems to be the older?" but "Which had the greater use for its kind of prolixity?"; and the answer is clear enough. If the series "wine, strong drink" were compacted into a single member, the effect of the change on "Do not drink wine nor strong drink" (Lev. 10:9) would be negligible, whereas if the word pair "wine/ strong drink" were so compacted the effect on "Wine is a mocker, strong drink is raging" (Prov. 20:1) would be devastating. Elements used in series met no requirement; used as word pairs they met a crucial requirement, for the poetry *consisted in* parallelism. Not their use in series, but their use as word pairs, caused elements to recur together; the contrary conclusion would be illogical. So it was not from the influence of the prose that so many sets like "wine/strong drink" became somewhat invariable in psalm, proverb, and prophecy.

Here again the second explanation—that the word pairs aided the memory of the poet—is much the less probable. Unable to marshal the verses of a passage, they did line up the hemistichs of a distich, though only with a parallelism, usually synonymous or antithetical, so uncomplicated that it could no more easily be remembered than made anew. And now we see the answer we were looking for: the word pairs became formulaic because they assisted the poet in *composing* by answering for him the question he faced continually: "Having had the luck to come upon this fine idea, how can I most readily express it a second time, a bit differently?" Let

us test our deduction by noting the word pair ʾ*elōhîm* "God"/
YHWH "Lord" in such verses as:

God is gone up with a shout,
the Lord with the sound of a trumpet (Ps. 47:5)

Then shalt thou understand the fear of the Lord,
and find the knowledge of God (Prov. 2:5)

for they know not the way of the Lord,
nor the judgment of their God (Jer. 5:4)

Therefore I will look unto the Lord;
I will wait for the God of my salvation (Mic. 7:7)

(For additional examples see Job 1:9, Ps. 18:6, 18:21, 20:1,
38:21, 55:16, 56:10, 68:16, 70:1, 91:2, 94:22, 104:33,
116:5, 146:2, and 147:7, Prov. 30:9, Isa. 2:3, 25:9, 35:2,
40:3, 45:5, 48:1, 49:4, 59:13, and 60:19, Hos. 5:4, and
Mic. 4:2.)

How are we to find a hemistich that will match "Hear the
word of the Lord, ye rulers of Sodom"? The word pair
"God/Lord" gives us part of our solution, and from similar
resources we produce the rest: "give ear unto the law of our
God, ye people of Gomorrah" (Isa. 1:10)—which we need
not worry about forgetting since it will occur to us unbidden.

(We have considered simple examples for the sake of developing a simple theory. Are the more sustained tours in
parallelism another problem entirely? No, it is gratifying to
see that they, too, can be explained in large part. The word
pair ʾ*arᵉbeh*/*yeleḳ* in Psalms 105:34 and Nahum 3:15 suggests
that "locust/cankerworm" was formulaic in an everyday
manner; the series ʾ*arᵉbeh*, *ḥāsîl* in 1 Kings 8:37 = 2 Chronicles 6:28 and the word pair ʾ*arᵉbeh*/*ḥāsîl* in Psalms 78:46
suggest the same for "locust/caterpiller." So we have con-

siderable insight into the process of thought behind Joel 1:4:

That which the palmerworm hath left hath the locust
   [*ar^eḇeh*] eaten;
and that which the locust hath left hath the cankerworm
   [*yeleḵ*] eaten;
and that which the cankerworm hath left hath the caterpiller
   [*ḥāsîl*] eaten.

ʾ*ᵃrî* and *kᵉpîr* occur in series in Isaiah 31:4 and as a word pair
in Psalms 17:12, Jeremiah 51:38, Ezekiel 19:6, Amos 3:4,
and Micah 5:8; ʾ*ᵃrî* and *lāḇîʾ* occur in series in Genesis 49:9
and as a word pair in Numbers 23:24 and 24:9 and Joel 1:6;
šaḥal and *kᵉpîr* are a word pair in Psalms 91:13 and Hosea
5:14; *kᵉpîr* and *lāḇîʾ* are a further word pair in Job 38:39
and Isaiah 5:29; and ʾ*ᵃrî* occurs in combination with both
kᵉpîr and *lāḇîʾ* in Ezekiel 19:2 and Nahum 2:11–12. Once
more, we can analyze much of the cadenza from ʾ*ᵃrî* to *šaḥal*
to *kᵉpîr* to *layiš* to *lāḇîʾ*, all referring to one kind of lion or
another, in Job 4:10–11:

The roaring of the lion,
and the voice of the fierce lion,
and the teeth of the young lions, are broken.
The old lion perisheth for lack of prey,
and the stout lion's whelps are scattered abroad.

Even this passage of virtuosity seems, from the evidently
commonplace word pairs it combines, to have been composed with rather little difficulty.)

   To sum up: parallelism was developed not for antiphonal
singing by opposed choirs, and not to aid the memory of
the audience, but only for its own impressive elegance; and
the word pairs of the poetry were established not from the

influence of the prose convention, and not to aid the memory of the poet, but only to assist him in creating parallelism. Evidence of the most complicated nature can be explained by these principles.

c. The word pairs raise the question of economy.

A passage of like kind will hold our attention in another manner; for there is a major difficulty that has never been paid its due respect. In Job 18:8–10 the half dozen hemistichs are all virtually identical in meaning; I cite as usual the Authorized Version (AV), but give in parentheses certain readings from the Revised Standard Version (RSV):

For he is cast into a net (net) by his own feet,
and he walketh upon a snare (pitfall).
The gin (trap) shall take him by the heel,
and the robber (snare) shall prevail against him.
The snare (rope) is laid for him in the ground,
and a trap (trap) for him in the way.

Ample though this supply of terms—*rešet*, *s*ᵉ*bākah*, *paḥ*, *ṣammîm*, *ḥebel*, and *mal*ᵉ*kō*det, respectively—would seem to be, there are further alternatives, and no word pair is sufficiently stereotyped to be predictable. *rešet*, from the first hemistich of the Job passage, occurs twice, in the verses quoted below, and is rendered as "net" in both AV and RSV. *paḥ*, from the third hemistich of the Job passage, occurs five times and is rendered as "snare" in AV, but as "snare" or "trap" in RSV. *m*ᵉ*ṣud*āh, foreign to the Job passage, is once "net" and once "snare" in both AV and RSV. *mô*ḳēš, also foreign to the Job passage, is once "trap" and twice "gin" in AV, but twice "trap" and once "snare" in RSV. To cite AV alone:

Let their table become a snare before them:
and that which should have been for their welfare, let it become a trap. (Ps. 69:22)

Keep me from the snare which they have laid for me,
and the gins of the workers of iniquity (Ps. 141:9)

as the fishes that are taken in an evil net,
and as the birds that are caught in the snare (Eccl. 9:12)

And I will spread my net upon him,
and he shall be taken in my snare (Eze. 17:20)

because ye have been a snare on Mizpah,
and a net spread upon Tabor (Hos. 5:1)

Can a bird fall in a snare upon the earth,
where no gin is for him? (Amos 3:5)

The inconsistency of the translators is adequate evidence that all these terms mean more or less the same thing. Why should there be so many? Even if the Job passage needed six of them, was there an additional need for the other two? And when we find two more besides—yākûš and mōneh in "they lay wait, as he that setteth snares; they set a trap, they catch men" (Jer. 5:26)—how can we begin to justify them? Nor is this collection unique; the other word pairs, though often highly regular, are even more often noticeably irregular.

(Not only are ʿānî "poor" and ʾebʿyôn "needy" commonly parallel to each other, they are also—now one, now the other —parallel to dal, which is translated as "needy" when with ʿānî [Isa. 10:2, 26:6], and as "poor" when with ʾebʿyôn

[Ps. 113:7, Isa. 14:30, 25:4, Amos 4:1, 8:6, cf. 1 Sam. 2:8].
Not only are *ᶜāwōn* "iniquity," *pešaᶜ* "transgression," and
ḥaṭṭāʾt "sin" all commonly parallel to each other, but *ᶜāwōn*
"iniquity" [Job 22:5] and *pešaᶜ* "transgression" [Lam.
1:22] are also parallel to *raᶜ*, which is translated as "wickedness" when parallel to *mᵉšubāh* "backslidings" [Jer. 2:19],
and as "evil" when parallel to *rešaᶜ* "wickedness" [Ps. 5:4]
—which is in turn parallel to *ᶜawᵉlāh* "iniquity" [Job 34:10,
Hos. 10:13].

   yārēḥ "moon" is parallel often to *šemeš* "sun" [Jos. 10:12,
Ps. 104:19, 121:6, Isa. 13:10, 60:19–20, Eze. 32:7, Joel
2:31] but once to *ʾôr* "sun" [Job 31:26], and *lᵉbānāh* "moon"
parallel twice to *ḥammāh* "sun" [S. of Sol. 6:10, Isa. 24:23].
bᵉhēmāh "beast" is parallel to *ᶜôp* "fowl" [Job 12:7, 35:11],
but the latter is parallel also to *ḥay* "beast" [Ps. 79:2, Eze.
31:6] and *zîz* "beast" [Ps. 50:11], and the former parallel
also to *ᶜayiṭ* "fowl" [Isa. 18:6]. *sᵉᶜārāh* "whirlwind" [Isa.
41:16] and *sûpāh* "whirlwind" [Hos. 8:7] are each parallel
to *rûaḥ* "wind"; *ḥāšaš* "chaff" is parallel to *qaš* "stubble"
[Isa. 5:24, 33:11], but *mōṣ* "chaff" to *teben* "stubble" [Job
21:18].)

An unfair selection of the evidence caused the word pairs
to appear more highly stereotyped than they are now seen to
be in fact. Yet the argument for a traditional diction is not
refuted, but merely challenged, and in reply we make two
special remarks. First, though the poet seldom needed more
than one word pair for any concept, the larger number of
available terms suggested to him, from time to time, that the
parallelism might be maintained longer than usual, and,
when it was indeed maintained longer than usual, terms that
would otherwise have corroded were repolished for further
circulation. The continuing of an idea throughout several
hemistichs, as in the snare passage (Job 18:8–10) and the

lions passage (Job 4:10–11), was not only a result, but to some extent also a safeguard, of the great number of synonyms in the poetic vocabulary. Neither ʾarᵉbeh "locust"/yeleḳ "cankerworm" nor ʾarᵉbeh "locust"/ḥāsîl "caterpillar" has replaced the other, for all three terms were occasionally used together, as in the three hemistichs of Joel 1:4, and when so used were kept from being forgotten. Secondly, since parallelism depends upon sense alone, and not—as with the Homeric meter, the Old English alliteration, and the Old French assonance—upon sound, the Old Testament poets had a relatively high degree of freedom, when choosing from among several terms, to suit their own regional or local preferences. The Aramaic word pair šᵉbîb/nûr, which would perhaps have been understood as "spark/light" in Hebrew, means "flame/fire" in Daniel 7:9, and probably replaces lehābāh "flame"/ʾēš "fire" (Num. 21:28 = Jer. 48:45, Job 41:19–21, Ps. 83:14, 106:18, Isa. 5:24, 10:17, 43:2, 47:14, Joel 1:19, 2:3, Obad. 18). Yet šᵉbîb/nûr does not actually compete with lehābāh/ʾēš, for the poetic style, owing to its being based upon the balance of concepts, is exceptional in not being impaired by translation.

d. The word pairs may all have been traditional.

The imperfect economy of the Old Testament formular system is as a matter of fact similar in kind to what we encounter in the poems of comparable nature. There is no reason, from either sound or sense, why in the *Iliad* Zeus should be both the ἐρίγδουπος πόσις Ἥρης "loud-thundering husband of Hera" (four times) and the Ὀλύμπιος ἀστεροπη-τής "Olympian lightener" (three times), or why in the fourth book Menelaus should be both Μενέλαον ἀρήϊον

'Ατρέος υἱόν "Menelaus warlike son of Atreus" (lines 98 and 205) and Μενέλαον ἀρήιον ἀρχὸν 'Αχαιῶν "Menelaus warlike leader of the Achaeans" (lines 115 and 195), or why in *Beowulf* providence should be *ece drihten* "eternal lord" (108) as well as *ylda waldend* "men's ruler" (1661), or why the epic hero should be a *rof oretta* "renowned warrior" (2538) as well as a *rices hyrde* "kingdom's shepherd" (3080), or why in the *Song of Roland* there should be competition between *cheval corant* "running horse" (3112 and a half dozen other instances) and *cheval tot blanc* "horse all white" (3369), or why the line *La bataille est merveillose e pesant* "The battle is terrible and heavy" (1412 and 3381) should once appear as *La bataille est e merveillose e grant* "The battle is both terrible and great" (1653). It is true (in my opinion, but I give no proof) that the Old Testament and Old English systems of formulas are less economical than the Homeric and Old French systems—in the former two the prosodic requirements were less exacting (more highly standardized phrases never had been needed and never would be), or the diction had not come to maturity (they were needed but not yet fully developed), or it had long since come to maturity (they were needed once but no longer)—but the difference is only a matter of degree. Unless we accept the argument for a traditional idiom in the Old Testament we cannot do so for *Beowulf* and cannot without misgivings do so even for the *Iliad* and the *Song of Roland*.

Hebrew had the particle *waw* "and" as almost its only connective; Homeric Greek had syllables of just two different lengths; Old English had the accent at the beginning of the word; and Old French had the accent at the end of the word and the clause. The one poetic style was therefore based upon parallelism, the second upon meter, the third upon alliteration, and the fourth upon assonance. In speaking of moun-

tains the one poet therefore used the word pair *hārîm*
"mountains"/*gᵉbā⁽ôt* "hills":

The mountains skipped like rams,
and the little hills like lambs (Ps. 114:4)

he cometh leaping upon the mountains,
skipping upon the hills (S. of Sol. 2:8)

and weighed the mountains in scales,
and the hills in a balance (Isa. 40:12)

I beheld the mountains, and, lo, they trembled,
and all the hills moved lightly (Jer. 4:24)

They sacrifice upon the tops of the mountains,
and burn incense upon the hills (Hos. 4:13)

contend thou before the mountains,
and let the hills hear thy voice (Mic. 6:1)

(See also Ps. 72:3, Prov. 8:25, S. of Sol. 4:6, Isa. 2:14,
41:15, 54:10, and 65:7, Jer. 3:23, Hos. 10:8, Joel 3:18,
Amos 9:13, Mic. 4:1, and Nah. 1:5.)

The second poet used such terms as ὄρος αἰπύ "steep mountain," μέγα . . . ὄρος "large mountain," and ὄρος ἀκριτόφυλ-
λον "thick-leaved mountain" for their meter; the third used
such terms as *brimclif*, *holmclif*, and *ecgclif* for their alliteration; and the fourth used such terms as *mont*, *montaigne*, and
lariz for their assonance. In precisely the same manner *sús*
"horse"/*hᵃmôr* "ass" (Prov. 26:3, Eze. 23:20) corresponds
to ἵππος ἀεθλοφόρος "prize-winning horse," πόδας αἰόλος
ἵππος "horse swift of foot," etc., to *hors*, *mearh*, etc., and to
destrier, *cheval corant*, etc. *mayim* "waters"/*nāhār* "flood" (Job
14:11, S. of Sol. 8:7, Eze. 31:15) corresponds to πόντος,
πόντος ἁλὸς πολιῆς, θάλασσα, etc., to *swanrad*, *merestræt*, *flod*,

etc., and to *ewe dolce, ewe corant, mer*, etc. *melek* "king"/*śar*
"prince" (Job 3:14–15, Ps. 148:11, Prov. 8:15–16, Eccl.
10:16, Isa. 32:1, 49:7, Hos. 7:3, 8:4) corresponds to ἄναξ,
βασιλεύς, etc., to *cyning, folces hyrde*, etc., and to *emperedre
magnes, rei*, etc. The difference is that an Old Testament
formula could occur whenever its meaning was right, whereas a Homeric, Old English, or Old French formula could
occur only when its sound was right besides; so it is in accord with expectation that a single word pair can be found
relatively more often than any specific one of its analogues.

The Hebrew poetic diction, insofar as it is formulaic, was
traditional, and now (having worked out a fourfold analogy)
we may—from current theory about Homeric, Old English,
and Old French poetry—reason out two further hypotheses.
First, the diction became formulaic because it was developed
by oral poets, who composed on the instant and therefore
needed word pairs, such as "wine/strong drink" and "death/
grave," that came immediately to mind; men of letters, with
the leisure to be more original, would not have *had the incentive* to express themselves all in the same manner. Secondly,
the poets were (a dozen times? a thousand times?) more
numerous than those we can speak of by name; men few in
number and widely separated would not by the laws of
chance have *been likely* to express themselves all in the same
manner. Yet we cannot be sure that the Hebrew or Homeric
or Old English or Old French diction, after it had already
been developed as a national property, was not also used by
those who were literate and working in isolation. It is wrong
to assert either that Job and the *Iliad* and *Beowulf* and the
Song of Roland are in every sense, or that they are not in any
sense, oral poems retold from the past.

Our conclusion has perhaps not been drawn before. When
a word pair occurs on a single occasion only—as does *zānā*b

"tail"/$p^e ḥādayim$ "stones" (Job 40:17), both terms referring, it seems, to the male sexual members—there is, though never a certainty, always a very good possibility, better than in nonformulaic poetry, that it was commonplace at one time. Even those word pairs that do not recur in what remains may well have been made orally and once shared by many poets as traditional formulas.

II. Hemistichs and distichs

a. They are not limited to specific *Gattungen*.

Old Testament poetry does not describe a march of events; its subjects have a different nature entirely. Hermann Gunkel, *Einleitung in die Psalmen* (Göttingen 1933) facing p. 1, classified passages from the Psalms by categories (*Gattungen*): chiefly, Hymns, Songs of the Lord's Enthronement, Communal Laments and Personal Laments, Royal Psalms, and Songs of Thanksgiving. By taking account of cult worship in ancient Mesopotamia and Egypt he also sought to define for each category its special place in life (*Sitz im Leben*). This approach has both advantages and disadvantages. It postulates the existence of a uniform culture over a wide area and associates the literature we possess with the religious life of the community, but requires the Psalms to have been liturgical from the first and regards them as always the source of those *Gattungen* that appear also in the wisdom and prophetic poetry. We are not concerned with these issues, however, so much as with the procedure itself; for in actual practice the classification of a poem can seldom be made without uncertainty. Typical scenes, or themes, or motifs, are found in Homeric, Old English, and Old French poetry, and a close look at them is often rewarding, but to analyze the *Iliad* or *Beowulf* or the *Song of Roland* exhaustively, by categories, would be disillusioning. The meaning is intractable, too complex for reduction into parts, and no less intractable is the meaning of Job or Isaiah. This is the first of the three vitiating limitations in the Gunkel technique:

1. There are no objective criteria that once and for all define with respect to each other a usefully small number of different *Gattungen*.
2. The classification does not observe that certain poems or passages, though different in the *Gattungen* to which they must be assigned, have nevertheless a hemistich or distich in common.
3. There is no road from the classification to any further theory concerning the origin of the poetry.

The second and third of these are now our concern; we are interested, as we were before, less in the composites than in the components. For the Gunkel *Gattungen* have failed in the same way as did the Lowth kinds of parallelism, and the supplementary analysis we aim at should therefore be the same also. Do hemistichs and distichs ever recur, in the manner of many word pairs, as formulas? There are two reasons why we foresee, rightly, that the answer will be yes, they do indeed.

First, though Homeric poetry (in its lines), Old English poetry (in its half-lines), and Old French poetry (in its lines) are paratactic—in contrast not only with Virgil and Milton but even with Dante and Chaucer—Nahum and Habbakuk are paratactic to a yet greater degree. Some hemistichs, and all distichs, go far towards being complete assertions which may or may not have much to do with what precedes or follows. There is little enjambment between hemistichs, and almost none between distichs, and only when several terms meaning much the same are brought together, as in Job 18:8–10 (about snares) and Job 4:10–11 (about lions), is a single idea considered throughout a verse paragraph or rhetorical period. From this discontinuity appears the likelihood that hemistichs and distichs from one passage will occur in another.

Secondly, if Old Testament poetry resembles Homeric, Old English, and Old French poetry in the recurrence of briefer elements, it ought to resemble them further in the recurrence of longer ones. With respect to the proportion of repeated lines and the number of different repeated lines, the *Iliad* and *Odyssey* far surpass all works of similar length in the whole range of literature, *Beowulf* surpasses the *Canterbury Tales* or *Paradise Lost*, and the collection of which the *Song of Roland* is the best example far surpasses the *Aeneid* or the *Divine Comedy*, ranking in fact second only to Homer. So some repetition in Job and the Psalms and Isaiah is to be expected.

We need only enough evidence to confirm our predictions, not a catalogue in any way complete; several examples will be taken from the marginal notes of the Authorized Version (which have been multiplied tenfold since the 1611 printing), and a few more will be noticed in commentaries or discovered by chance. We reject phrases—like *urbs antiqua fuit* (*Aeneid* 1.12) and *urbs antiqua ruit* (*Aen.* 2.363), or "Alas, poor Yorick!" (*Hamlet* 5.1.203) and "Alas, poor York!" (*3 Henry 6*, 1.4.84)—that would impress only a foreigner, and never a native, as being formulaic; and as a rule we look for phrases that are at least as substantial and impressive as "all thy waves and thy billows are gone over me" (Ps. 42:7, Jon. 2:3). Even specimens of the first quality—such as "Yet a little sleep, a little slumber, a little folding of the hands to sleep" (Prov. 6:10 and 24:33)—will not be accepted unless they occur in more than one book: this is a restriction of great severity which we impose to shut out as many accidental recopyings and deliberate plagiarisms as possible. Our concern is not with the repeated passage—2 Samuel 22 and Psalm 18, 1 Chronicles 16:23–33 and Psalm 96—but with the verse, or the half-verse, that has found its way into different passages. (I quote from the Authorized Version but look to the Hebrew text; identical verses that have in translation become only similar are sometimes noted, but not the only similar verses that have become identical. Jot-or-tittle variations, in word order or inflection, are disregarded.)

The Lord is my strength and song,
and he is become my salvation (Ex. 15:2, Ps. 118:14, Isa. 12:2)

For there is a fire gone out of Heshbon,
a flame from the city of Sihon (Num. 21:28, Jer. 48:45)

For the Lord shall judge his people,
and repent himself for his servants (Deut. 32:36, Ps. 135:14)

the earth trembled, and the heavens dropped . . . before the Lord [God],
even that Sinai from before the Lord [God, the] God of Israel (Jud. 5:4–5, Ps. 68:8)

He raiseth up the poor out of the dust,
and lifteth up the beggar from the dunghill,
to set them among princes (1 Sam. 2:8, Ps. 113:7–8)

He maketh my feet like hinds' feet:
and setteth me upon my high places (2 Sam. 22:34, Ps. 18:33, cf. Hab. 3:19)

He poureth contempt upon princes . . .
and causeth them to wander in a wilderness, where there is no way (Job 12:21–24, Ps. 107:40)

They conceive mischief,
and bring forth vanity (Job 15:35, Isa. 59:4, cf. Ps. 7:14)

the word of the Lord [God] is tried:
he is a buckler to all those that trust in him (Ps. 18:30,
    Prov. 30:5)

For I have heard the slander of many:
fear was on every side (Ps. 31:13, Jer. 20:10)

. . . from sea to sea,
and from the river unto the ends of the earth (Ps. 72:8,
    Zec. 9:10)

Pour out thy wrath upon the heathen that have not known
    thee,
and upon the kingdoms [families] that have not called upon
    thy name.
For they have devoured Jacob, and laid waste his dwelling
    place (Ps. 79:6–7, Jer. 10:25)

all the ends of the earth have seen the salvation of our God
    (Ps. 98:3, Isa. 52:10)

O give thanks unto the Lord; call upon his name:
make known his deeds among the people (Ps. 105:1, Isa.
    12:4)

For he hath broken the gates of brass,
and cut the bars of iron in sunder (Ps. 107:16, Isa. 45:2)

He turneth the wilderness into a standing water:
and dry ground into watersprings (Ps. 107:35, Isa. 41:18)

I will not give sleep to mine eyes,
or slumber to mine eyelids (Ps. 132:4, Prov. 6:4)

He causeth the vapours to ascend from the ends of the earth;
he maketh lightnings for the rain;
he bringeth the wind out of his treasuries (Ps. 135:7, Jer.
    10:13)

For their feet run to evil,
and make haste to shed blood (Prov. 1:16, Isa. 59:7)

and they shall beat their swords into plowshares,
and their spears into pruninghooks (Isa. 2:4, Mic. 4:3, cf.
   Joel 3:10)

on all their heads shall be baldness,
and every beard cut off (Isa. 15:2, Jer. 48:37)

And gladness is taken away,
and joy out of the plentiful field (Isa. 16:10, Jer. 48:33)

The fathers have eaten a sour grape,
and the children's teeth are set on edge (Jer. 31:29, Eze.
   18:2)

I have heard a rumour from the Lord,
and an ambassador is sent unto the heathen (Jer. 49:14,
   Obad. 1)

I will kindle a fire in the wall of Damascus
[I will send a fire into the house of Hazael],
and it shall consume the palaces of Benhadad (Jer. 49:27,
   Amos 1:4)

A day of darkness and of gloominess,
a day of clouds and of thick darkness (Joel 2:2, Zep. 1:15)

he is gracious and merciful, slow to anger, and of great
   kindness,
and repenteth him of the evil (Joel 2:13, Jon. 4:2)

The Lord also shall roar out of Zion,
and utter his voice from Jerusalam (Joel 3:16, Amos 1:2)

Our predictions are satisfied. In the length and complexity
of its formulas the Old Testament does not match the *Iliad*,
but surpasses *Beowulf*, and approaches the *Song of Roland*.
Furthermore, as the recurring lines from the other cultures

are not limited to passages of any special nature (except that
no line occurs where it would make nonsense), the recurring
hemistichs and distichs from the Old Testament are not
limited to special *Gattungen*. Certainly the following passages
have little in common other than the distich they share
between them:

Then they cried unto the Lord in their trouble,
and he saved them out of their distresses.
He brought them out of darkness and the shadow of death,
and brake their bands in sunder.
Oh that men would praise the Lord for his goodness,
and for his wonderful works to the children of men!
For he hath broken the gates of brass,
and cut the bars of iron in sunder.
Fools because of their transgression,
and because of their iniquities, are afflicted.
Their soul abhorreth all manner of meat;
and they draw near unto the gates of death.
(Ps. 107:13–18)

Thus saith the Lord to his anointed,
to Cyrus, whose right hand I have holden,
to subdue nations before him;
and I will loose the loins of kings,
to open before him the two leaved gates;
and the gates shall not be shut;
I will go before thee,
and make the crooked places straight:
I will break in pieces the gates of brass,
and cut in sunder the bars of iron:
And I will give thee the treasures of darkness,
and hidden riches of secret places,
that thou mayest know that I, the Lord,
which call thee by thy name, am the God of Israel.
(Isa. 45:1–3)

We therefore abandon the *Gattungen* as we did the kinds of parallelism. And it seems likely that the same explanation of recurrence will hold for the hemistichs and distichs as did for the word pairs.

b. The hemistichs and distichs may all have been traditional.

The nineteenth-century scholars who studied the tenth book of the *Iliad* decided that it was not Iliadic but Odyssean. Not Iliadic, because the Towneley scholium on its first line says that Homer, though he created the book, did not intend it for the *Iliad*. Odyssean, because certain lines from the book, used nowhere else in the *Iliad*, do occur in the *Odyssey*: for example, *Il.* 10.292–294 = *Od.* 3.382–384. (For a list of thirty works on the subject, one of them Dutch and all the others German, see A. Shewan, "Repetition in Homer and Tennyson," *The Classical Weekly* 16 [1922–1923] 155, n. 5.) The not-Iliadic conclusion is acceptable if the testimony it depends on is reliable, but the Odyssean conclusion is acceptable only if the argument it depends on is rigorous—a condition no longer regarded as fulfilled. For the tenth book of the *Iliad* could have given, rather than taken, the lines it shares with the *Odyssey*; there is no way of showing by logic that either alternative is preferable to the other. Every considerable part is related in so many ways to the corpus as a whole, furthermore, that the patchwork theory can be as well applied to one book as to another. (See the fine papers by John A. Scott, "Odyssean Words Found in but One Book of the *Iliad*" and "Words Found in the *Iliad* and in but One Book of the *Odyssey*," *Classical Philology* 5 [1910] 41–49 and 6 [1911] 48–55.) Homerists nowadays hold, more sensibly, that a repeated passage, line, or phrase, was not, as a rule, copied from here to there, but was instead an element that just came readily to mind.

In an outstanding monograph that had the misfortune of being refuted the following year by a mediocre article, Gregor Sarrazin, *Beowulf-Studien* (Berlin 1888) 117 and 132, argued that the similarities between *Beowulf* and the poems attributed to Cynewulf led to a consideration of only three possibilities. The *Beowulf* poet imitated Cynewulf, or Cynewulf imitated the *Beowulf* poet, or the two men were the same. J. Kail, "Über die Parallelstellen in der angelsächsischen Poesie," *Anglia* 12 (1889) 32, proposed instead that the formulas, as Sarrazin had called them, were not marks of a personal style, but stock elements of a diction used by all poets as a matter of course. Further attempts to identify a phrase as specifically Beowulfian or Cynewulfian, or to trace the influence of one work on another, summoned forth further rejoinders, and today the issue is closed. It was an intelligent idea, which occurred to M. Wilmotte, "La Chanson de Roland et la Chançun de Willame," *Romania* 44 (1915–1917) 55, that the *Song of William* had "échos directs et fidèles" from the *Song of Roland*, but not a single scholar of the present time admits to holding a like opinion.

The old and perhaps not yet outmoded orthodoxy in biblical studies is that the books are to be dated with respect to each other (from the historical events they claim to describe, or the dialects they employ, or the degrees of sophistication they show in the use of a phrase shared between them), and that the earlier instance of a phrase is to be regarded as the literary source of the later one. This view is represented by Theodore H. Robinson, *The Poetry of the Old Testament* (London 1947) 80–81, who believes that, for dating the Book of Job, the slight but famous similarity of "What is man, that thou shouldest magnify him . . . and try him every moment?"

to "What is man, that thou art mindful of him?" is "one
interesting piece of direct evidence. In Job 7:17f we have a
bitter parody of phrases found in Ps. 8:4. The book is, therefore, later than Ps. 8. But when was Ps. 8 written? All we
know is that it may not be put late in the post-exilic period."
But does the evidence really lead to this conclusion? If the
relative ages of the books were known to be those given by,
and here abridged from, the *Dictionary of the Bible*, ed. James
Hastings, revised ed. (New York 1963) 104—

1. Amos
2. Hosea, Isaiah 1–39, and Micah
3. Nahum, Zephaniah, Jeremiah, and Habakkuk
4. Obadiah, Ezekiel, Isaiah 40–55, Haggai, and Zechariah
   1–8
5. Isaiah 56–66, Malachi, and Psalms 1–72
6. Proverbs, Job, Psalms 73–89, and Joel
7. Zechariah 9–14, Ecclesiastes, and the Song of Solomon
8. Psalms 90–150

—it would indeed be easy to argue for the copying of "I have
heard a rumour from the Lord, and an ambassador is sent
unto the heathen" from Jeremiah 49:14 into Obadiah 1, or
of "A day of darkness and of gloominess, a day of clouds and
of thick darkness" from Zephaniah 1:15 into Joel 2:2, or of
"For he hath broken the gates of brass, and cut the bars of
iron in sunder" from Isaiah 45:2 into Psalms 107:16. Such
decisions as these may occasionally be accurate, of course,
for when the canon took shape lines from one scroll could
be copied into another; but in general the philosophy of
composition is unacceptable since it means that, though of
the same kind to outward appearances, deutero-Zechariah
and Amos were not created in the same way at all, the

Zechariah poet having borrowed now from one work and now from another, the Amos poet not having been able to borrow a single aleph—except perhaps from the Ugaritic tablets which celebrated a god different from his own.

The new orthodoxy in biblical studies is more and more given to saying, sometimes with an inconsistent return to the idea of patterns and copies, that neither instance of a repeated hemistich or distich need have been taken from the other. N. H. Tur-Sinai (H. Torczyner), *The Book of Job* (Jerusalem 1957), though speaking about "the quotation of detached sentences from ancient literary sources" (p. 208) and though suggesting that Job 31:1 served as the model for Ecclesiasticus 9:5 (p. 435 n.), observes that the diction is stereotyped in general and consequently doubts whether Job 3:3–11 was either borrowed from or lent to Jeremiah 20:14–17 (p. 46 n.). So we find to our satisfaction that specialists in Old Testament, Homeric, Old English, and Old French poetry are somewhat agreed upon the use not only of briefer formulas but of longer ones as well. The cause of the standardization is also held, for each of the four cultures, to have been the oral tradition lying behind the literary remains. We conceive of a time when there were no records to show who was original and who was not, when poets borrowed freely from each other until their songs were a good deal alike, and when a man aimed less at individuality than at making the finest poetry possible from all available resources. In commenting upon not only the repeated word pairs, but also the repeated hemistichs and distichs, we must always allow that possibly, but can never insist that probably, some late author searched through a room full of documents and appropriated whatever he had a need for; the likelihood is that both instances of the element had a common source which was never written down. The tradition is a single monument, a single house of many mansions, and the three classes spoken of in Jeremiah 18:18—the priest, the wise, and the prophet (whom we may associate with psalm, proverb, and prophecy, respectively)—cannot have been mutually independent. All poets tended to use not only the same word pairs but also the same hemistichs and distichs; not only the kinds of parallelism, but also the *Gattungen*, mislead us away from the treasury of formulas.

Once again we arrive at a conclusion that has not, perhaps, been drawn by any Old Testament scholar, even though it is of considerable importance. Because the poetic diction could not well have become so regular if a far greater collection had not once existed than the small quantity we are now able to study, even the hemistichs and distichs that do not recur in what survives—such as "He that refuseth instruction despiseth his own soul" (Prov. 15:32)— are likely to have been commonplaces in an earlier time. To say that a given verse is Isaianic (or Iliadic) ought to mean only that it is found in no book of our library besides Isaiah (or the *Iliad*); there is certainly no way of saying that the verse was created—i.e., *first* created—for the passage where it occurs, and in every single instance we must doubt that it was. This is significant for anyone who believes that Old Testament poetry sometimes foretells—"Surely he hath borne our griefs, and carried our sorrows"—the life of Jesus Christ. For the prophecy of what was to come must now be ascribed to the tradition as a whole.

Six / Biblical poetry has its frame of reference in the prose.

We are interested in only the first of the major types of Old Testament prose (story, law, and record), but in all the major types of the poetry (psalm, proverb, and prophecy). Our objectives are to describe the prose and the poetry with respect to each other, and then to say how they relate to each other when occurring side by side.

I. The Old Testament is marked by a complete separation of styles.

In the first chapter of *Mimesis*—hereafter cited from the English translation by Willard R. Trask (Princeton 1953), but with the page numbers from the German edition (Bern 1946) in brackets—Erich Auerbach contrasted the narrative about Odysseus' scar (from the nineteenth book of the *Odyssey*) with the narrative about Abraham's offering of Isaac (from the twenty-second chapter of Genesis). The analysis is brilliant; and yet the two texts do not seem wholly comparable. For Homeric epic is no more analogous to Old

Testament prose than to the poetry; it is episodic like the one, but formulaic like the other—the argument from style that Homeric epic derived ultimately from an oral culture cannot be extended to Old Testament prose but can in large measure be extended to the poetry. So the passage about Odysseus' scar answers, in one way, to the passage about the offering of Isaac, but in another way, equally good, to a chapter from Habakkuk. In considering how Old Testament prose may be unlike the poetry, we shall keep Homeric epic as a touch-stone, and bring Auerbach, quoting him as extensively as need be, under judgment.

a. Old Testament poetry lacks distinctive characteriza-tion.

Herein lies the reason why the great figures of the Old Testa-ment are so much more fully developed, so much more fraught with their own biographical past, so much more distinct as individuals, than are the Homeric heroes. Achilles and Odysseus are splendidly described in many well-ordered words, epithets cling to them, their emotions are constantly displayed in their words and deeds—but they have no development, and their life-histories are clearly set forth once and for all. So little are the Homeric heroes presented as developing or having developed, that most of them— Nestor, Agamemnon, Achilles—appear to be of an age fixed from the very first. Even Odysseus, in whose case the long lapse of time and the many events which occurred offer so much opportunity for biographical development, shows almost nothing of it. Odysseus on his return is exactly the same as he was when he left Ithaca two decades earlier. But what a road, what a fate, lie between the Jacob who cheated his father out of his blessing and the old man whose favorite son has been torn to pieces by a wild beast!—between David

the harp player, persecuted by his lord's jealousy, and the old king, surrounded by violent intrigues, whom Abishag the Shunnamite warmed in his bed, and he knew her not! The old man, of whom we know how he has become what he is, is more of an individual than the young man; for it is only during the course of an eventful life that men are differentiated into full individuality; and it is this history of a personality which the Old Testament presents to us as the formation undergone by those whom God has chosen to be examples. Fraught with their development, sometimes even aged to the verge of dissolution, they show a distinct stamp of individuality entirely foreign to the Homeric heroes.
(*Mimesis* 17–18 [22–23])

It will be convenient to borrow from Auerbach, for the sake of showing how far we agree with him, two spatial metaphors. The one concerns depth: it contrasts a background (of matters in obscurity) with a foreground (where all is made clear). The other contrasts verticality (or succession in time) with horizontality (or contemporaneity). Let us apply both metaphors to Old Testament prose and Homeric epic (after the manner of *Mimesis*), and then to Old Testament poetry as well.

Content. Old Testament prose implies a background and develops with suspense. The prosateur sets down only whatever matters are crucial; no ancillary material is allowed to claim attention for itself. Many things that might be expressed are left to be inferred. Nor can we accurately predict much of what is about to happen.

And Rebekah took goodly raiment of her eldest son Esau, which were with her in the house, and put them upon Jacob her younger son: And she put the skins of the kids of the goats upon his hands, and upon the smooth of his neck: And

she gave the savoury meat and the bread, which she had
prepared, into the hand of her son Jacob. And he came unto
his father, and said, My father: and he said, Here am I;
who art thou, my son? And Jacob said unto his father, I am
Esau thy firstborn; I have done according as thou badest me:
arise, I pray thee, sit and eat of my venison, that thy soul
may bless me. And Isaac said unto his son, How is it that
thou hast found it so quickly, my son? And he said, Because
the Lord thy God brought it to me. And Isaac said unto
Jacob, Come near, I pray thee, that I may feel thee, my son,
whether thou be my very son Esau or not. And Jacob went
near unto Isaac his father; and he felt him, and said, The
voice is Jacob's voice, but the hands are the hands of Esau.
    (Gen. 27:15–22)

Homeric epic occurs in the foreground and has less suspense.
The poet works into the narrative by one device or another
whatever seems likely to hold the interest of his audience.
He understands everything fully and leaves nothing obscure.
We can predict some events because they are explicitly
foretold.

And warm tears were flowing from their brows to the ground
as they grieved in longing for their charioteer, and their rich
manes were stained as they streamed from the yoke-pads by
the yoke on both sides. Seeing the two of them in grief, the
son of Cronus pitied them, and shaking his head he said to
himself: Ah, wretched ones, why did we give you to lord
Peleus, a mortal, when you yourselves are ageless and im-
mortal? Was it that among unhappy men you should have
your own sorrows? For I suppose that of all the things that
breathe and creep on the earth there is nothing more
miserable than man. But Hector Priamides is certainly not
going to mount on you and the resplendent chariot; I will
not allow it. Isn't it enough that as things are he has the arms

and prides himself on them? But I shall send courage into
your knees and your heart, so that you may save Automedon
from the war and bring him to the hollow ships. For I shall
still stretch out glory to the Trojans to slay, until they come
to the well-benched ships, and the sun sets and the sacred
darkness comes on.   (*Il.* 17.437–455)

Old Testament poetry occurs in the foreground and has no
suspense. Not details about political intrigues but truths
known to every generation, not new facts but new insights,
engage the poet's special eloquence. We lack any incentive
to predict; nothing will take place that is memorable as
history.

   (Having long been barren, Hannah conceived a son;
when he was weaned she prayed as follows:)

My heart rejoiceth in the Lord,
mine horn is exalted in the Lord:
my mouth is enlarged over mine enemies;
because I rejoice in thy salvation.
There is none holy as the Lord:
for there is none beside thee:
neither is there any rock like our God.
Talk no more so exceeding proudly;
let not arrogancy come out of your mouth:
for the Lord is a God of knowledge,
and by him actions are weighed.
The bows of the mighty men are broken,
and they that stumbled are girded with strength.
They that were full have hired out themselves for bread;
and they that were hungry ceased:
so that the barren hath born seven;
and she that hath many children is waxed feeble.
The Lord killeth, and maketh alive:

7+

he bringeth down to the grave, and bringeth up.
The Lord maketh poor, and maketh rich:
he bringeth low, and lifteth up.
He raiseth up the poor out of the dust,
and lifteth up the beggar from the dunghill,
to set them among princes,
and to make them inherit the throne of glory:
for the pillars of the earth are the Lord's,
and he hath set the world upon them.
He will keep the feet of his saints,
and the wicked shall be silent in darkness;
for by strength shall no man prevail.
The adversaries of the Lord shall be broken to pieces;
out of heaven shall he thunder upon them:
the Lord shall judge the ends of the earth;
and he shall give strength unto his king,
and exalt the horn of his anointed.   (1 Sam. 2:1–10)

Old Testament prose is vertical in showing a procession of
figures after the usual fashion of a chronicle, and in showing
that a long passage of time has affected certain figures in the
usual way. But Homeric epic is horizontal since the casts of
the *Iliad* and *Odyssey* are somewhat identical, and since the
passage of time—each poem taking place in a few days, and
only ten years lying between them—is too brief for much
aging. And Old Testament poetry is horizontal in rather like
manner: no great while is needed for the dialogue in Job,
and everyone is the same at the end as at the beginning.

Style. Old Testament prose suggests a background by using
only such descriptive elements as cannot be spared, and
stands vertical because these elements always give point to
the moment at hand; character is drawn without the use of
clichés. But Homeric epic evenly illuminates its foreground
with descriptive elements that are interesting for their own

sake, and lies horizontal because these elements are timeless. Being loaded now with treasure to ransom the body of Hector (*Il.* 24.189), and now with clothing that Nausicaa and her handmaids will wash at the shore (*Od.* 6.72), a wagon is a "wagon well-wheeled, mule-drawn" ἄμαξαν εὔτροχον ἡμιονείην. Character is sketched by assigning to everyone certain traits and titles that may be repeatedly mentioned without regard for their appropriateness in any particular passage. Not that all are alike: Achilles and Odysseus, since their names are identical in meter, could have shared their epithets between them, and the same is true for Hector and Ajax, or Athene and Apollo. But there is no change: there is never a time when we are sure that Achilles will not be called "swift-footed," and those who are prominent in both poems—Odysseus, Nestor, Menelaus, and Helen—are described in the same way early and late. Old Testament poetry creates a foreground of Homeric leisure and serenity by restating every concept, and lies horizontal because its idiom has a Homeric timelessness and inevitability. A mountain of any kind brings mention of a hill: "I will get me to the mountain of myrrh, and to the hill of frankincense" (S. of Sol. 4:6); "contend thou before the mountains, and let the hills hear thy voice" (Mic. 6:1). Character is not here an important subject, yet "Jacob" and "Israel," synonymous names, are balanced in forty verses; there is no development, no contrast.

It may be helpful to extend what Tolstoi, *What is Art? and Essays on Art*, trans. Aylmer Maude (London n.d.) 208, remarked about Wagnerian opera: "There is one fixed combination of sounds, or *leit-motiv*, for each character, and this *leit-motiv* is repeated every time the person whom it represents appears; and when anyone is mentioned the *motiv* is heard which relates to that person. Moreover each article also has its own *leit-motiv* or chord. There is a *motiv* of the ring, a *motiv* of the helmet, a *motiv* of the apple, a *motiv* of fire, spear, sword, water, etc., and as soon as the ring, helmet, or apple is mentioned, the *motiv* or chord of the ring, helmet, or apple, is heard." None of this pertains to Old Testament prose, but if we change *leitmotiv* to *epithet* there are resemblances to Homeric epic, and if we change it to the *synonym*, or antonym, completing a word pair—there are resemblances to Old Testament poetry. With regard to background versus foreground, and verticality versus horizontality, both metaphors being applied in particular to characterization, Old Testament prose belongs on the left, Homeric epic and Old Testament poetry belong together on the right. Without debating whether, if all the factors were weighed, the figures of the Old Testament really would seem to have, as Auerbach claimed for them, an individuality foreign to the Homeric heroes, we observe that even the analysis behind this conclusion is valid only for the prose and not in the least for the poetry.

In contrasting Old Testament prose, on the one hand, with Homeric epic and Old Testament poetry, on the other, we say nothing about which is the nobler or has the more forcible effect on the mind. We say only that certain differences can be noted: the reportorial against the creative, the naturalistic against the nonnaturalistic, the suggestiveness of what is withheld as internal against the handsomeness of what is revealed as external, the nonformulaic against the formulaic, low against high style. To give these qualities in a slightly different order we may notice that, in contrasting Old Testament prose with Homeric epic, Auerbach defined the latter by its "fully externalized description, uniform illumination, uninterrupted connection, free expression, all events in the foreground, displaying unmistakable meanings, few elements of historical development and of psychological perspective" (*Mimesis* 23 [18]). Every term in the list applies also to Old Testament poetry.

b. Old Testament poetry consists of nonnaturalistic speech.

With the utmost fullness, with an orderliness which even passion does not disturb, Homer's personages vent their inmost hearts in speech; what they do not say to others, they speak in their own minds, so that the reader is informed of it. Much that is terrible takes place in the Homeric poems, but it seldom takes place wordlessly: Polyphemus talks to Odysseus; Odysseus talks to the suitors when he begins to kill them; Hector and Achilles talk at length, before battle and after; and no speech is so filled with anger or scorn that the particles which express logical and grammatical connections are lacking or out of place. (*Mimesis* 6 [10])

One fact Auerbach failed to discuss is that, unlike Old Testament prose, Homeric epic and Old Testament poetry had special requirements, and became circumlocutory, and formulaic, as a consequence. A concept had to be expressed under exacting conditions (of meter in the one, parallelism in the other), and these conditions were fulfilled in perhaps the easiest way possible (by such means as the use of epithets to create phrases of the desired meter in the one, by the use of synonyms and antonyms to create word pairs of the desired parallelism in the other). And whenever the same problem recurred the poet ordinarily supplied the same answer because it came most quickly to mind. For this reason, Thetis, Diomedes, Andromache, and Eumaeus all speak with like epithets to accompany like nouns; Hannah, Job, Lemuel, and Isaiah all speak with the same word pairs. It was not from any wish for decorum, but primarily for the sake of convenience, that the poet never allowed his figures, no matter how strong the passions that might govern them, to mar their eloquence with solecisms, stammerings, and anacolutha. No one in Homeric epic used "swift-footed" because he was intended to emphasize that term in particular, but solely because the poet needed to stretch out the name "Achilles"; no one in Old Testament poetry used "hills" because he was intended to be interested in them, but solely because the poet needed to complement the noun "mountains." Whether "swift-footed" or "hills" occurs in a line is accordingly somewhat fortuitous, the deciding factors being "Achilles" and meter, or "mountains" and parallelism. Here is a further aspect, not in Old Testamant prose but in Homeric epic and Old Testament poetry, of an analogy with the *leitmotiv*: W. H. Auden, "Mimesis and Allegory," *English Institute Annual, 1940* (New York 1941) 5–6, remarks that it "was Wagner who showed the surrealists that the primitive, the illogical, the chance-determined was the true revolutionary art and who preceded Sibelius and Gertrude Stein in the discovery that if you repeat the same thing four times it has little effect, but that a remarkable effect can be gained by repeating it four hundred times."

Some speech in the Old Testament is prose, some poetry; but all the poetry—a fact noticed by few besides Paul Dhorme, O.P., *Le Livre de Job*, 2nd ed. (Paris 1926) li—is speech. In the historical books the main narrative, in prose, is broken only for the quotation of a blessing (Gen. 49:1–27), a song of victory (Jud. 5), a prayer of thanksgiving (1 Sam. 2:1–10), or one of the other subjects of poetry. In Job the prologue and epilogue are in prose (except that Satan speaks in poetry: "From going to and fro in the earth, and from walking up and down in it"), and the assignment of the

speeches and the introduction of Elihu are in prose; but Job
and his friends converse in poetry, Elihu gives his monologue
in poetry, and the Lord speaks in poetry from the whirlwind.
In the books of psalms and proverbs prose is used for attri-
buting, now and then, a passage of poetry to an author, or
for naming the circumstances behind its creation; and in the
books of prophecy prose introduces, comments upon, and
otherwise gives continuity to the words of the prophets,
which are characteristically in poetry. The distinction between the forms, low against high style, is exact and uniform.
In Homeric epic there is nothing comparable: the narrator
speaks in the idiom of his heroes: the words of Priam resemble
those of Telemachus, and both are like what the poet says as
spectator; the high style is never interrupted. In this respect
there is a distinction between the Old Testament and Homer,
and it is precisely the opposite of what was asserted by
Auerbach—who so far has been censurable only for having
possibly misled us by giving all his attention to Old Testament prose and none to the poetry, but here for once is
certainly mistaken:

From the rule of the separation of styles which was later
almost universally accepted and which specified that the
realistic depiction of daily life was incompatible with the sub-
lime and had a place only in comedy or, carefully stylized, in
idyl—from any such rule Homer is still far removed. And
yet he is closer to it than is the Old Testament.   (*Mimesis*
22 [28])

This assertion, which stands near the close of the first chapter, is not peripheral or incidental to the arguments Auerbach
developed throughout his book, for it reappears near the
middle of the third chapter: "In the Judaeo-Christian tradition, as we have previously pointed out, there was no

separating the elevated style from realism" (63 [68]). The assertion is not peripheral but central, and it is wrong. For the separation of styles is not further to seek in the Old Testament than in Homeric epic; it is immeasurably closer at hand; indeed it is obvious. Prose is used for the naturalistic description of events, poetry for all speech that is elevated or sustained.

II. The prose assigns to the poetry its speaker and occasion.

Whether the prose, like the poetry, has a style that can be argued as having been created in an oral culture, is one question. Whether all the prose, or all the poetry, was orally transmitted in something like its present shape, is another. Whether the two forms were orally transmitted *together* is a third: and this is the subject before us. Remembering that prose is never used for sustained speech, poetry always for speech alone, we note that now the former predominates, now the latter. When the prose predominates, a passage of poetry often seems a set piece inserted for its intrinsic merits, like the song "It was a lover and his lass" from *As You Like It*. When the poetry predominates, the prose resembles the stage directions of a verse play like *Macbeth*—and here we ask: Why did not the Old Testament tradition develop formulas for introducing a speaker, such as τὸν δὲ μέγ' ὀχθήσας προσέφη ξανθὸς Μενέλαος "to him greatly troubled said sandy Menelaus" (*Il.* 17.18, *Od.* 4.30, 4.332)? There being no answer, we assume initially that, rather than having been orally transmitted together, the prose and the poetry did not stand side by side until they were put into writing. To prove this much is well nigh impossible, however, and

we shall aim only at showing the two forms to be, in most
contexts, unrelated.

  a. The poetry refers only vaguely to its context.

Job. At the beginning of the prologue Job has seven sons
and three daughters, 7,000 sheep, 3,000 camels, 500 yoke of
oxen, and 500 she asses; at the end of the epilogue he has
seven sons and three daughters, 14,000 sheep, 6,000 camels,
1,000 yoke of oxen, and 1,000 she asses—the same number of
children and twice as many animals. Either the author of the
prologue referred forward to the epilogue, or the author of
the epilogue referred back to the prologue; almost certainly
both parts are by the same hand. But the relationship of the
poetry to this prose framework is less certain. In the dialogue
Job speaks of the time when his children were still about him
(29:5, cf. 8:4), but also speaks of children in general as if his
own were still living (17:5, 21:19, 27:14; cf. 19:17). The
prologue makes clear, and the epilogue tends to confirm, that
Job is innocent; so he refers fittingly to his innocence (16:17,
23:12) but surprisingly to his transgression (7:21, 14:17).
It hardly seems that the dialogue is closely connected with
the special circumstances it purports to be considering: a
great deal is as well suited to numerous other situations as to
the one before us—and the marginal notes (to Job 3:3, 4:8,
7:17, 15:35, 28:15, and 28:28, Ps. 107:40, and Prov. 5:21
and 24:20) of the Authorized Version show in fact that the
thought, now and then even the wording, of several hemistichs and distichs may be found elsewhere:

Let the day perish, wherein I was born,
and the night in which it was said,
      there is a man-child conceived . . .
Why died I not from the womb? (Job 3:3–11)
  7*

Cursed be the day wherein I was born . . .
Cursed be the man who brought tidings to my father, saying,
    A man child is born unto thee . . .
Because he slew me not from the womb (Jer. 20:14–17)

they that plow iniquity, and sow wickedness, reap the same
    (Job 4:8)

He that soweth iniquity, shall reap vanity (Prov. 22:8)

Ye have plowed wickedness, ye have reaped iniquity
    (Hos. 10:13)

They conceive mischief, and bring forth vanity (Job 15:35)

they conceive mischief, and bring forth iniquity (Isa. 59:4)

and hath conceived mischief, and brought forth falsehood
    (Ps. 7:14)

[wisdom] cannot be gotten for gold,
neither shall silver be weighed for the price thereof . . .
for the price of wisdom is above rubies (Job 28:15–18)

For the merchandise of [wisdom] is better than the mer-
    chandise of silver,
and the gain thereof, than fine gold.
She is more precious than rubies (Prov. 3:14–15)

Receive my instruction, and not silver;
and knowledge rather than choice gold.
For wisdom is better than rubies (Prov. 8:10–11)

the fear of the Lord, that is wisdom,
and to depart from evil, is understanding (Job. 28:28)

Poetry and Prose Framework

The fear of the Lord is the beginning of wisdom,
and a good understanding have all they that do his com-
   mandments (Ps. 111:10)

The fear of the Lord is the beginning of knowledge:
but fools despise wisdom and instruction (Prov. 1:7)

The fear of the Lord is the beginning of wisdom:
and the knowledge of the holy is understanding (Prov. 9:10)

He poureth contempt upon princes . . . and causeth them to
   wander
in a wilderness, where there is no way (Job 12:21-24)

He poureth contempt upon princes: and causeth them to
   wander
in the wilderness, where there is no way (Ps 107:40)

For his eyes are upon the ways of man,
and he seeth all his goings (Job 34:21)

For the ways of man are before the eyes of the Lord,
and he pondereth all his goings (Prov. 5:21)

How oft is the candle of the wicked put out? (Job 21:17)

but the lamp of the wicked shall be put out (Prov. 13:9)

the candle of the wicked shall be put out (Prov. 24:20)

None of these is sharply pertinent to any specific unusual
event; each belongs to the once undifferentiated collection
we now know as psalm, proverb, and prophecy. Consider
only the first from the list: what Sir Thomas Browne in the
last chapter of *Hydriotaphia* remembered of Job—"who cursed
not the day of his life, but his nativity: content to have so far

been, as to have a title to future being; although he had lived here but in an hidden state of life, and as it were as abortion" —happens to be quite wrong; for Job did curse the night in which he was conceived. But the elegant comment would apply to the lament of Jeremiah, and Browne may merely have had the wrong passage in mind, a confusion for which the recurrence of hemistichs and distichs was responsible.

There has perhaps been a disarrangement, not only of certain chapters—H. H. Rowley, "The Book of Job and its Meaning," *John Rylands Library Bulletin* 41 (1958–1959) 187, observes that chapter twenty-six, assigned to Job by a prose introduction, would be better said by one of the friends—but of certain verses as well. The prologue makes clear, and the dialogue often confirms, that Job is an innocent man whom God has agreed not to answer for a while; so why Job should say in chapter twenty-seven that God does not hear the cry of the *hypocrite* (verse 9) is unclear; but the chapter cannot be reassigned in its entirety, for the phrase "all ye yourselves" (verse 12) is better said by Job to the friends than by one of them to him. But even if we attempt to repair the arrangement by reassigning the verses singly, the issue of relevance will remain unsettled. Chapter twenty-eight, though very grand, has nothing to do with the case, no matter who the speaker may be.

Without regarding the poetry as a treatise arriving at firm conclusions, let us draw up two double summations for the sake of seeing where they lead. The first: *Job asserts that he is innocent* (which we know from the prologue to be a fact), *and finds no alternative to believing* (what is so far uncertain) *that God does not favor the innocent.* The second: *his friends assert that God does indeed favor the innocent* (which is so far uncertain), *and find no alternative to believing* (what we know from the prologue to be false) *that Job is not innocent after all.* Neither

argument is wholly satisfactory—and no choice is made between them. For the Lord announces from the whirlwind
that neither premise (Job is innocent; God favors the innocent) leads necessarily to its supposed conclusion (God does
not favor the innocent; Job is not innocent): the whole truth
is that man cannot fathom the divine plan.

By the close of the poetical section, Job has been reproved
for, and has repented of, speaking about things beyond man's
understanding. Since in cursing his existence he did not
blaspheme, furthermore, the Lord has won the wager made
with Satan in the prologue. If the story ended here, the reward to Job for his uprightness would be no more than the
revelation to him of his meagerness, and his life would represent a game played by powers higher than himself; he
would have been right in saying that he was innocent and
that God did not favor the innocent. The story therefore
needed to be completed, though it turns out not to be simpli-
fied, by an epilogue. Job is declared to have spoken better
than the friends—and we have two reasons for saying that he
did: he asserted his innocence but they denied it, and he came
to repent of speaking about things beyond man's understanding but they did not—and he is made more fortunate in
the end than he was in the beginning (which means that he
was wrong and the friends right about whether God favored
the innocent).

The problems raised by the book have been solved, first in
the poetry and then in the prose, in ways that are reasonably
harmonious but not the same—and this is an aspect of the
fact that Old Testament poetry (being high style, philosophical, and general) and Old Testament prose (being low
style, historical, and specific) have little to do with each other
as a rule. Traditional and universal elements of phrasing—
word pairs, hemistichs and distichs, perhaps even passages—

have been restricted to a particular study; a framework has made them dramatic. Some of these (used by Job) are from one viewpoint; others (used by the friends) are from another; and yet others (used by the Lord) are from another still. But the poetry has not been carefully adapted for the prose; *the formulaic idiom has not been modified so as to speak distinctly about the specific calamities of Job*; and most of the verses in the book claim attention primarily for their own beauty and power.

The Psalms. A number of psalms—3, 7, 18, 34, 51, 52, 54, 56, 57, 59, 60, 63, and 142—seem at first to be dramatic monologues; for they are introduced by allusions in prose to specific events from the life of David: one of these (Ps. 18) occurs also in the chronicle (2 Sam. 22); the others do not. The question is not whether the poems in this small group contain formulaic word pairs and formulaic hemistichs and distichs; for obviously they do. The question is whether they were (1) composed by David under the circumstances that the headings refer to, or (2) composed earlier by David or someone else but sung by him as fitting under the circumstances referred to, or (3) not in fact sung by David under the circumstances but only ascribed to him and to them by some compiler. There may be no final way to decide among the possibilities; yet the first is the least probable, the last the most. For in none of these psalms is there mention of any name or detail that points to a definite time, place, or occurrence. Consider Psalm 3, which is said by its heading to be "A Psalm of David, when he fled from Absalom his son":

Lord, how are they increased that trouble me!
many are they that rise up against me.
Many there be which say of my soul,
There is no help for him in God. Selah.
But thou, O Lord, art a shield for me;

my glory, and the lifter up of mine head.
I cried unto the Lord with my voice,
and he heard me out of his holy hill. Selah.
I laid me down and slept;
I awaked; for the Lord sustained me.
I will not be afraid of ten thousands of people,
that have set themselves against me round about.
  Arise, O Lord;
  save me, O my God:
for thou hast smitten all mine enemies upon the cheek bone;
thou hast broken the teeth of the ungodly.
Salvation belongeth unto the Lord:
thy blessing is upon thy people. Selah.

Where is the testimony from the poetry that would support
the prose at its beginning? Why is not Absalom spoken of by
these verses? Clear and strong in wording, the psalm is vague
about history; and so are they all. The poetry and the prose
are not so clearly connected as their juxtaposition in our
texts makes them seem at first.

The Books of Prophecy. The four rolls of the latter prophets
—Isaiah, Jeremiah, Ezekiel, and (together) the twelve minor
prophets—contain prose headings which, accurately or not,
name the authors and the kings under whose reigns they
lived. But the poetry itself is in a way anonymous and timeless; for the word pairs, and the hemistichs and distichs, that
are repeated in what has survived—and also those that are
likely to have been repeated in what has not survived—belonged to the culture as a whole. Consider "The word of the
Lord which came unto Zephaniah the son of Cushi, the son
of Gedaliah, the son of Amariah, the son of Hizkiah, in the
days of Josiah the son of Amon, king of Judah" (Zep. 1:1).
Can we apply this ascription to the distich "Surely Moab
shall be as Sodom, and the children of Ammon as Gomorrah"

(Zep. 2:9)? The parallelism of *Sodom* and *Gomorrah* was certainly conventional: should we say the same for the disrepute of Moab and Ammon? Yes, there is no alternative. The Moabites were descended from the elder daughter of Lot and worshipped Chemosh; the Ammonites from the younger daughter and worshipped Molech (Gen. 19:37–38, 1 Kings 11:7). When the Israelites needed bread and water, the Moabites and Ammonites hired Balaam to curse them; for this reason they were excluded from the congregation of the Lord (Num. 22:5–6, Deut. 23:3–4, Neh. 13:1–2). The Israelites warred with the Moabites and Ammonites again and again (Jud. 3:12–13, 2 Chr. 20:1); there is no evidence of temporary friendship between them. So to prophesy against Moab and Ammon, by comparing them with Sodom and Gomorrah, required no originality; the distich has been credited to Zephaniah and the days of Josiah, but must really be regarded as traditional.

Nineveh was prominent before Babylon, and it would therefore be disagreeable to deny that the verses about the one were composed before, and intended to be fulfilled before, those about the other; still, the enemies of the Jewish nation have never been hard to identify—the verses against Damascus and Egypt can perhaps be taken as not fulfilled yet. Except for the few geographical terms, furthermore, the poetry of the prophecies is entirely general. Isaiah refers in his prose to a specific moment when the sun returned ten degrees (38:8); but he does not refer in his poetry to a specific forest fire (10:17: "And the light of Israel shall be for a fire, and his Holy One for a flame: and it shall burn and devour his thorns and his briers in one day") or a specific earthquake (13:13: "Therefore I will shake the heavens, and the earth shall remove out of her place"). There are no riddles here, no hexameters of the Delphic oracle or quatrains of Nostradamus, but figures used by the Hebrew poets without any single occurrence in mind:

A fire goeth before him,
and burneth up his enemies round about.
His lightnings enlightened the world;
the earth saw, and trembled. (Ps. 97:3-4)

b. Jesus was a traditional poet.

We are concerned about the reliability of our literary theory rather than the orthodoxy of our theology, and speak in a somewhat Nestorian fashion about Jesus (the historical figure) rather than Christ (the Son of God). We accept for the sake of convenience the story of his life at its face value; whether what has been set down actually happened is not a part of our inquiry. We wish to consider Jesus as a scholar, and then as a poet; to affirm or deny any item of a religious nature does not lie before us.

The synoptic gospels contain half or entire verses that are identified as quoted from the Old Testament. Several of these are prose: for example, the Sadducees refer to what was said or written by Moses (Matth. 22:24, Mark 12:19, Luke 20:28; Deut. 25:5), and Jesus refers to what was said in the old time (Matth. 5:21; Ex. 20:13, Deut. 5:17); but prose is not our present concern. Several other verses are poetry: for example, Satan justly claims to cite Scripture (Matth. 4:6, Luke 4:10-11; Ps. 91:11-12), and the evangelist as narrator—once crediting to Jeremiah what belongs now to Zechariah (Matth. 27:9; Zech. 11:13)—cites the prophecies, some of them from the Psalms, that he regards as being fulfilled; but Satan and the evangelist himself are likewise not our present concern. What we want to take account of is the poetry explicitly quoted from the Old Testament by Jesus. These verses are of two kinds: some are ascribed to a specific prophet (e.g. Matth. 15:8, Mark 7:6; Isa. 29:13) or psalmist (e.g. Matth. 22:44; Ps. 110:1); others merely speak of what may be read (Matth. 21:42, Mark 12:10, Luke 20:17; Ps. 118:22)—and we are interested in both together. For it was our purpose only to remark that Jesus might here be regarded as a scholar.

The gospels also contain half or entire verses of poetry that, though not announced as quotations, bring the Old Testament to mind: the Septuagint will give us the advantage of comparing Greek with Greek. Thus the angel in foretelling the birth of John the Baptist in Luke 1:17 seems to be using a phrase from Malachi 4:6—but this instance we elect to leave undiscussed, since the angel is not our special interest. What we would consider instead is a brief series (which might easily be lengthened) of examples from the words of Jesus:

Matth. 5:5, μακάριοι οἱ πραεῖς, ὅτι αὐτοὶ κληρονομήσουσιν τὴν γῆν: Ps. 37:11, οἱ δὲ πραεῖς κληρονομήσουσι γῆν "But the meek shall inherit the earth"

Matth. 5:34–35, μήτε ἐν τῶι οὐρανῶι, ὅτι θρόνος ἐστὶν τοῦ Θεοῦ· μήτε ἐν τῆι γῆι, ὅτι ὑποπόδιόν ἐστιν τῶν ποδῶν αὐτοῦ: Isa. 66:1, Ὁ οὐρανός μου θρόνος, καὶ ἡ γῆ ὑποπόδιον τῶν ποδῶν μου "The heaven is my throne, and the earth is my footstool"

Matth. 7:23, (ἀποχωρεῖτε ἀπ' ἐμοῦ) οἱ ἐργαζόμενοι τὴν ἀνομίαν, Luke 13:27, ἀπόστητε ἀπ' ἐμοῦ πάντες (ἐργάται ἀδικίας): Ps. 6:8, ἀπόστητε ἀπ' ἐμοῦ πάντες οἱ ἐργαζόμενοι τὴν ἀνομίαν "depart from me, all ye workers of iniquity"

Matth. 24:29 = Mark 13:24, ὁ ἥλιος σκοτισθήσεται, καὶ ἡ σελήνη οὐ δώσει τὸ φέγγος αὐτῆς: Isa. 13:10 (cf. Joel 2:10 and 3:15), καὶ σκοτισθήσεται τοῦ ἡλίου ἀνατέλλοντος, καὶ ἡ σελήνη οὐ δώσει τὸ φῶς αὐτῆς "the sun shall be darkened in his going forth, and the moon shall not cause her light to shine"

Mark 9:48, ὁ σκώληξ αὐτῶν οὐ τελευτᾶι καὶ τὸ πῦρ οὐ σβέννυται: Isa. 66:24, ὁ γὰρ σκώληξ αὐτῶν οὐ τελευτήσει, καὶ τὸ πῦρ αὐτῶν οὐ σβεσθήσεται "for their worm shall not die, neither shall their fire be quenched"

Luke 23:30, τοῖς ὄρεσιν Πέσατε ἐφ' ἡμᾶς, καὶ τοῖς βουνοῖς Καλύψατε ἡμᾶς: Hos. 10:8, τοῖς ὄρεσι Καλύψατε ἡμᾶς, καὶ τοῖς βουνοῖς Πέσατε ἐφ' ἡμᾶς "to the mountains, Cover us; and to the hills, Fall on us"

Either we should here again regard Jesus as a scholar who spoke from Scripture because of its sanctity, or else we should regard him as a poet who reworked such hemistichs and distichs as lay among his resources: we cannot yet tell which.

The gospels furthermore contain half or entire verses of poetry that cannot (except in rough likeness) be found in the Old Testament. One belongs to an angel (Luke 1:14), another to Mary (Luke 1:52), a third to Zacharias (Luke 1:71), a fourth to John the Baptist (Matth. 3:12, cf. Luke 3:17), a fifth to the evangelist himself (Matth. 17:2, cf. Mark 9:3, Luke 9:29), and a sixth to a woman unnamed (Luke 11:27). But the most stimulating ones to consider are those spoken by Jesus; these are the best evidence of the continuity between the Testaments. Let us choose out only the following examples from among many:

Matth. 7:7 = Luke 11:9, "Ask, and it shall be given you; seek, and ye shall find"

Matth. 7:14, "strait is the gate, and narrow is the way"

Matth. 7:16 (cf. Luke 6:44), "Do men gather grapes of thorns, or figs of thistles?"

Matth. 11:17 (cf. Luke 7:32), "We have piped unto you, and ye have not danced; we have mourned unto you, and ye have not lamented"

Matth. 11:30, "my yoke is easy, and my burden is light"

Matth. 25:24 (cf. Luke 19:21), "reaping where thou hast not sown, and gathering where thou hast not strawed"

Matth. 25:35, "I was an hungred, and ye gave me meat: I was thirsty, and ye gave me drink"

We have arrived at the heart of our inquiry, for as the speaker here Jesus is no longer to be regarded as a scholar, but as a poet. Every one of these examples, though Greek in actual language, is Hebrew (or Aramaic) in form: the two Testaments are not more obviously alike only because of a linguistic circumstance which we shall try to discount.

Biblical poetry has the mark of parallelism—though sometimes the relationship between the hemistichs is obscure: "Yet man is born unto trouble, as the sparks fly upward" (Job 5:7)—but not all biblical parallelism is a mark of poetry. Let us distinguish between the parallelism of poetry and the parallelism of prose. The one is known by its use of synonyms and antonyms, the other by its repetition of the same word. This distinction may not be acknowledged by everyone, but it is straightforward and will be useful.

C. F. Burney, *The Poetry of Our Lord* (Oxford 1925) 63, believed that the parallelism of poetry was to be found in Mark 10:38 (cf. Matth. 20:22):

can ye drink of the cup that I drink of?
and be baptized with the baptism that I am baptized with?

We disagree; the parallelism is good, and the phrases "can

ye drink?" and "can ye be baptized?" might have occurred as parallel elements in a distich of poetry; but the threefold use in the latter clause of the only term participating in parallelism is perhaps characteristic less of poetry than of prose. The construction is Semitic, for it resembles Jeremiah 23:28 (where *dābar* "speak" is a verbal form of *dābār* "word"):

The prophet that hath a dream, let him tell a dream;
and he that hath my word, let him speak my word faithfully.

But the repetitions *bapt- bapt- bapt-* and *dbr dbr dbr* belong to prose, or to a category between prose and poetry, and they are printed as prose by those versions—Revised Standard Version and Jerusalem Bible—that print the poetry as verse. It would not be difficult, by maiming the sense somewhat, to write either example as poetry of the usual kind: "can ye drink of the cup I bring to my mouth? and be baptized at the waters I stir with my hand?"; "The prophet that hath a dream, let him interpret it; and he that hath my word, let him pronounce it." And we need not even go so far: "baptize with baptism" or "say a saying"—or "drink a drink" or "dream a dream"—would be acceptable for poetry so long as the phrase were not the only member of its clause that participated in parallelism. There is no flaw in the poetry of Joel 2:28: "your old men shall dream dreams, your young men shall see visions."

Eduard Norden, *Agnostos Theos* (Leipzig 1913) 356, believed that the parallelism of poetry (of the Psalms, in his words) was to be found in 1 Corinthians 7:4:

The wife [γυνή] hath not power of her own body, but the husband [ἀνήρ]:
8

and likewise also the husband [ἀνήρ] hath not power of his
own body, but the wife [γυνή].

We disagree again; the parallelism is perfect, and either
clause alone might have occurred in a distich of poetry, but
the double use of the only word pair, or set of elements that
are parallel without being identical, does not accord with the
conventions of poetry. Once more the construction is Semitic,
for it answers to Ezekiel 18:20:

The son (*bēn*) shall not bear the iniquity of the father (ʾ*āb*),
neither shall the father (ʾ*āb*) bear the iniquity of the son (*bēn*)

But the repetition of γυνή/ἀνήρ (as ἀνήρ/γυνή) and *bēn*/ʾ*āb* (as
ʾ*āb*/*bēn*) belongs to prose, and the verses are printed as prose
by the Revised Standard Version and the Jerusalem Bible.
They would be typical of poetry as we might emend them:
"The wife hath not power of her body, but the husband: and
likewise also the *man* hath not power of his body, but the
woman"; "The son shall not bear the iniquity of the father,
neither shall the *old man* bear the iniquity of the *young man.*"
They would even be fairly typical as "The wife hath not
power of her own body, but the husband: and likewise also
the husband hath not *claim on* his own body, but the wife";
"The son shall not bear the iniquity of the father, neither
shall the father bear the *transgression* of the son." But in their
present form they are prose. Elegant variation has been
avoided rather than sought after.

   This comparison of the parallelism of poetry and the
parallelism of prose has made us for the moment especially
sensitive to iteration. We are now all the more able to con-
demn certain distichs of poetry as defective. These do not
repeat the one word pair consisting of different elements, as

do Ezekiel 18:20 (with "son/father" and "father/son") and
1 Corinthians 7:4 (with "wife/husband" and "husband/
wife"). But some, each containing no more than a single
word pair whose members are parallel without being identical, repeat the same element as both members of the second
word pair we are accustomed to look for. These distichs are
not good prose, like Ezekiel 18:20 and 1 Corinthians 7:4,
Jeremiah 23:28 and Mark 10:38; they are merely bad
poetry, boring and pointless. Consider Psalms 118:16:

The right hand [*yāmîn*] of the Lord is exalted:
the right hand [*yāmîn*] of the Lord doeth valiantly.

Right calls for *left*, so we looked for *yāmîn* to be balanced by
śĕmō᾽wl, as in Song of Solomon 8:3:

His left hand should be under my head,
and his right hand should embrace me.

But other variations in Psalms 118:16 would have done just
as well: "Lord" might have been balanced by "God," or
*yā*d "hand" and *ka*p "hand" might have replaced *yāmîn*
altogether, as in Jeremiah 15:21:

And I will deliver thee out of the hand of the wicked,
And I will redeem thee out of the hand of the terrible.

The threefold variation here—"deliver/redeem," *yā*d
"hand"/*ka*p "hand," and "wicked/terrible"—is excellent,
but double variation would have sufficed. The repetition of
*yā*d is not a flaw in Psalms 123:2:

as the eyes of servants look unto the hand of their masters,
and as the eyes of a maiden unto the hand of her mistress.

So there are several ways in which Psalms 118:16 might be improved: *yā*d "hand"/*ka*p "hand," or "Lord/God," or "right hand/left hand," could any one of them be brought into the verse; and either double variation as in Psalms 123:2, or threefold variation as in Jeremiah 15:21, would be acceptable. But in its present condition Psalms 118:16 is unattractive. In attempting to domicile the poetry of the New with that of the Old Testament, we must refuse such examples, and ask every distich to contain at least four different elements participating in parallelism.

We have noticed that *yā*d and *ka*p are both translated as "hand," a fact indicating that, in the transfer from one language to another, some instances of variation have been lost; the same is true for all the following:

If I have made gold [*zāhā*b] my hope,
or have said to the fine gold [*ketem*], Thou art my confidence
    (Job 31:24)

His bones [*ᶜeṣem*] are as strong pieces of brass;
his bones [*gerem*] are like bars of iron (Job 40:18)

Yet a little sleep [*šᵉnôt*], a little slumber,
a little folding of the hands to sleep [*šākab*] (Prov. 6:10)

For my mouth [*ḥēk*] shall speak truth;
and wickedness is an abomination to my lips.
All the words of my mouth [*peh*] are in righteousness;
there is nothing froward or perverse in them (Prov. 8:7–8)

The way [*derek*] of the slothful man is as an hedge of thorns:
but the way [*ʾōraḥ*] of the righteous is made plain (Prov. 15:19)

when I looked that it should bring forth grapes [*ᶜᵃnābîm*],
brought it forth wild grapes [*bᵉʾušîm*]? (Isa. 5:4)

Can a bird fall in a snare upon the earth [ʾereṣ],
where no gin is for him?
shall one take up a snare from the earth [ʾᵃdāmāh],
and have taken nothing at all? (Amos 3:5)

as a lion [ʾᵃrî] among the beasts of the forest,
as a young lion [kᵉpîr] among the flocks of sheep (Mic. 5:8)

Some of the word pairs noted in this list recur as formulas,
but none so impressively as ʾᵉnôš "man¹"/ʾādām "man²":

Every man² may see it;
Man¹ may behold it afar off (Job 36:25)

What is man¹, that thou art mindful of him?
and the son of man², that thou visitest him? (Ps. 8:4)

They are not in trouble as other men¹;
neither are they plagued like other men² (Ps. 73:5)

Thou turnest man¹ to destruction;
and sayest, Return, ye children of men² (Ps. 90:3)

Lord, what is man², that thou takest knowledge of him!
or the son of man¹, that thou makest account of him!
  (Ps. 144:3)

I will make a man¹ more precious than fine gold;
even a man² than the golden wedge of Ophir (Isa. 13:12)

that thou shouldest be afraid of a man¹ that shall die,
and of the son of man² which shall be made as grass
  (Isa. 51:12)

Blessed is the man¹ that doeth this,
and the son of man² that layeth hold on it (Isa. 56:2)

What we miss here is not any change in sense (for the Hebrew
words mean more or less the same), but a change in sound;

so in some ways it would be better English to say "man/
mortal," or "man/human being"—at least in the wretched
verse

What is man [$^{\,e}n\hat{o}\check{s}$], that is a worm [$rimm\bar{a}h$]?
and the son of man [$^{\,}\bar{a}d\bar{a}m$], which is a worm [$t\hat{o}l\bar{e}^{c}\bar{a}h$]?
  (Job 25:6)

And the Authorized Version is not unique for its failure to
keep the variation in the word pairs, since "man¹/man²" is
ordinarily translated by the Septuagint as ἄνθρωπος/ἄνθρω-
πος (Psalms 8:4, 73:5, 90:3, 144:3, Isa. 51:12). So to our
earlier statement that the trait of Old Testament poetry to
be looked for in the New Testament is not just parallelism
but a parallelism characterized less by repetition than by the
use of synonyms, we must now add that these were liable to
be lost when sayings were put into Greek from Aramaic.

The Greek nouns in the series $\d{s}\bar{a}r\bar{a}h$ "trouble" θλῖψις,
$\d{s}\hat{u}\d{k}\bar{a}h$ "anguish" στενοχωρία (Isa. 30:6, cf. 8:22) derive from
the same roots as the Greek adjectives in the word pair
τεθλιμμένη "narrow"/στενή "strait" (Matth. 7:14). So by
comparing the Greek New Testament with the Septuagint,
and then referring back to the Hebrew Old Testament, we
can begin to recover the Aramaic spoken by Jesus in the
verse "strait is the gate, and narrow is the way." We could
not do the like in English; we could not trace "strait/narrow"
back to "anguish, trouble"; but we can do it plausibly in
Semitic, for the primary sense of $\d{s}\hat{u}\d{k}\bar{a}h$ and $\d{s}\bar{a}r\bar{a}h$ is "con-
striction, compression, crampedness, tightness." The Greek
New Testament is held to have been brought into agreement
with the Septuagint in the quotation of the prophecies, but
in the "strait/narrow" word pair it has not been changed
and is authoritative in its own right. The poetry of Jesus can

be discerned not just when it is identified as quoted from the Old Testament, or when without being so identified it is to first appearances quoted from the Old Testament, or when without in any way seeming to be quoted it has the parallelism of the Old Testament, but also when it contains an evidently traditional word pair that was more likely to be lost than to be created by translation.

The Septuagint effaces not only (by rendering different words from a given distich in the same way) the variation within the word pairs, but also (by rendering the same word from scattered distichs in different ways) the formulaic character of the word pairs. Let us examine certain elements of Matthew 25:24: "*reaping* where thou hast not *sown*, and *gathering* where thou hast not strawed." The English terms "sow" and "reap" regularly occur together—either in the same hemistich or as a word pair in successive hemistichs— and always point back to $z\bar{a}ra^c$ and $k\bar{a}sar$ from the Hebrew Old Testament, or $\sigma\pi\epsilon\acute{\iota}\rho\omega$ and $\theta\epsilon\rho\acute{\iota}\zeta\omega$ from the Greek New Testament (Job 4:8, Ps. 126:5, Prov. 22:8, Eccl. 11:4, Isa. 37:30, Jer. 12:13, Hos. 8:7 and 10:12, and Mic. 6:15; Matth. 6:26 and 25:24, and Luke 12:24 and 19:21). In the Septuagint, however, $\sigma\pi\epsilon\acute{\iota}\rho\omega$—for $z\bar{a}ra^c$—may be accompanied not by $\theta\epsilon\rho\acute{\iota}\zeta\omega$—for $k\bar{a}sar$—but by $\dot{a}\mu\acute{a}\omega$ (Isa. 37:30, Mic. 6:15), $\dot{\epsilon}\kappa\delta\acute{\epsilon}\chi o\mu a\iota$ (Hos. 8:7), or $\tau\rho\upsilon\gamma\acute{a}\omega$ (Hos. 10:12) instead. So it is no surprise that $\theta\epsilon\rho\acute{\iota}\zeta\omega$—for $k\bar{a}sar$—is again replaced by $\dot{a}\mu\acute{a}\omega$ in Isaiah 17:5, where the word pair we are interested in, $\theta\epsilon\rho\acute{\iota}\zeta\omega$ "reap"/$\sigma\upsilon\nu\acute{a}\gamma\omega$ "gather" from Matthew 25:24, appears as $\dot{a}\mu\acute{a}\omega$ "reap"/$\sigma\upsilon\nu\acute{a}\gamma\omega$ "gather." We can still say that "reap/gather" is a traditional formula (a supplement to "sow/reap"), even though the Septuagint has rubbed out the line of continuity.

In addition, the Septuagint sometimes appears to be either an inaccurate translation of a good text, or an accurate translation of a bad text. The word pair ζυγός "yoke"/ φορτίον "burden" from Matthew 11:30, "my yoke is easy, and my burden is light," might have been expected to render the word pair ʿōl "yoke"/subāl "burden" in Isaiah 10:27 and 14:25; but we find ζυγός/φόβος "fear" and ζυγός/κῦδος "glory" instead. To explain these readings is not our purpose here; but they are no impediment to our believing, even though we cannot prove, that ζυγός/φορτίον in the New represents a formula from the Old Testament tradition.

Some of our results satisfy expectation in a manner that needs no discussion. ὀρχέομαι "dance" and κόπτομαι "lament"—which form a word pair in Matthew 11:7 (cf. Luke 7:32): "We have piped to you and ye have not danced, we have mourned and ye have not lamented"—occur as elements in one of the hemistichs of the Septuagint version of Ecclesiastes 3:4: "a time to lament and a time to dance." αἰτέω "ask" and ζητέω "seek"—which form a word pair in Matthew 7:7 = Luke 11:9: "ask and ye shall receive, seek and ye shall find"—occur again as parallel to each other, though possibly not as a word pair, in the Septuagint version of Isaiah 58:2: "Yet they seek me daily . . . they ask of me the ordinances of justice."

The formulaic character of the elements in Matthew 25:35 may be clearer yet:

For I was an hungred, and ye gave me meat:
I was thirsty, and ye gave me drink
ἐπείνασα γὰρ καὶ ἐδώκατέ μοι φαγεῖν,
ἐδίψησα καὶ ἐποτίσατέ με

ἐπείνασα and ἔφαγον from the one hemistich are also complementary in Isaiah 65:13, "my servants shall eat, but ye shall be hungry"; ἐδίψησα and ἐπότισα from the other are complementary in (Ps. 69:21 and) Prov. 25:21, "and if he be thirsty, give him water to drink"; and the word pair ἐπείνασα "I was hungry"/ἐδίψησα "I was thirsty" occurs again in (Prov. 25:21, Isa. 65:13, and) Isaiah 32:6, "to make empty the soul of the hungry, and he will cause the drink of the thirsty to fail." σταφυλαί "grapes"/σῦκα "figs," finally, is a word pair not only in the gospels but in the prophets as well:

Matth. 7:16: "Do men gather grapes of thorns, or figs of thistles?"

Luke 6:44: "For of thorns men do not gather figs, nor of a bramble bush gather they grapes"

Jer. 8:13: "there shall be no grapes on the vine, nor figs on the fig tree"

Hos. 9:10: "I found Israel like grapes in the wilderness; I saw your fathers as the firstripe in the fig tree at her first time"

Since we do not hold the Septuagint in high esteem, why have we given it such close attention? Just to guard against coincidence: having found word pairs—not in English only but in Greek as well—that are the same in the two Testaments, we can say with greater confidence than we could before (when our only evidence lay in the use of parallelism) that Jesus was a poet in the line from Amos onwards. He resembles the prophets in using parables (e.g. Jer. 13:1–11, Luke 15:4–7), but his particular parables are not theirs. He resembles them further in using the two kinds of parallelism that we have regarded as being less poetry than prose (see Jer. 23:28 and Matth. 7:2, Ezek. 18:20 and Matth. 10:39); but again it is the forms of expression—rather than the actual words—that are identical. He resembles them further still in using the parallelism of poetry; but once more his hemistichs and distichs are not theirs except when we know (for it is so declared: see Isa. 29:13 and Matth. 15:8) or may at least believe (the relationship between Isa. 66:24 and Mark 9:48 being so far undecided) that he is intentionally quoting from them. Jesus resembles the prophets finally in his choice of word pairs, such as "grapes/figs," and here, where it does not make sense to speak about quoting, we can say that he is one of their number.

What part of his work was original, and what part appropriated? It must be established that the idea of literary property does not seem to have been the same then as it is now. Jeremiah (23:30) denounced, but was himself among, the prophets who stole words "every one from his neighbor"; any noble expression was likely to become the possession of all poets in common. We have concluded that Jesus spoke of "grapes/figs" (Matth. 7:16) without the idea of referring specifically to Jeremiah (8:13) or Hosea (9:10), and we are now prepared to assert that he said "Where their worm dieth not, and the fire is not quenched" (Mark 9:48) without the idea of quoting specifically from Isaiah (66:24). Elsewhere he is a scholar; in these two examples—among many—he is a poet: this word pair (Matth. 7:16) and this distich (Mark 9:48) were taken from the past only as elements of the standard Semitic poetic diction. There is no logical reason to exclude Jesus from a continuous tradition that had begun perhaps a thousand years before. So "appropriated" is the wrong term; the question must be recast.

What part of his work was original, and what part traditional? But this cannot possibly be answered, whether it is asked about Jesus, or about Amos, or Isaiah, or any other poet of the Bible. We have argued that the poetic idiom could not have been normalized to such a degree in the first place if the poetic craft had not been undertaken by a greater number of men than those we know by name, and the Dead

Sea scrolls support our contention that every generation produced, not just a few poems by an isolated figure of unusual wisdom and prescience, but a much vaster collection of poetry than it has been fashionable to believe in. So some things from the preaching of Jesus that strike us as unique, and beyond the capability of anyone else, may in actuality have been said before. The task of reforming the precepts of morality, in the interests of ever greater justice and charity, had belonged to the prophets also. They replaced "The fathers have eaten sour grapes, and the children's teeth are set on edge" with "The son shall not bear the iniquity of the father, neither shall the father bear the iniquity of the son" (Eze. 18:2–20, cf. Jer. 31:29–30)—as he replaced "[God] shall reward evil unto mine enemies: cut them off in thy truth" (Ps. 54:5) with "Love your enemies, bless them that curse you, do good to them that hate you, and pray for them which despitefully use you, and persecute you" (Matth. 5:44, cf. Luke 6:27–28). Jesus was not the first poet to be a reformer, a lawgiver—and even those sayings of his that cannot be found elsewhere may well have been anticipated in part by the lost poems that lie below our plumb line. And yet there is one respect in which his poetry does indeed appear to be unique. For some of it—"Love your enemies, bless them that curse you"—defines, according to the gospel account, his own special practice. This relationship between a poem and its prose context is the most important one that we have encountered, or could encounter.

The poetry of Jesus is very nearly universal, pertinent to the world of today or tomorrow. Concerning not events that happened once only, in a special time and place, and containing almost no proper names, it lacks historical perspective and fails to describe personal character—it does not refer explicitly, exclusively, to himself or anyone else. Being often similar, in its word pairs and its hemistichs and distichs, to Old Testament psalm, proverb, and prophecy, it gives the impression of having in large measure been said by other poets as well, throughout a long tradition. In all these ways the poetry of Jesus resembles that of Job—and in one more besides: both owe part of their impact upon us to the extraordinary prose that has made them not just words of depth and beauty, but the words of a certain great man, spoken under stated, momentous circumstances. One difference: the poetry of Jesus is the smaller part, though that of Job almost the entirety, of what he is recorded as saying. And another: the gospel context claims the words of Jesus, though the prologue and epilogue do not claim those of Job, to be for us the way, the truth, and the life.

c. It is unclear whether the oral poem was dictated.

Jesus may be regarded as an oral poet because he used formulas that were to every appearance developed for the making of poetry in an oral culture, and also because the prose context of his poetry seems to say that he composed by ear and mouth rather than by eye and hand. So any answer to the question "How were his poems transcribed?" may help us to answer the larger question "How was any oral poem transcribed?"

In a major article published thirty-five years ago Rhys Carpenter, "The Antiquity of the Greek Alphabet," *American Journal of Archaeology* 37 (1933) 29, suggested that the *Iliad* and *Odyssey* were dictated, and in an important book published forty years ago William Witherle Lawrence, *Beowulf and Epic Tradition* (Cambridge, Mass. 1928) 10, suggested that *Beowulf* was dictated; but the general theory about the dictation of formulaic poetry belongs to Albert B.

Lord, *The Singer of Tales* (Cambridge, Mass. 1960) 124–128 and throughout. Having come upon this idea during the course of studying the Yugoslav epic songs created by bards of our own day, Lord applies it to Homeric, Old English, and Old French poetry, though not to the poetry of the Bible. Now dictation has been used from time to time even by literate men (such as St. Paul: see Rom. 16:22) and was used at least once to record a poem on the grand scale (*Paradise Lost*), so the idea is reasonable; we merely wish to know whether it is more than that. Since Lord neither acknowledges the existence of any evidence against his theory, nor brings forward any ancient or medieval testimony in its favor, a summary of the few relevant facts will be in order.

The *Iliad* and *Odyssey* mention writing only in a passage (*Il.* 6.168–169) that implies it to be an obscure and mysterious thing, and the *Song of Roland* (1442, 1684–1685, 2095, 3262, 3742, 4002) refers to charters and documents, or the *geste* or *geste Francor*, chiefly as if to claim that the events being described really did occur, not as if to acknowledge the sources from which the material was taken. For evidence against the dictation theory, we must look not to the Homeric and Old French traditions, but to the Old English and biblical traditions, instead. *Beowulf* may have been dictated, but the runic signatures of Cynewulf argue that he wrote with his own hand the poems where they appear: *Fates of the Apostles*, *Elene*, *Christ*, and *Juliana* (though concerning the first three there is some question: see George Philip Krapp and Elliott V. K. Dobbie, ed. *The Anglo-Saxon Poetic Records* [New York 1931–1953] 2 xxxviii and xl, and 3 xxix and xxxvi). And since Richard Kistenmacher, *Die wörtlichen Wiederholungen im Bêowulf* (Greifswald 1898) 42, found that *Elene* was formulaic to the same extent as *Beowulf*, Arthur Gilchrist Brodeur, *The Art of Beowulf* (Berkeley and Los

Angeles 1959) 4, is right in saying that if the one was written down by its author the other may have been too. Similarly, some of the poetry in the Bible may have been dictated, but the alphabetic poems (especially Ps. 119, Prov. 31:10–31, and Lam. 1–4) cannot be the work of an illiterate, even though they use several formulas that we find elsewhere: "For the sins of her prophets, and the iniquities of her priests" (Lam. 4:13). The theory has these feet of clay: can we strengthen it with a crutch?

There is no testimony whatsoever that any Homeric, Old English, or Old French poem was even in part set down by means of dictation, but the thirty-sixth chapter of Jeremiah declares explicitly that the prophet dictated to Baruch, and according to the gospel account the poetry of Jesus was always spoken by him, never written. Our conclusion would therefore seem to be this: it is an open question how the *Iliad, Beowulf,* and the *Song of Roland* were first recorded, but in some ways the beatitudes from the Sermon on the Mount may be regarded, even though they exist in two versions (Matth. 5:2–12 and Luke 6:20–23), as an oral dictated text.

Appendix / Work to be done

It is widely, though not universally, held that the *Iliad* and Job, *Beowulf* and the *Song of Roland*, contain late additions. Why do such theories matter? Primarily because they teach us that the poems are not flawless as unities. Secondarily because they imply a kind of literary activity that shakes faith in the idea of a bard's dictating to a scribe. Since the additions are most clearly visible, or most nearly visible, when isolated by evidence of different kinds, the following arguments are unusually commendable. Denys Page, *History and the Homeric Iliad* (Berkeley 1963) 297–302 and 327–328, invites us to observe that for three reasons Phoenix cannot have been originally a part of the Embassy episode in the *Iliad*: (1) Odysseus and Ajax are described in several lines as going without him to the place of Achilles; (2) whereas ordinarily in Homeric poetry it is the gods who govern what man does, Phoenix speaks as if Achilles himself were morally responsible; and (3) some of the words used by Phoenix either are not to be found elsewhere as elements of the epic dialect or are to be regarded as Ionian or Odyssean. Samuel Rolles Driver and George Buchanan Gray, *A Critical and Exegetical*

Commentary on the Book of Job (Edinburgh 1921) xl–xlvii, thought that the Elihu section of Job was interpolated: the rest of the book ignores Elihu entirely, and his address is noticeably full of Aramaisms. Kenneth Sisam, "Beowulf's Fight with the Dragon," *Review of English Studies* N. S. 9 (1958) 130, regards lines 3069–3073 of *Beowulf* as an interpolation, partly because they grated on the ear of Eduard Sievers, but chiefly because they impute to the hoard a curse that evidently does not apply to the epic hero. Finally, Robert Hall, "Linguistic Strata in the *Chanson de Roland*," *Romance Philology* 13 (1959) 159, believes that different strata in the *Roland* can be identified not only from inconsistencies (for nominating him to command the rear guard, Roland thanks Ganelon in laisse 59 but denounces him in laisse 60; and the hanging foretold in laisse 109 is carried out as a quartering in laisse 288) but also from the sound changes that occurred in the first half of the twelfth century (laisse 59 is late, laisse 60 is early; 109 is late, 288 is early).

Now it is not my intention either to approve of these arguments or to raise any objection against them; I would only suggest a method, not yet tried, by which they, or similar arguments, could perhaps be made stronger yet. Let someone compile, in as detached a manner as possible, a complete list of all the violations of economy, preferably in one or another of the four traditions, or, second best, in one or another of the four poems. (Whoever undertakes the task will have to set down clearly what general principles he is following. For to say what does, and what does not, constitute a violation, is in practice not so easy. Probably we should refuse to recognize, as violations, these four examples among many: "evil-named sons of the Achaeans" δυσώνυμοι υἷες Ἀχαιῶν [*Il.* 6.255] with "long-haired Achaeans" κάρη κομόωντες Ἀχαιοί [*Il.* 2.323, 2.472, 3.43, etc.]; "Almighty" *šadday*/ "adversary" [Job 31:35] with "Almighty" *šadday*/ "God" *ʾēl* or *ʾelōah* [Job 5:17, 6:4, 8:3, etc.]; "nobleman spiritless" *æþeling unfrom* [*Beowulf* 2188] with "nobleman good from far back" *æþeling ærgod* [*Beowulf* 130, 1329, 2342]; and [*Ed une ymágene Apolin*] *lo felon* [*Roland* 3268] with [*Desor l'alter saint Séverin*] *lo baron* [*Roland* 3685].) If the violations are clustered thickly in certain areas, these will be the places where, other matters being equal, additions are to be looked for. Whether this method will yield positive results, I do not know; but even negative results may be valuable.

It would be interesting to know what expressions were used by Hesiod (the Job poet, Cynewulf, the *Raoul* poet) instead of what expressions used in Homeric poetry (Isaiah, *Beowulf*, the *Song of Roland*). The problem amounts to finding where there are violations of economy in a tradition but not in any specific poem.

We need a convention for assigning to a passage its formular coefficient. Without such a convention it is not helpful to describe a passage as being forty, or sixty, or ninety percent formulaic. What does one hundred percent represent? Does it mean that the entire passage is a formula? The rules to be devised should give greater weight to elements that are (1) repeated letter for letter than to those that merely have analogues; (2) lengthy than to those that are brief (and the progression ought to be geometric rather than arithmetic); (3) repeated often than to those that are repeated seldom; and (4) guiltless of, than to those that are involved in, violations of economy.

Once the rules are agreed upon, let them be applied to passages from the *Iliad*, Job, *Beowulf*, and the *Song of Roland*—

and also, for a truer perspective, to passages from Chaucer
and Byron, to passages from Browne and Gibbon and
Darwin, and to recordings of ordinary speech. All language is
formulaic, or based upon analogy, and a table of formular
coefficients might help us to distinguish the unusual from the
commonplace.

We do not know enough about how the expressions for the
different concepts are related. What are the chief formula
types for the following: Homeric common nouns; Old Testament word pairs that are neither synonymous nor antithetical; Old English common nouns that contain, or do not
contain, the standard Germanic prefixes, such as *wæl-*; Old
French proper names and common nouns.

The formulas deserve attention in the making of translations. Richmond Lattimore's *Iliad*, Homeric in many ways,
is more highly formulaic in Modern English than *Beowulf* is
in Old English, but not quite so formulaic as Homer in
Greek. πολύμητις 'Οδυσσεύς is rendered as "resourceful
Odysseus" in 3.216, 4.329, 4.349, 10.148, 10.382, 10.400,
10.423, 10.488, 10.554, 14.82, 19.154, and 19.215, but as
"crafty Odysseus" in 1.311 and as "Odysseus of the many
designs" in 1.440. Furthermore, the lines 5.175–176 =
16.424–425 are worded now in one way, now in another:

at this strong man, whoever he be, who does so much evil
to the Trojans, since many and great are those whose knees
   he has broken

who this is who has so much strength and has done so much
   evil
to the Trojans, since many and brave are those whose knees
   he has unstrung

The Authorized Version is faithful to the same high but imperfect degree. Answering to *māwet* "death," *šeʾôl* is rendered
as "hell" in 2 Samuel 22:6, Psalms 18:5, Proverbs 5:5 and
7:27, Isaiah 28:15 and 28:18, and Habakkuk 2:5, but as
"grave" in Psalms 6:5, 49:14, and 89:48, Song of Solomon
8:6, Isaiah 38:18, and Hosea 13:14. Then too, though
"vanity" and "iniquity" translate *ʾāwen* equally well, the
same choice ought to have been made in Job 15:35, "They
conceive mischief, and bring forth vanity," as in Isaiah
59:4, "They conceive mischief and bring forth iniquity."
E. Talbot Donaldson's *Beowulf* surpasses its competitors now
for readability, now for accuracy, but *hæle hildedeor* is
"warrior dear to battle" in 1646, "the man dear to war" in
1816, and "man brave in battle" in 3111. Dorothy Sayers'
Song of Roland has the assonance as well as the force of the
original, but a specific assonance in Old French has not been
assigned a specific counterpart in English, and consequently
lines that were once the same, such as 1071–1072 = 1703–
1704, are now different:

Charles in the passes will hear it as he goes,
Trust me, the French will all return right so

When Carlon hears, passing through Gate of Spain,
I pledge my word, the French will turn again

Are we speaking here about lapses, failures, *faults*? No, the
formular character of a translation matters less than almost
any other quality. But for the sake of distorting the originals
to the least degree possible, those who make versions in the
future might take the formulas into account.

Let it be determined mathematically whether the varieties
of dactylic meter (parallelism, alliteration, assonance) are

arranged from line to line in the *Iliad* (distich to distich in Job, line to line in *Beowulf*, laisse to laisse in the *Roland*) as if by chance. On the basis of formula theory alone we should assume that any admirable lack of monotony, in the sequence of the varieties, resulted only from luck. But the assumption may turn out to be wrong.

We need an analysis of the relationship between the "theme," or motif, and the formula. Homeric poetry, being highly formulaic and stichic, would lend itself best. Old French poetry, which is also highly formulaic, raises special problems because, consisting of laisses that differ in assonance, it is not purely stichic but also stanzaic. Old Testament and Old English poetry raise special problems because they are perhaps less than highly formulaic.

When the poet repeats an element to nearly the last syllable, what is the value in saying that the element is a theme? Why not just say that it is a formula? Let no one reply that themes are long and uncommon whereas formulas are short and common. It is true that $\pi\rho o\sigma\acute{e}\phi\eta$ "he (she) said," which is restricted in all but two of its two hundred thirteen occurrences in the *Iliad* and *Odyssey* to the part of the line between the middle of the third foot and the middle of the fourth, is highly formulaic and certainly short and common. But many phrases, such as the last five feet of *Il.* 15.479 = *Od.* 22.122, are just as highly formulaic though longer and rarer. Many an unusual line or pair of lines is a formula; the passage *Od.* 2.96–110 = 19.141–156 = 24.131–146 is a formula; and passages of even greater length might have been identifiable as formulas at an earlier day. And to argue that a formula is also a theme is to complicate matters unnecessarily.

The question is whether the poet intended to repeat a

theme when he used different words to express much the same idea in passages that might be interchanged without harm to the meter. If he himself regarded the idea as being the same, why did he not (as we should have expected from the law of economy) use the same words? Is the theme just an imperfectly developed formula?

The Homeric words *sakos* and *aspis*, both meaning "shield," provide for different metrical needs (as we should have expected them to) and yet are not used as synonyms (as we learn to our great surprise). It would be highly interesting to know of other words, from any of the four traditions, that have a comparably exceptional nature.

No less interesting would be a clear answer to the question whether the consistent use of *sakos* and *aspis* indicates that the *Iliad* was in some sense by a single poet. Our first impulse is to say, yes, by arranging *sakos* and *aspis* in a special manner, the poet of the *Iliad* did indeed leave his personal mark upon his work. But then we notice that both the *Odyssey* and, what is more remarkable, the Hesiodic *Shield of Heracles* seem to have the words in the Iliadic fashion.

It is perhaps a principle that the choice between two tenses sometimes depends in the *Iliad* on meter and in the *Roland* on assonance. A comparative study defining this principle with exactitude (or showing it to be unreliable) would be welcome.

It is clear that the Homeric, Old English, and Old French poets were prepared to express many a basic concept in various ways, according to the changes rung in meter, alliteration, and assonance. Were they prepared to express the thought of many an entire passage in various ways? The question has little moment for the *Iliad* or *Beowulf*, since the meter or alliteration of an entire passage seldom appears significant. But it has considerable moment for the *Roland*, where the assonance is sustained throughout a laisse. Was the Old French poet able to turn a series of ideas as well into one assonance as into another? The *laisses similaires* seem to indicate that he was indeed. But our initial impression is perhaps not to be trusted. Has the practice of composing in laisses led now and then to a correlation between a specific assonance and a specific subject?

In my opinion the formulaic descriptive elements for the heroes of the *Iliad* differ in at least one way from those for the heroes of *Beowulf*: the former are more significantly true to individual character than accurate to context; the latter are more significantly accurate to context than true to individual character. If this generalization is sound, what problems does it suggest? The first is whether the formulaic descriptive elements for the heroes of the *Roland*, or of other Old French poems, pertain to character or to context, or neither or both.

The second problem, a twofold one, is whether the *Odyssey* resembles the *Iliad*, and whether the other Old English poems resemble *Beowulf*. Part of what we are asking here can perhaps be answered quickly, part not. Several epithets in the *Odyssey* are true to individual character, though fewer than in the *Iliad* are exemplified, or illustrated, in memorable episodes. And the kennings in the other Old English poems are as a rule accurate to context, but whether they are ever interchanged with precision—in the manner of the *Beowulf h . . . h* half-lines *har hilderinc* "old battle-warrior" (first for Hrothgar, then for Beowulf) and *hæle hildedeor* "hero battle-fierce" (first for Beowulf, then for Wiglaf), or *f* half-lines *folces hyrde* "shepherd of the people" (Hrothgar, then

Beowulf) and *feþecempa* "foot-warrior" (Beowulf, then
Wiglaf)—has not yet been studied, and sometime ought to be.

To many a North American or Western European, the
traditions dealt with in this book—Homeric and Old Testament poetry, Old English and Old French poetry—are the
most interesting, as well as the most accessible, representa-
tives of their genre. But the problems they present are sometimes solved best by analogy with yet further materials.
Consider the guidelines drawn by Albert B. Lord's studies
of Yugoslav poetry and James A. Notopoulos's studies of
Cretan poetry: for example, Lord, *The Singer of Tales* (Cambridge, Mass. 1960) 99 and 127 (on the importance of music),
and Notopoulos, "Studies in Early Greek Oral Poetry,"
Harvard Studies in Classical Philology 68 (1964) 1–18 (on the
length of recitation). Collections of Mongolian poetry and
the Ainu poetry of Japan may also come to appear directly
relevant. Such less well known traditions will perhaps prove
to be the most valuable resource for testing and clarifying
the hypotheses about the better-known traditions; the formula theorist who is in addition a comparatist has still a
great deal of worthwhile work before him; few literary subjects offer so large a supply of dissertation topics.

How do formulas relate to characterization, and to their
contexts, in the Balkan poetry of our own time? Do the
modern traditions, as judged by their degree of economy,
resemble the *Iliad* and the *Roland*, or do they more closely resemble Job and *Beowulf*? How many whole repeated lines
are there in the modern traditions, and how do these totals
compare with those for the formulaic poems of antiquity and
the Middle Ages? Are any two lengthy modern epics as
similar in diction as the epics of Homer are? Is it true that the
more exacting the prosodic requirements—compare Yugoslav

poetry, marked by isosyllabism, with Old French poetry, marked by isosyllabism and assonance—the greater the tendency towards syllable-for-syllable recurrence? Are there, in any modern formulaic poem known to have been created by a single poet, such clustered violations of economy as might ordinarily be thought to indicate a break in authorship?

Index

THE CENTER FOR HELLENIC STUDIES

*The Center
for Hellenic Studies, located
at 3100 Whitehaven Street, Washington, D.C.,
is a residential center for research in the
fields of ancient Greek history, literature, and
philosophy. The land upon which the Center
stands was devised to the Old Dominion
Foundation by Marie Beale and the Center was
established and endowed in 1961 by a grant
from the Old Dominion Foundation to the
Trustees for Harvard University. Eight
resident fellows are appointed each year,
from America and from abroad; the publications
of the Center present work begun or completed
by them during their tenure of the
fellowship.*

CHS

Publications of the Center for Hellenic Studies

Theocritus' Coan Pastorals: A Poetry Book, by Gilbert Lawall, 1967
Theopompus and Fifth-Century Athens, by W. Robert Connor, 1968
Formula, Character, and Context: Studies in Homeric, Old English, and Old Testament Poetry, by William Whallon, 1969